STECK-VAUGHN
GED Literature and the Arts

STECK-VAUGHN ADULT EDUCATION ADVISORY COUNCIL

Donna D. Amstutz
Assistant Professor
Adult Education
Northern Illinois
University
DeKalb, Illinois

Sharon K. Darling
President, National Center
for Family Literacy
Louisville, Kentucky

Roberta Pittman
Director, Project C3 Adult
Basic Education
Detroit Public Schools
Detroit, Michigan

Elaine Shelton
President, Shelton
Associates
Consultant, Competency-
Based Adult Education
Austin, Texas

STECK-VAUGHN
COMPANY
A Subsidiary of National Education Corporation

STAFF CREDITS

Supervising Editor: Ron Lemay
Editor: Bob Fullilove
Design Director: D Childress
Editorial Consultant: Donna Amstutz

Contributing Writers/Editor: Virginia Lowe, Joan Rosenblatt, Sylvia P. Bloch

Design/Production: Fuller Dyal & Stamper Inc.
Cover Photograph: David C. Mackenzie

Editorial Development: McClanahan & Company, Inc.
Project Director: Mark Moscowitz

Photograph Credits: p. 36 © Rafael Macia/Photo Researchers
p. 134 © 1990 Martha Swope
p. 200 © Barbara Rios/Photo Researchers

ISBN   0-8114-4704-9

Printed in the United States of America.

Table of Contents

What You Should Know About the GED Test

What is the GED Test?

You are taking a very big step toward changing your life with your decision to take the GED test. By opening this book, you are taking your second important step: to prepare for the test. You may feel nervous about what is ahead, which is only natural. Relax and read the following pages to find out the answers to your questions.

The GED, the test of General Educational Development, is given by the GED Testing Service of the American Council on Education for adults who did not graduate from high school. When you pass the GED, you will receive a certificate that is the equivalent of a high school diploma. It is regarded as being the same as a high school diploma. Employers in private industry and government, as well as admissions officers in colleges and universities, accept the GED certificate as they would a high school diploma.

The GED tests cover the same subjects people study in high school. The five subject areas are: Writing Skills, Interpreting Literature and the Arts, Social Studies, Science, and Mathematics. In Writing Skills Part II, you will be asked to write a short essay on a specific subject. You will not be required to know all the information that is usually taught in high school. You will, however, be tested on your ability to read and process information. In some states you may be required to take a test on the U.S. Constitution or on your state government. Check with your local adult education center to see if your state requires this test.

Each year hundreds of thousands of adults take and pass the GED test. The *Steck-Vaughn GED Series* will help you to develop and refine your reading and thinking skills in order to pass the GED test.

What You Should Know About GED Scores

After you complete the GED test, you will get a score for each section and a total score. The total score is an average of all the other scores. The highest score possible on a single test is 80. The scores needed to pass the GED test vary, depending on where you live. The chart on page 2 shows the minimum state score requirements. A minimum score of *40 or 45* means that no test score can be less than 40, or if one or more scores is less than 40, an average of at least 45 is required. Scores of *35 and 45* mean that no test score can be less than 35, and an average of at least 45 is required.

GED Score Requirements

Area	Minimum Score on Each Test		Minimum Average on All Five Tests
UNITED STATES			
Alabama, Alaska, Arizona, Colorado, Connecticut, District of Columbia, Georgia, Hawaii, Idaho, Illinois, Indiana, Iowa, Kansas, Kentucky, Maine, Massachusetts, Michigan, Minnesota, Missouri, Montana, Nevada, New Hampshire, North Carolina, Ohio, Pennsylvania, Rhode Island, Tennessee, Vermont, Virginia, Wyoming	35	and	45
Arkansas, California, Delaware, Florida, Maryland, New York, Oklahoma, Oregon, South Dakota, Utah, Washington, West Virginia	40	and	45
Louisiana, Mississippi, Nebraska, Texas	40	or	45
New Jersey (42 is required on Test 1; 40 is required on Tests 2, 3, and 4; 45 is required on Test 5; and 225 is required as a minimum test score.)			
New Mexico, North Dakota	40	or	50
South Carolina	–		45
Wisconsin	40	and	50
CANADA			
Alberta, British Columbia, Manitoba, Northwest Territories, New Brunswick (35 and 45 for French), Nova Scotia, Prince Edward Island, Saskatchewan, Yukon Territory	45		–
Newfoundland	40	and	45
U.S. TERRITORIES & OTHERS			
Guam, Kwajalein, Puerto Rico, Virgin Islands	35	and	45
Canal Zone, Palau	40	and	45
Mariana Islands, Marshall Islands	40	or	45
American Samoa	40		–

THE TESTS OF GENERAL EDUCATIONAL DEVELOPMENT

Test	Content Areas	Number of Items	Time Limit (minutes)
Writing Skills Part I	Sentence Structure Usage Mechanics	55	75
Writing Sample Part II	Essay	1	45
Social Studies	U.S. History Geography Economics Political Science Behavioral Science	64	85
Science	Life Science Earth Science Physics Chemistry	66	95
Interpreting Literature and the Arts	Popular Literature Classical Literature Commentary	45	65
Mathematics	Arithmetic Algebra Geometry	56	90

The chart tells you what will be on each test. When you take the simulated GED test in this book, see how well you do within the time limit. In some states you do not have to take all sections of the test on the same day. If you take the test one section at a time, this chart can help you decide how much time you will need for each test. If you want to take all the test sections in one day, you will find that the GED test will last an entire day. Check with your local adult education center for the requirements in your area.

Where Do You Go to Take the GED Test?

The GED test is offered year-round throughout the United States, its possessions, U.S. military bases worldwide, and in Canada. To find out where and when a test is being held near you, contact one of the following institutions in your area:

- An adult education center
- A continuing education center
- A private business school or technical school
- A local community college
- The public board of education
- A library

In addition, these institutions can give you information regarding necessary identification, testing fees, and writing implements. Schedules vary: some testing centers are open several days a week; others are open only on weekends.

Why Should You Take the GED Test?

A GED certificate can help you in the following ways:

Employment
Employees without high school diplomas or GED certificates are having much greater difficulty changing jobs or moving up in their present companies. In many cases, employers will not consider hiring people who do not have a high school diploma or its equivalent.

Education
If you want to enroll in a college or university, a technical or vocational school, or even an apprenticeship program, you often must have a high school diploma or its equivalent.

Personal
The most important thing is how you feel about yourself. You have the unique opportunity to turn back the clock by making something happen that did not happen in the past. You can now attain a GED certificate that not only will help you in the future, but will help you feel better about yourself now.

How to Prepare for the GED Test

Classes for GED preparation are available to anyone who wants to take the GED. The choice of whether to take the class is entirely up to you; they are not required. If you prefer to study by yourself, the *Steck-Vaughn GED Series* has been prepared to guide your study. *Steck-Vaughn Exercise* books are also available to give you practice on all of the tests, including the writing sample.

Many people are taking classes to prepare for the GED test. Most programs offer individualized instruction and tutors who can help you identify areas in which you may need help. Most adult education centers offer free day or night classes. The classes are usually informal and allow you to work at your own pace and with other adults who also are studying for the GED. Attendance is usually not taken. In addition to working on specific skills, you will be able to take practice GED tests (like those in this book) in order to check your progress. For more information about classes available near you, call one of the institutions listed on page 3.

What You Need to Know to Pass
Test Four: Literature and the Arts

This test focuses on reading comprehension and analysis. In other words, you will be tested on how well you understand what you read and on how you can use and apply that information. You will not be tested on your knowledge about literature. The test takes 65 minutes. It has 45 questions divided among three types of literature: Popular Literature, Classical Literature, and Commentary.

Popular Literature

Fifty percent of the passages you will read are taken from popular literature. Popular literature is recently published prose nonfiction, novels, short stories, plays, poems, and magazines. The selections are examples of good writing and cover many subjects.

Classical Literature

Twenty-five percent of the passages are from classical literature. Classical literature is prose nonfiction, novels, short stories, plays, and poetry that literary experts regard as superior writing. All the selections are examples from the 1800s and 1900s. The classics, such as the play *Death of a Salesman*, have stood the test of time.

Commentary

Twenty-five percent of the passages are taken from commentary found in current publications. Commentary includes reviews of books, movies, television, music, art, dance, or theater.

The test questions require you to think about the reading passages in several different ways. To answer the questions, you will be using four basic reading skills. The *Steck-Vaughn GED Interpreting Literature and the Arts* text will train you in applying these skills.

Literal Comprehension

You must read carefully to understand the facts and the details that support those facts. You may be asked to identify and restate specific information. You may be asked to show a general understanding of what the author is saying. Here you need to gather information from several parts of the passage to answer the question.

Inferential Comprehension

Although this skill may sound difficult, it is actually something you do every day. To infer simply means to make decisions based on stated or suggested information. You make inferences when you read, because authors do not always state their ideas directly. Think about the sentence "Allison hissed and dug her claws into the rug." Since you know that cats hiss and have claws, you can infer that Allison is not a person but a cat.

Application

You will be asked to take the information you learned through literal or inferential comprehension and view it another way. To answer an application question correctly, you must first understand an idea and then use (apply) it in another situation. For example, you may read that two people dislike each other. Then you may be asked how they would act if they were stuck in an elevator together. So, you will be taking information and applying it to new contexts.

Analysis

To analyze something means to take it apart to see how it works. Analysis in reading means that you look at the ways the author makes a point. For analysis questions, you ask yourself *how* and *why*, rather than *what*.

Sample Passage and Questions

The following is a sample passage with questions. These are similar to actual GED questions. An explanation of the correct answer follows each question. The sample passage is much shorter than those on the test. Passages for the Interpreting Literature and the Arts test are about 400 words in length, which is a lot of information to read and absorb. Remember that there are more comprehension questions than application or analysis questions.

The purpose question in bold type above the passage helps you focus on what the author is trying to say. Every passage in this book and on the GED test has a purpose question above it.

Items 1 to 3 refer to the following paragraph.

WHAT IS HAPPENING TO THIS BOY?

All this time, of course (while he lay in bed), he had kept his eyes closed, listening to the nearer progress of the postman, the muffled footsteps thumping and slipping on the snow-sheathed cobbles; and all the other sounds—the double knocks, a frosty far-off voice or
(5) two, a bell ringing thinly and softly as if under a sheet of ice—had the same slightly abstracted quality, as if removed by one degree from actuality—as if everything in the world had been insulated by snow. But when at last, pleased, he opened his eyes, and turned them towards the window, to see himself this long-desired and now
(10) so clearly imagined miracle—what he saw instead was brilliant sunlight on a roof; and when, astonished, he jumped out of bed and stared down into the street, expecting to see the cobbles obliterated by the snow, he saw nothing but the bare, bright cobbles themselves.

1. Which of the following best describes what this boy is doing through most of the passage?

    (1) He is lying in bed awake.
    (2) He is looking out the window.
    (3) He is sound asleep.
    (4) He is watching the snow fall.
    (5) He is having a nightmare.

Answer: **(1) He is lying in bed awake.**

Explanation: This question is an example of literal comprehension. You can find the information you need in the first sentence of the passage, which states "(while he lay in bed)." You can tell he was awake because he "kept his eyes closed," meaning he was making an effort not to open them. A person asleep or looking out the window would not be described this way.

2. The description of what the boy is thinking about suggests that

    (1) he does not want to wake up
    (2) he is under a magic spell
    (3) he is going mad
    (4) he is daydreaming about winter
    (5) he is frightened

Answer: **(4) he is daydreaming about winter**

Explanation: This is an example of a question about inferential comprehension. The information needed to answer the question is provided but not stated directly. Here you must understand that he is thinking about something that is not really happening. The mention of snow helps you to understand what he imagines. However, the clear day, which he sees out the window, is the reality of the situation.

3. According to the information in this passage, which of the following would this boy enjoy most?

    (1) staying in bed until noon
    (2) playing in the snow
    (3) having a vacation at the beach
    (4) being a postman
    (5) seeing the streets clean

Answer: **(2) playing in the snow**

Explanation: This is an example of an application question. You must first understand that the boy is wishing it were winter. Then you can decide which thing he would most like to do, even though it is not directly mentioned in the passage. You will need to be careful of misleading choices, such as options (4) and (5), which do refer to something mentioned in the passage. Read carefully.

4. The author helps you to understand what the boy is thinking about by

    (1) using the word "winter"
    (2) saying that he jumped out of bed
    (3) referring to a miracle
    (4) using the word "actuality"
    (5) using such words as "ice" and "snow-sheathed"

Answer: **(5) using such words as "ice" and "snow-sheathed"**

Explanation: This is an example of an analysis question. You must determine the answer by using information that is not clearly stated in the passage. In this case, the author uses words we all associate with winter.

The *Steck-Vaughn GED Series* helps you develop the necessary skills by giving detailed explanations for the answers to every question in the book. All options, correct and incorrect, are accounted for.

Test-Taking Skills

Most people become nervous when they are faced with taking a test. Try to keep yourself as calm and relaxed as possible. Treat preparation for the GED as you would preparation for an important job interview. Feel good about yourself. Get plenty of sleep the night before the test, and have a good meal before you take the test. Wear something comfortable, because you will be sitting for a long time. Be sure to take important items, such as your watch or tissues, because you will not be allowed to leave your seat while the test is in progress.

Answering the Test Questions

The GED is not the kind of test you can "cram" for. You will be tested on your reading skills, not on specific information that you can know about beforehand. There are, however, some ways you can improve your performance on the test. (It would be helpful to practice some of these as you work through this book.)

♦ Never skim the instructions. Read the directions carefully so that you know exactly what you are being asked to do. For example, you do not want to circle answers if you are supposed to be filling in the circles. If you are unsure, ask the test-giver if the directions can be explained.

♦ First skim the reading passage to get a general idea of what it is about and read the questions through once. Then go back and read the passage carefully before answering the questions.

♦ Be sure to read all the options closely, even if you think you know the right answer. Some answers may not necessarily seem wrong. However, one answer will be better than the others.

♦ Try to answer as many questions as you can. Wrong answers will not be subtracted from your score. If you cannot find one correct answer, eliminate all the answers you positively know are wrong. Now the number of possible correct answers is smaller. Then read the passage again to see if you can find the correct answer. If you still cannot find the correct answer, as a last resort, make your best guess.

♦ Remember that this is a timed test. Do not take a long time on each question. Answer each question as best you can and go on. If you finish before the time is up, go back to the questions you were unsure of and give them more thought.

Test-Taking Tips for the Interpreting Literature and the Arts Test

- When you read to find the main idea, if you do not find a directly stated main idea, it is probably implied in the details and examples. To understand the unstated main idea, ask yourself the following questions: Who is doing something? What is being done? When is it happening? Where is it happening? Why is it being done? These questions will help you find the details that will add up to the main idea.

- Remember that restating an idea does not mean just repeating it. Each time the author adds another detail or example, the central idea of the passage is made clearer. Each supporting detail helps you to understand the author's purpose. The details help to bring the idea to life, much as the adding of color to a black and white cartoon makes it more exciting.

- When you are trying to draw a conclusion from the reading passage, you will have to use reasoning skills as well as comprehension skills. Before you come to a conclusion, be sure to identify the main idea and determine the meaning of unfamiliar words from the context.

- A writer's choice of style and structure depends on the subject being presented and the attitude the author has about the subject. As you read, ask yourself why the writer chose certain words and why the ideas were organized into a certain pattern.

- When reading to determine the mood of a passage, try to imagine yourself in the scene or situation. How would you feel? Imagine yourself as several of the characters. Would you feel the same as each one?

- When you are asked to read a poem, pay attention to the details in the same way you would if you were reading a passage from a novel or short story.

- When you read a passage from a play, pay attention to the stage directions, even if the questions do not ask you to. The stage directions can give you information about the characters and the situation.

And last but not least:

- Before you answer a question, be sure you have found evidence in the reading passage that supports your choice. Do not rely on things you know outside the context of the passage.

Study Skills

Organize your time.

- If you can, set aside an hour every day to study. If you do not have time every day, set up a schedule of the days you can study and stick to that schedule. Be sure to pick a time when you will be the most relaxed and least likely to be bothered by outside distractions.

- Let others know your study time. Ask them to leave you alone for that period. It helps to explain to others why this is important.

- You should be relaxed when you study, so find an area that is comfortable and quiet. If this is not possible at home, go to a local library. Many libraries have areas for reading and studying. If there is a college or university near you, check the library there. Most college libraries have spaces set aside for studying.

Organize your study materials.

- Be sure to have sharp pencils, pens, and paper for any notes you might want to take.

- Keep all of your books together. If you are taking an adult education class, you probably will be able to borrow some books or other study material. Keep them separate from your own books so that there is no mix-up.

- Make a separate notebook or folder for each subject you are studying. A folder with pockets is useful for storing loose papers.

- If you can study at home, keep all of your material near your study area so you will not waste time looking for it each time you study.

Read!

- Read the newspaper, read magazines, read books. Read whatever appeals to you—but read! If it sounds as though this idea has been repeated a lot, you are right. Reading is the most important thing you can do to prepare for the tests.

- Go to your local library. If you are not familiar with the library, ask the librarian for help. If you are not sure what to read, ask the librarian to suggest something. Be sure to tell the librarian the kinds of things you are interested in. Ask for a library card if you do not have one.

- Try to read something new every day.

Take notes.

- Take notes on things that interest you or things that you think might be useful.

- When you take notes, do not simply copy the words directly from the book. Restate the information in your own words.

- You can take notes any way you want. You do not have to write in full sentences. Just be sure that you will be able to understand your notes later.

- Use outlines, charts, or diagrams to help you organize information and make it easier to learn.

- You may want to take notes in a question-and-answer form, such as: What is the main idea? The supporting details are . . .

Improve your vocabulary.

- As you read, do not skip over a word you do not know. Instead, try to figure out what the difficult word means. First, omit it from the sentence. Read the sentence without the word and try to put another word in its place. Is the meaning of the sentence the same?

- Make a list of unfamiliar words, look them up in the dictionary, and write down the meanings.

- Since a word may have several meanings, it is best to look up the word while you have the passage with you. You can then try out the different meanings in the sentence.

- When you read the definition of a word, restate it in your own words. Use the word in a sentence or two.

Make a list of subject areas that give you trouble.

- As you go through this book, make a note whenever you do not understand something.

- Go back and review the problem when you have time.

- If you are taking a class, ask the teacher for special help with the problem areas.

Use the glossary at the end of this book to review the meanings of the key terms.

- All of the words you see in boldface type are defined in the back of the book.

- In addition, definitions of other important words are included.

Self-Inventory of Study Skills

Ask yourself the following questions:

- Am I organized?
- Do I have a study schedule?
- Do I stick to my study schedule?
- Do I have a place to study?
- Do I have a place for my study material?
- Do I have a notebook and a pencil or pen?
- Do I read something at least once a day?
- Do I take notes on what I read?
- Do I review my notes later?
- Do I pay attention to words I don't know?
- Do I look up words in the dictionary and write down their meanings?
- Do I know where my local public library is?
- Do I have a library card so that I can check out books to read?
- Do I keep a list of things that give me trouble?
- Do I ask for help when I need it?

If you said yes to all the questions, good for you! If there were a few no's, why not give those areas a try?

PRETEST

Interpreting Literature and the Arts

Directions

The Interpreting Literature and the Arts Pretest consists of excerpts from classical and popular literature and articles about literature or the arts. Each excerpt is followed by multiple-choice questions about the reading material.

Read each excerpt first and then answer the questions following it. Refer back to the reading material as often as necessary in answering the questions.

Each excerpt is preceded by a "purpose question." The purpose question gives a reason for reading the material. Use these purpose questions to help focus your reading. You are not required to answer these purpose questions. They are given only to help you concentrate on the ideas presented in the reading materials.

You should spend no more than 65 minutes answering the questions on this pretest. Work carefully, but do not spend too much time on any one question. Be sure you answer every question. You will not be penalized for incorrect answers.

Record your answers on the answer sheet provided on page 276 or on a separate piece of paper. Be sure all requested information is properly recorded on the answer sheet. To record your answers, mark the numbered space on the answer sheet beside the number that corresponds to the question on the pretest. You may make extra copies of page 276.

Example: It was Susan's dream machine. The metallic blue paint gleamed, and the sporty wheels were highly polished. Under the hood, the engine was no less carefully cleaned. Inside, flashy lights illuminated the instruments on the dashboard, and the seats were covered by rich leather upholstery.

The subject ("It") of this excerpt is most likely

(1) an airplane
(2) a stereo system
(3) an automobile
(4) a boat
(5) a motorcycle

The correct answer is "an automobile"; therefore, answer space 3 would be marked on the answer sheet.

Do not rest the point of your pencil on the answer sheet while you are considering your answer. Make no stray or unnecessary marks. If you change an answer, erase your first mark completely. Mark only one answer space for each question; multiple answers will be scored as incorrect. Do not fold or crease your answer sheet.

Pretest

Directions: Choose the best answer to each item.

Items 1 to 5 refer to the following passage from a play.

WHY IS ENID SO WORRIED?

ENID: One thing is certain—if you can't go back to school till July,
you sure as hell are going to get a job.

PAUL: W-what d-do you mean?

ENID: Work, my boy—a position—some way of contributing to the
(5)   present and preparing for the future.

PAUL (*Scared*): Like w-what?

ENID: You don't think this is how we like it? For you to piddle away
your years locked in your bedroom with silk handkerchiefs
disappearing up your sleeves.

(10) PAUL: I'll find a job.

ENID: What? What specifically will you do?

PAUL (*Takes a step backwards toward the table*): I d-don't know yet.

ENID: That's what I thought. You've never even given any thought
to a position or goal? (*She picks up her drink*)

(15) PAUL: N-no . . . except . . .

ENID (*Interested*): Yes?

PAUL: T-to b-be a m-magician.

ENID: Oh, well, that's the best news I've had all week. Paul, are you
aware I can't support us forever? What do you envision

(20)   happening when your father moves out with his little tramp?

PAUL: I said I'd f-find a job.

ENID: A magician is hardly what I had in mind for your life's work.

PAUL: If he l-leaves, will you r-remarry?

ENID: Sure. Immediately. First day. Why? You have someone for me?

(25) PAUL: N-no, I don't m-mean that.

ENID: Where do you think I should go to meet new men? What
should I do, grab them off the floor at Macy's?

1. If Paul had said he wanted to be a singer, his mother would probably

    (1) support him enthusiastically
    (2) ask him to sing something for her
    (3) arrange for an audition with a record producer
    (4) reject his idea as impractical
    (5) tell his father to discuss it with him

2. From what you know about Paul in this passage, which of these jobs would <u>not</u> be suitable for him?

    (1) word processor
    (2) librarian
    (3) radio announcer
    (4) clerk in a magic store
    (5) typist

3. The author uses Paul's stutter to show that he

    (1) is a good magician
    (2) doesn't like his mother
    (3) doesn't want to get a job
    (4) fears losing his father
    (5) lacks confidence

4. From what you know about Enid in this passage, what will she probably do when she sees her husband?

    (1) say she wants to plan a vacation
    (2) ask him for money
    (3) welcome him warmly
    (4) tell him to help Paul with his tricks
    (5) tell him that she has met another man

5. Enid's remark about "piddle away your years" (lines 7–9) shows that she

    (1) hates Paul for his laziness
    (2) respects Paul's ability to do magic tricks
    (3) is worried about her son's future
    (4) has been planning to get rid of her son
    (5) wants to protect her son from the world

WHAT IS THIS MAN REMEMBERING?

My Cousin Agatha

to Jesús Villalpando

My godmother used to invite my cousin Agatha
to spend the day with us
and my cousin would arrive
dressed in a contradiction
(5) of starch and terrible
ceremonious black.

Agatha would appear, rustling
with starch, and her green
eyes and ruddy cheeks
(10) protected me against the awful
black . . .

I was young
and knew the *o* by its roundness,
and Agatha knitting
(15) meekly and perseveringly in the echoing
corridor gave me
unknown chills . . .
(I'm sure to this day I owe to her
my heroically insane habit of talking alone.)

(20) At dinnertime, in the quiet
half-light of the dining room,
I was captivated by a brittle
intermittent ringing of dishes
and the endearing timbre
(25) of my cousin's voice.

Agatha was
(black, green pupils and ruddy
cheeks) a polychrome basket
of apples and grapes
(30) on the ebony of an aged cabinet.

6. Which of the following statements best describes the relationship of the speaker in the poem to Agatha?

    (1) Agatha was about the same age as the speaker.
    (2) Agatha was much younger than the speaker.
    (3) Agatha was much older than the speaker.
    (4) Agatha was much older than the godmother.
    (5) Agatha appeared to be both younger and older than the speaker.

7. How did the speaker in the poem feel toward Agatha when she was knitting?

    (1) The speaker hated her.
    (2) The speaker thought she was funny.
    (3) The speaker loved her.
    (4) The speaker felt a little afraid of her.
    (5) The speaker was angry at her.

8. Which of these is true about Agatha?

    (1) She lived with the speaker's godmother.
    (2) She was an occasional guest at the house where the speaker lived.
    (3) She taught the speaker to write.
    (4) She kept house for the speaker and his godmother.
    (5) She replaced the speaker's godmother.

9. Which statement best sums up the main idea of the poem?

    (1) The speaker was fascinated by Agatha.
    (2) The speaker did not understand the friendship between Agatha and the speaker's godmother.
    (3) The speaker became insane when Agatha came to visit.
    (4) Agatha was the speaker's best friend.
    (5) Agatha was like a mother to the speaker.

10. The speaker in the poem compares Agatha to

    (1) apples and grapes
    (2) starch and black
    (3) the letter *o*
    (4) the sound of dishes rattling
    (5) quiet half-light

11. Which of the following is the best meaning for "polychrome" (line 28)?

    (1) fragile
    (2) mysterious
    (3) old
    (4) colorful
    (5) frightening

Items 12 to 17 refer to the following passage.

WHAT DOES HUCK LEARN ABOUT THE MEANING OF "FEUD"?

One day Buck and me was away out in the woods, hunting, and heard a horse coming. We was crossing the road. Buck says:

"Quick! Jump for the woods!"

We done it, and then peeped down the woods through the
(5) leaves. Pretty soon a splendid young man come galloping down the road, setting his horse easy and looking like a soldier. He had his gun across his pommel. I had seen him before. It was young Harney Shepherdson. I heard Buck's gun go off at my ear, and Harney's hat tumbled off from his head. He grabbed his gun and rode straight to
(10) the place where we was hid. But we didn't wait. We started through the woods on a run. The woods warn't thick, so I looked over my shoulder, to dodge the bullet, and twice I seen Harney cover Buck with his gun; and then he rode away the way he come—to get his hat, I reckon, but I couldn't see. We never stopped running till we
(15) got home. The old gentleman's eyes blazed a minute—'twas pleasure, mainly, I judged—then his face sort of smoothed down, and he says, kind of gentle:

"I don't like that shooting from behind a bush. Why didn't you step into the road, my boy?"

(20) "The Shepherdsons don't, father. They always take advantage."

Miss Charlotte she held her head up like a queen while Buck was telling his tale, and her nostrils spread and her eyes snapped. The two young men looked dark, but never said nothing. Miss Sophia she turned pale, but the color came back when she found the
(25) man warn't hurt.

Soon as I could get Buck down by the corncribs under the trees by ourselves, I says?

"Did you want to kill him, Buck?"

"Well, I bet I did."

(30) "What did he do to you?"

"Him? He never done nothing to me."

"Well, then, what did you want to kill him for?"

"Why, nothing—only it's on account of the feud."

"What's a feud?"

(35) "Why, where was you raised? Don't you know what a feud is?"

"Never heard of it before—tell me about it."

"Well," says Buck, "a feud is this way. A man has a quarrel with another man, and kills him; then that other man's brother kills *him*; then the other brothers, on both sides, goes for one
(40) another; then the *cousins* chip in—and by-and-by everybody's killed off, and there ain't no more feud. But it's kind of slow, and takes a long time."

"Has this one been going on long, Buck?"

"Well, I should *reckon!* It started thirty years ago, or som'ers

(45) along there. There was trouble about something, and then a lawsuit to settle it; and the suit went agin one of the men, and so he up and shot the man that won the suit—which he would naturally do, of course. Anybody would."

12. How do the events of the first half of the passage relate to the ideas in the second half?

(1) as a commentary on them
(2) as a contradiction to them
(3) as an argument against them
(4) as an introduction to them
(5) as a distraction from them

13. The two boys are chased by

(1) an older brother of Buck's
(2) the son of a rival family
(3) the old gentleman
(4) an underage soldier
(5) the local sheriff

14. From Sophia's reaction, it is clear that she

(1) cares about Harney
(2) wishes Harney dead
(3) finds the feud boring
(4) wishes she were a boy
(5) admires her brother

15. According to Buck, a feud

(1) has its own rules and codes of conduct
(2) is lots of fun for everyone
(3) has nothing to do with him
(4) is something that Huck should join
(5) is better than a lawsuit

16. The character who does not fulfill the role in the feud that Buck expects is

(1) Huck, because he does not know what a feud is
(2) the old gentleman, because he is pleased with Buck
(3) Harney Shepherdson, because he does not shoot at Buck
(4) Charlotte, because she does not want to hear about the incident
(5) Sophia, because she turns pale

17. No direct value judgment is made about feuds. How do you think the author regards them?

(1) as too bad but necessary
(2) as a test of family honor
(3) as an exercise in manhood
(4) as proof of family loyalty
(5) as foolish and wasteful

DOES ELVIS PRESLEY LIVE ON TV?

On the money would not be a bad little signifier for ABC's new half-hour drama, *Elvis*, or at least for its applicability to late '80s/early
(5) '90s thought. Not that I don't worship and revere the program like unto the gospel of a living god. I do. In fact, my feeling is that American children should be
(10) required to watch *Elvis*, the TV series, while being forcibly made to consume large quantities of Batman: The Cereal and wearing swimwear designed by Jerry
(15) Hall. You've got to have a dream, after all. Or what would be really avant is if we began to designate things as *Elvis*, which were not only not the real thing, but
(20) actually bore no relationship to the real Elvis whatsoever, as in "Honey, did you remember to pick up Elvis the milk?" "No, sweetheart, I'll get it on my way
(25) home from Elvis the group therapy. Should I wear these pants with Elvis the belt, or just plain?" Only then would I feel our culture to be truly owning up to
(30) the Elvis that lies just beneath the surface in us all.

But I digress. My point is that I can't help noticing that a certain *materialism* has crept
(35) into this particular version of the greatest story ever told. And I'm sure, given the post-MTV, the corporate, steel-wheels-they-keep-on-turnin' direction of late-
(40) 20th century rock, it makes sense to the youth of today that Elvis had to become a rock star because his Mama needed a new couch and his Daddy hurt his

(45) back too bad to keep working and he was haunted by the memory of when Vernon forged a check and got thrown in jail. Why else would anyone go into that
(50) particular line of work? ABC obviously can't think of a reason—the first two episodes deal with the age-old conflict of whether one's monetary
(55) responsibility to one's family can be better served by becoming an electrician or taking a chance that your record might be a hit, you know, that old overtime
(60) versus rehearsal-time thing that played such hell with the nascent careers of all the greats, especially Phil Collins.

Still, it makes great
(65) television. While not filmed in the pure lucid-nightmare style of *thirtysomething*, it looks unlike most TV enough to have been hailed (by critics) as seeming
(70) "like a finely crafted, detailed movie" and described (by my roommate) as "having the heightened perfectness of a Steven Spielberg movie that went
(75) through the trash compactor." I leave it to you to assign value judgments to these quotes—I can only say, with all the authority of the visually insensitive, that it
(80) looks okay to me, kinda like MTV, with tight close-ups of people's shoes and stuff. I like the pink writing they use for the title. Pink is my favorite color.

18. How does the author feel about the *Elvis* show?

    (1) The author really likes the show.
    (2) The author thinks it's the best show on TV today.
    (3) The author thinks it's true to life.
    (4) The author doesn't like the actor who plays Elvis.
    (5) The author thinks it doesn't tell the true story about Elvis.

19. The author thinks that ABC does not understand

    (1) how to make a good TV show
    (2) what happened to Elvis in his later life
    (3) why Elvis became a rock and roll singer
    (4) the importance of MTV
    (5) Elvis's parents

20. By saying "Not that I don't worship and revere the program like unto the gospel of a living god. I do" (lines 5–8), the author is

    (1) making fun of Elvis
    (2) making fun of the show
    (3) rejecting material values
    (4) praising the talent of Elvis
    (5) praising ABC

21. The author thinks the show looks about the same as

    (1) a finely crafted movie
    (2) the show *thirtysomething*
    (3) a Steven Spielberg movie
    (4) a nightmare
    (5) MTV

22. The author implies that Elvis became a rock star

    (1) because he wanted to be like Phil Collins
    (2) because he wanted to leave home
    (3) for reasons other than those given on the show
    (4) to avoid being thrown in jail
    (5) because he could not be an electrician

23. The author feels that by using such terms as "Elvis the belt" (lines 27–28), we would be saying that Elvis is

    (1) part of our popular culture
    (2) alive
    (3) of no importance
    (4) well dressed
    (5) a hit TV show

HOW DOES PURA FE MAKE A NEW KIND OF MUSIC?

The scene is Brooklyn's Prospect Park amphitheater: the summer night is cool, the moon an elegant sliver. Across the stage waft clouds of sage as members of Pura Fe, a Native American jazz-fusion ensemble, prepare for a performance, burning herbs and circling
(5) together backstage in prayer. Dressed in beads, vests and other traditional garb, the seven musicians look as if they're pioneer folk, but their music—plaintive Indian chants jazzily arranged for three female voices and syncopated with flutes, drums, rattles and bells— sounds surprisingly hip; in fact, many of their tunes could easily
(10) slip onto the pop charts, sandwiched somewhere between Ladysmith Black Mambazo's South African gospel and the more jazz-oriented licks of Take 6. Their lyrics, however, set Pura Fe apart from the mainstream. With an ear tuned to history, they have adapted songs and chants they learned from their grandparents, from other elders
(15) at powwows, and even from their own visions and dreams. "We are not relics. . . not souvenirs . . . not echoes of the past" goes one song. ". . . We are here and now/proud Indian nation/with ancestor spirits . . . together the power of prayer/brings the medicine back."

Ten years ago, an Indian-arts group like Pura Fe—grounded in
(20) tradition but artistically progressive—would have been unthinkable in contemporary America. Victimized by a racial repression that proved nearly fatal, whole generations of Native Americans either denied their identity out of shame or retreated into tribal separatism. It wasn't until 1978 that the American Indian Religious
(25) Freedom Act even allowed native peoples to practice—in public or in private—their spiritual rituals. But the youngest generation of Native American performance artists, actively challenging stereotypes and discrimination, are finding new ways to connect with their heritage and still remain urban. By establishing themselves
(30) as caretakers of a culture that has been all but lost, they have become a bridge between two seemingly incongruous worlds.

The music of the Pura Fe ensemble is not just by Indians for Indians, insists Frank Menusan, who came to perform the music of his ancestry only after an in-depth study of music and instruments
(35) from other cultures. Among the instruments he plays professionally are the East Indian sitar and vina, the Turkish oud and string lutes from Afghanistan, as well as all kinds of Latin percussion. While the Pura Fe groups uses only authentic Indian instruments such as peyote rattles, tree-trunk drums, pre-Columbian ocharinas and
(40) Amerindian flutes, it's Menusan's wide-ranging musicianship that brings a freshness to the group's arrangements. "We are trying very hard to keep the integrity of our music," he says, "while opening it up to be more universal. A lot of people, even Indians, have stereotyped their own music as a monotonous drumbeat with a lot of

(45) wailing. But we received the blessings from elders of many tribal affiliations who believe in what we're doing and condone it. If it touches them, they say, they're sure it will touch others."

24. One way that Pura Fe creates a new sound is by

  (1) using only traditional Indian instruments
  (2) singing plaintive chants
  (3) using jazzy arrangements
  (4) rejecting syncopation
  (5) using instruments from Asian countries, such as the sitar

25. The author compares Pura Fe to Ladysmith Black Mambazo and Take 6 (lines 10–12) in order to

  (1) say that Pura Fe is better than both groups
  (2) give an idea of what Pura Fe's music sounds like
  (3) suggest to Pura Fe the sounds they should imitate
  (4) make fun of Pura Fe's attempts to sound hip
  (5) tell whose music Pura Fe has adapted

26. Which of the following words best reflects the author's opinion of Pura Fe's music?

  (1) interesting
  (2) romantic
  (3) authentic
  (4) slow
  (5) boring

27. According to the review, if Pura Fe heard a traditional Indian chant they had not heard before, they might

  (1) play it using Turkish and Afghani instruments
  (2) arrange it in a modern style
  (3) teach it to their grandparents and other elders
  (4) play it to educate the audience about Indian history
  (5) play it only for other Indians

28. The author includes some information about Native Americans in order to

  (1) explain why Pura Fe has been prohibited from performing until now
  (2) influence the reader to feel sorry for Pura Fe
  (3) explain how Pura Fe developed a unique style
  (4) explain why Pura Fe uses instruments from other countries in their arrangements
  (5) show how Pura Fe fits into the youngest generation of Native Americans

Items 29 to 33 refer to the following excerpt from a play.

DO MAGS AND FANNY VIEW DADDY IN THE SAME WAY?

FANNY: (*pulling* MAGS *next to her onto the sofa*) I'm so glad you're finally here, Mags. I'm very worried about Daddy.

MAGS: Mummy, please, I just got here.

FANNY: He's getting quite gaga.

(5) MAGS: Mummy! . . .

FANNY: You haven't seen him in almost a year. Two weeks ago he walked through the front door of the Codmans' house, kissed Emily on the cheek and settled down in the maid's room, thinking he was home!

(10) MAGS: Oh come on, you're exaggerating.

FANNY: He's as mad as a hatter and getting worse every day! It's this damned new book of his. He works on it around the clock. I've read some of it, and it doesn't make one word of sense, it's all at 6s and 7s . . .

29. Fanny blames Daddy's behavior on

(1) the fact that Mags has not seen him for almost a year
(2) the fact that he is moving to a new house
(3) his new book
(4) Emily Codman
(5) herself

30. Fanny shows by her words that she wants to

(1) impress Mags with Daddy's book
(2) leave Daddy in someone else's care
(3) convince Mags that Daddy needs help
(4) get Mags to leave again soon
(5) get out more socially with Daddy

31. Mags shows by her words that she wants to

    (1) deny Fanny's worries about Daddy
    (2) read Daddy's book
    (3) have a long talk with Fanny
    (4) move back home
    (5) believe Fanny about Daddy

32. As evidence for her conclusions about Daddy, Fanny says that he

    (1) mistook his neighbor's house for his own home
    (2) works on his book night and day
    (3) spends time counting by 6s and 7s
    (4) pays no attention to her
    (5) has ignored his daughter for a year

33. From the evidence given in this passage, you can infer that

    (1) Fanny may be the one who needs help
    (2) Daddy may in fact be going senile
    (3) Mags is imagining this whole scene
    (4) Emily Codman is trying to cause trouble for Fanny
    (5) Daddy wants to leave Fanny

Items 34 to 39 refer to the following passage.

WHAT DO YOU THINK OF WHEN YOU HEAR AN OLD SONG?

"On second thought," said Helen, "I want to sing one for Francis for buying me that flower. Does your friend know 'He's Me Pal,' or 'My Man'?"

"You hear that, Joe?"

(5) "I hear," said Joe the piano man, and he played a few bars of the chorus of "He's Me Pal," as Helen smiled and stood and walked to the stage with an aplomb and grace befitting her reentry into the world of music, the world she should never have left, oh why did you leave it, Helen? She climbed the three steps to the platform,

(10) drawn upward by familiar chords that now seemed to her to have always evoked joy, chords not from this one song but from an era of songs, thirty, forty years of song that celebrated the splendors of love, and loyalty, and friendship, and family, and country, and the natural world. Frivolous Sal was a wild sort of devil, but wasn't she

(15) dead on the level too? Mary was a great pal, heaven-sent on Christmas morning, and love lingers on for her. The new-mown hay, the silvery moon, the home fires burning, these were sanctuaries of Helen's spirit, songs whose like she had sung from her earliest days, songs that endured for her as long as the classics she had commit-

(20) ted to memory . . . in her youth, for they spoke to her, not abstractly of the aesthetic peaks of the art she had once hoped to master, but directly, simply, about the everyday currency of the heart and soul. The pale moon will shine on the twining of our hearts. My heart is stolen, lover dear, so please don't let us part. Oh love, sweet love, oh

(25) burning love—the songs told her—you are mine, I am yours, forever and a day. You spoiled the girl I used to be, my hope has gone away. Send me away with a smile, but remember: you're turning off the sunshine of my life.

Love.

(30) A flood tide of pity rose in Helen's breast. Francis, oh sad man, was her last great love, but he wasn't her only one. Helen has had a lifetime of sadnesses with her lovers. Her first true love kept her in his fierce embrace for years, but then he loosened that embrace and let her slide down and down until the hope within her died. Hope-

(35) less Helen, that's who she was when she met Francis. And as she stepped up to the microphone on the stage of The Gilded Cage, hearing the piano behind her, Helen was a living explosion of unbearable memory and indomitable joy.

34. When Helen sings she imagines she is singing

    (1)   to Francis about her sorrow
    (2)   a song her mother used to sing
    (3)   a song she never knew before
    (4)   a song about a pale moon
    (5)   an era of songs celebrating love

35. As used in line 22, what does "currency" mean?

    (1)   the money Helen makes singing
    (2)   the value of the heart and soul
    (3)   the cost of her musical education
    (4)   her standard of living
    (5)   the money Francis spent on flowers

36. Which of the following characteristics best describe Helen?

    (1)   pathetic but proud
    (2)   young and pretty
    (3)   jolly and off key
    (4)   foolish and loud
    (5)   hopeful but naive

37. With which of the following statements would the author most likely agree?

    (1)   Helen should never have given up music.
    (2)   Helen's life is better than the lives in songs.
    (3)   It was all for the best that Helen gave up singing.
    (4)   Those old songs are all sad.
    (5)   Old songs are not worth taking seriously.

38. The author uses the phrase "unbearable memory and indomitable joy" (line 38) to emphasize that

    (1)   Helen has not sung before
    (2)   Francis changed Helen's life
    (3)   Helen is fooling herself
    (4)   Helen is too romantic
    (5)   Francis is a happy man

39. If Francis were in trouble, Helen would probably

    (1)   write a song for him
    (2)   give up the situation as hopeless
    (3)   leave him for a man she could lean on
    (4)   try to get her past lover to help him
    (5)   try to help him

Items 40 to 45 refer to the following passage.

WHY DOES LEE CHONG MAKE A DEAL WITH MACK?

Lee Chong stiffened ever so slightly when Mack came in and his eyes glanced quickly about the store to make sure that Eddie or Hazel or Hughes or Jones had not come in too and drifted away among the groceries.

(5) Mack laid out his cards with a winning honesty. "Lee," he said, "I and Eddie and the rest heard you own the Abbeville place."

Lee Chong nodded and waited.

"I and my friends thought we'd ast you if we could move in there. We'll keep up the property," he added quickly. "Wouldn't let

(10) anybody break in or hurt anything. Kids might knock out the windows, you know—" Mack suggested. "Place might burn down if somebody don't keep an eye on it."

Lee titled his head back and looked into Mack's eyes through the half-glasses and Lee's tapping finger slowed its tempo as he

(15) thought deeply. In Mack's eyes there was good will and good fellowship and a desire to make everyone happy. Why then did Lee Chong feel slightly surrounded? Why did his mind pick its way as delicately as a cat through cactus? It had been sweetly done, almost in a spirit of philanthropy. Lee's mind leaped ahead at the

(20) possibilities—no, they were probabilities, and his finger tapping slowed still further. He saw himself refusing Mack's request and he saw the broken glass from the windows. Then Mack would offer a second time to watch over and preserve Lee's property—and at the second refusal, Lee could smell the smoke, could see the little

(25) flames creeping up the walls. Mack and his friends would try to help to put it out. Lee's finger came to a gentle rest on the change mat. He was beaten. He knew that. There was left to him only the possibility of saving face and Mack was likely to be very generous about that. Lee said, "You like pay lent my place? You like live there

(30) same hotel?"

Mack smiled broadly and he was generous. "Say—" he cried. "That's an idear. Sure. How much?"

Lee considered. He knew it didn't matter what he charged. He wasn't going to get it anyway. He might just as well make it a really

(35) sturdy face-saving sum. "Fi' dolla' week," said Lee.

Mack played it through to the end. "I'll have to talk to the boys about it," he said dubiously. "Couldn't you make that four dollars a week?"

"Fi' dolla'," said Lee firmly.

(40) "Well, I'll see what the boys say," said Mack.

And that was the way it was. Everyone was happy about it. And if it be thought that Lee Chong suffered a total loss, at least his mind did not work that way. The windows were not broken. Fire did not break out, and while no rent was ever paid, if the tenants

(45) ever had any money, and quite often they did have, it never occurred to them to spend it any place except at Lee Chong's grocery.

40. You can infer that Lee Chong makes sure that Eddie and the others are not with Mack because

(1) Lee Chong thinks they will buy out his store
(2) Lee Chong thinks they will steal groceries
(3) Lee Chong wants some excuse to avoid talking to Mack
(4) Lee Chong would ask Eddie to get rid of Mack
(5) Lee Chong wants to make a deal with Eddie and the others

41. You know from this passage that Lee Chong

(1) has never seen Mack before but knows Eddie
(2) expects to get a lot of money from Mack
(3) is naive about what Mack wants
(4) is trying to figure out what kind of man Mack is
(5) knows Mack and understands him quite well

42. When Mack offers to "keep up the property" (line 9) and ". . . keep an eye on it" (line 12), he is actually

(1) trying to strike up a friendship
(2) trying to become a community leader
(3) asking for a job
(4) threatening Lee Chong
(5) trying to cheat his friends

43. Lee Chong and Mack pretend to bargain over the deal to

(1) preserve their dignity
(2) try to cheat each other
(3) scare each other
(4) prove that they are really friends
(5) insult each other

44. If someone ever sets fire to Lee Chong's grocery, Mack and his friends will probably

(1) move out of the Abbeville place
(2) add fuel to the flames
(3) try to help put out the fire
(4) run away
(5) steal the groceries before they burn

45. The author would probably describe the deal between Lee Chong and Mack as

(1) practical
(2) immoral
(3) unfair to Mack
(4) pathetic
(5) silly

Answers and Explanations

Literature Pretest, pages 14–29

1. (Application) **(4) reject his idea as impractical** Enid is very practical about money and knows that a singer does not bring in a regular paycheck, so options (1), (2), and (3) are wrong. Enid does not count on her husband, so option (5) is incorrect.

2. (Application) **(3) radio announcer** Paul's stutter makes him unlikely to speak in public. Options (1), (2), (4), and (5) are jobs that do not require extensive public speaking.

3. (Analysis) **(5) lacks confidence** We do not know if Paul is a good magician or not, so option (1) is incorrect. Paul seems to want to please his mother and clearly wants to get a job, so options (2) and (3) are not supported by the passage. While Paul may fear losing his father, option (4), his stutter does not seem to be connected to this fact.

4. (Application) **(2) ask him for money** Enid's biggest worry is money. Because her husband is about to move out, option (3) is incorrect. Enid doesn't want Paul to be a magician, so it is unlikely she would ask her husband to help him, option (4). Options (1) and (5) are not supported by the passage.

5. (Inferential Comprehension) **(3) is worried about her son's future** Lines 7–9 show that Enid wants a good life for her son, not that she hates him, option (1), or wants to get rid of him, option (4). Option (2) is not supported by the passage. Although Enid may want to protect her son, option (5), this is not the thrust of lines 7–9.

6. (Literal Comprehension) **(3) Agatha was much older than the speaker.** The speaker says in line 12 that the speaker was young and in line 30 refers to Agatha's body as "an aged cabinet," because she dresses and acts like an adult, so options (1) and (2) are wrong. There is no evidence for options (4) or (5).

7. (Literal Comprehension) **(4) The speaker felt a little afraid of her.** The speaker says again that Agatha's knitting "gave me unknown chills" (lines 16–17). The speaker does not mention hating her, option (1), or that she was funny, option (2). Options (3) and (5) are not supported by the poem.

8. (Literal Comprehension) **(2) She was an occasional guest at the house where the speaker lived.** The answer is found in the first two lines of the poem. There is no evidence for options (1), (3), (4), and (5).

9. (Inferential Comprehension) **(1) The speaker was fascinated by Agatha.** The poem describes the impression that Agatha's visits made. The friendship between Agatha and the speaker's godmother is not described, so option (2) is wrong. Though the speaker mentions "my heroically insane habit of talking alone" (line 19), the speaker did not become insane, so option (3) is wrong. There is no support in the passage for options (4) and (5).

10. (Analysis) **(1) apples and grapes** In the last five lines of the poem, Agatha is described as a "basket of apples and grapes." Though she wore starch and black, Agatha is not described in these terms, so option (2) is wrong. Options (3), (4), and (5) are descriptions of other things in the poem, not Agatha.

11. (Inferential Comprehension) **(4) colorful** Line 27 gives a clue by mentioning the colors, black, green, and ruddy. Agatha may have been mysterious, option (2); old, option (3); and frightening, option (4); however, these do not have to do with the word "polychrome." There is no evidence that Agatha is fragile, option (1).

12. (Analysis) **(4) as an introduction to them** The incident in the woods is both an example of and an introduction to the ideas in the final three paragraphs. Options (1), (2), (3), and (5) do not describe this relationship.

13. (Literal Comprehension) **(2) the son of a rival family** Though he looks like a soldier, option (4), we know it is a young local civilian because the boys know his name (line 7). Options (1), (3), and (5) are not supported by the passage.

14. (Inferential Comprehension) **(1) cares about Harney** Sophia turns pale (line 24) when she thinks Harney might have been hurt, telling us that she cares for him. There is no evidence for options (2), (3), (4), and (5) in the passage.

15. (Literal Comprehension) **(1) has its own rules and codes of conduct** Buck does not say that he likes the feud, so options (2) and (5) are incorrect. He is clearly involved, but he never asks Huck to join, so options (3) and (4) are wrong.

16. (Inferential Comprehension) **(3) Harney Shepherdson, because he does not shoot at Buck** Although Buck is surprised that Huck does not know about feuds, he does not expect Huck to have a role, so option (1) is wrong. The male characters are not surprised at Charlotte's or Sophia's actions so options (4) and (5) are incorrect. Option (2) is the expected role of the old gentleman.

17. (Inferential Comprehension) **(5) as foolish and wasteful** Though Buck's family would agree with options (1), (2), (3), and (4), Bucks own description of the meaning of "feuds" (lines 35–46) reveals how foolish and wasteful the author thinks they are.

18. (Inferential Comprehension) **(5) The author thinks it doesn't tell the true story about Elvis.** The author points out how the show changes the facts about Elvis's life. Options (1), (2), and (3) are incorrect. Option (4) is not mentioned in the review.

19. (Inferential Comprehension) **(3) why Elvis became a rock and roll singer** In lines 47–50 ("Why else would anyone go into that particular line of work? ABC obviously can't think of a reason") the author suggests that ABC didn't understand Elvis's love of rock and roll. Option (1) is not supported by the passage. Options (2), (4), and (5) are incorrect.

20. (Analysis) **(2) making fun of the show** The rest of the passage shows that the author actually thinks the show is silly. The author does not describe the real Elvis, so options (1) and (4) are incorrect. Options (3) and (5) are not supported by the passage.

21. (Literal Comprehension) **(5) MTV** Options (1), (2), and (3) describe how others think the show looks; option (4) is not what the passage is about.

22. (Inferential Comprehension) **(3) for reasons other than those given on the show** Options (4) and (5) describe parts of the plot of the show, not the real Elvis. Options (1) and (2) are not supported by the passage.

23. (Literal Comprehension) **(1) part of our popular culture** Options (2), (3), (4), and (5) are not supported by the passage.

24. (Literal Comprehension) **(3) using jazzy arrangements** Options (1) and (2) name the elements of the group's traditional sound. Options (4) and (5) are not mentioned in the passage.

25. (Analysis) **(2) give an idea of what Pura Fe's music sounds like** The author says Pura Fe's tunes could be "sandwiched . . . between" the other groups' music; the author does not say Pura Fe is better, option (1), or should imitate them, option (3). Option (5) is not supported by the passage, and the author doesn't make fun of Pura Fe, option (4).

26. (Inferential Comprehension) **(1) interesting** Options (2), (4), and (5) are not supported by the passage. Although the author mentions the group's authenticity, option (3), this is not an opinion of their music.

27. (Application) **(2) arrange it in a modern style** Options (1), (3), (4), and (5) are not supported by the passage.

28. (Analysis) **(5) show how Pura Fe fits into the youngest generation of Native Americans** Options (1) and (2) are not supported by the passage. Pura Fe's musical style, options (3) and (4), have nothing to do with recent Native American history.

29. (Literal Comprehension) **(3) his new book** Daddy is *not* moving to a new house, so option (2) is incorrect. Mags, Emily Codman, and Fanny herself, are not blamed, so options (1), (4), and (5) are wrong.

30. (Inferential Comprehension) **(3) convince Mags that Daddy needs help** This is correct because she uses such words as "gaga" and "mad as a hatter." There is no evidence for option (1). Option (2) is not supported, although Fanny does seem to think Mags should spend more time at home, which also rules out option (4). Option (5) is unlikely motivation, as she would not want him to be seen in his condition.

31. (Inferential Comprehension) **(1) deny Fanny's worries about Daddy** This is correct because she makes light of Fanny's worries, which rules out option (5). Option (2) is not supported, and option (3) is wrong. Option (4) might be Fanny's wish, but Mags does not show any motivation for such a move.

32. (Literal Comprehension) **(1) mistook his neighbor's house for his own home** Although Fanny does mention Daddy working on his book, option (2), this is not given as evidence of his troubles. Options (3), (4), and (5) are not supported by the passage.

33. (Inferential Comprehension) **(2) Daddy may in fact be going senile** The incident where Daddy mistakes another house for his own is evidence that something is wrong. Although Fanny needs help, option (1), the help she needs is support from Mags. Options (3), (4), and (5) are not supported by the passage.

34. (Literal Comprehension) **(5) an era of songs celebrating love** There is no mention of singing about sorrow, option (1); nor of Helen singing a song her mother used to sing, option (2); nor a specific song about the moon, option (4). The songs are clearly ones she has known before, so option (3) is incorrect.

35. (Analysis) **(2) the value of the heart and soul** There is no mention of Helen being paid, option (1), nor of paying for anything, option (3). Her singing is not related to her standard of living, so option (4) is incorrect. She sings to thank Francis for flowers, but this does not involve currency, option (5). The author uses "currency" in line 22 to define the qualities or values of the heart.

36. (Inferential Comprehension) **(1) pathetic but proud** The last paragraph points out how hopeless Helen's life had been until she met Francis. She is proud to get up on the platform and sing. Helen could not be young, option (2), because she remembers the old songs. She does not seem jolly, option (3), and though singing, she is not foolish, option (4). Because she has lived through a great deal and looks back on the old songs, we know she is not naive, option (5).

37. (Analysis) **(1) Helen should never have given up music.** The author suggests that the world described in songs is more splendid than everyday life, making options (2), (4), and (5) incorrect. In line 8, the author writes that Helen should never have quit singing, so option (3) is wrong.

38. (Analysis) **(2) Francis changed Helen's life** The passage mentions how Francis had given Helen inspiration when she was hopeless. Option (1) is not true. The author is sympathetic to Helen, so options (3) and (4) are incorrect. Option (5) is not mentioned in the passage.

39. (Application) **(5) try to help him** It is clear that Helen feels that Francis has given her strength, so in turn she would want to help Francis. It isn't likely that Helen would give up, option (2); leave him, option (3); or seek out her past lover, option (4). No mention is made of Helen writing songs, option (1).

40. (Inferential Comprehension) **(2) Lee Chong thinks they will steal groceries** From the rest of the passage, you can tell that these people do not have much money, so option (1) is wrong. Although Lee Chong may not want to talk to Mack, options (3) and (4) are wrong because they probably would not work. Option (5) is wrong because Lee Chong clearly would rather not have to make a deal with anyone.

41. (Inferential Comprehension) **(5) knows Mack and understands him quite well** You can infer this by the way Lee Chong thinks about what Mack might do. Options (1), (2), (3), and (4) are not supported by the passage.

42. (Inferential Comprehension) **(4) threatening Lee Chong** The part of the passage giving Lee Chong's thoughts explains what Mack is doing. Mack is clearly not a friend, option (1), or a community leader, option (2). Options (3) and (5) are not supported by the passage.

43. (Literal Comprehension) **(1) preserve their dignity** The passage states that Lee Chong knows he must make a deal and wants a peaceful solution, so options (2), (3), and (5) are wrong. Lee Chong and Mack are not really friends, so option (4) is incorrect.

44. (Application) **(3) try to help put out the fire** The author explains how Mack and his friends made a deal with Lee Chong about living in the Abbeville place and protecting it. Because they want to stay there, it would be in their interest to protect Lee Chong's grocery, not harm it, so options (2) and (5) are incorrect. Options (1) and (4) are not supported by the passage.

45. (Analysis) **(1) practical** This is correct because everyone benefits from the deal. The author is not critical of the deal, so options (2) and (4) are incorrect. Options (3) and (5) are not supported by the passage.

PRETEST Correlation Chart

Interpreting Literature and the Arts

The chart below will help you determine your strengths and weaknesses in reading comprehension and in the content areas of popular and classical literature and commentary.

Directions

Circle the number of each item that you answered correctly on the Pretest. Count the number of items you answered correctly in each column. Write the amount in the Total Correct space for each column. (For example, if you answered 8 literal comprehension items correctly, place the number 8 in the blank above *out of 12*.) Complete this process for the remaining columns.

Count the number of items you answered correctly in each row. Write that amount in the Total Correct space for each row. (For example, in the Popular Literature row, write the number correct in the blank before *out of 22*.) Complete this process for the remaining rows.

Cognitive Skills / Content	Literal Comprehension	Inferential Comprehension	Application	Analysis	Total Correct
Popular Literature *(Pages 36–133)* Fiction Poetry Drama	34 6, 7, 8 29, 32	36 9, 11 5, 30, 31, 33	39 1, 2, 4	35, 37, 38 10 3	_____ out of 22
Classical Literature *(Pages 134–199)* Fiction	13, 15, 43	14, 16, 17, 40, 41, 42	44	12, 45	_____ out of 12
Commentary *(Pages 200–249)* Television Music	21, 23 24	18, 19, 22 26	27	20 25, 28	_____ out of 11
Total Correct	_____ out of 12	_____ out of 17	_____ out of 6	_____ out of 10	Total correct: ___ out of 45 1–36 → Need more review 37–45 → Congratulations! You're Ready

If you answered fewer than 45 questions correctly, determine which areas are hardest for you. Go back to the *Steck-Vaughn GED Interpreting Literature and the Arts* book and review the content in those areas. In the parentheses under the item type heading, the page numbers tell you where you can find specific instruction about that area of literature and the arts in the *Steck-Vaughn GED Interpreting Literature and the Arts* book.

POPULAR LITERATURE

♦ **fiction**
a story based on the writer's imagination; it may talk about real things, but it is not true

♦ **nonfiction**
writing that is based on facts; it is about real places, real people, or events that actually took place

So what *is* popular literature? Popular literature is what most people are reading today. When you read books or articles or short stories or poems that have been written recently, you are probably reading popular literature. If you see a play that has been written in the last few years, you are watching a play that might be called, in its written form, popular literature.

As you may have guessed already, popular literature is divided into several categories or types. As you study for the GED and when you take the GED test, you will be asked to read several kinds of writing. You will see prose **fiction** and prose **nonfiction**. (Prose is the ordinary language that is used in most writing.) In most cases, interpreting literature is simply understanding what is plainly written.

Reading the passages and answering a few questions to show you understand what you have read is the only work you will need to do. That's all. You won't need to remember any complicated terms. You won't need to know who wrote what or when it was written.

poetry
a special form of writing that is more rhythmical and imaginative than ordinary writing

drama
a story that is told through action and speech; it is meant to be performed

main idea
the most important point or central idea of a paragraph or passage

context
the ideas or descriptions that surround a word or phrase and can help to suggest its meaning

In addition to fiction and nonfiction, you will be reading and interpreting **poetry** and **drama**. If these forms of writing are less familiar to you, remember that this book is designed to teach you the skills you will need to understand what you read.

The passages in this book are similar to those you will find on the GED test. The questions you will answer are also similar to those that will appear on the test. Because understanding the passages may be difficult at first, a page of instructions and explanations is provided at the beginning of each chapter. Authors write because they have something to say. They want you to understand their ideas; they do not want to confuse you. The skills in each chapter will help you learn to understand what may at first seem complicated.

In lessons 1 and 2, you will start by reading for the author's basic meaning. The most important reading skill is knowing how to find the **main idea** of what you read. Writers make points as they go along, and these points can help you to find the main idea. Two related skills follow in lessons 3 and 4. Part of understanding what you read is being able to put it into your own words and to see when the author is repeating a basic idea. Sometimes this is difficult if the author uses a word you do not know. So, you will also learn to figure out the meaning of a word from the information around it. The **context** of a word or phrase can provide clues to how it is being used.

After you have mastered these skills, you will go on to learn how to make judgments about what you have read. You also will be introduced to the special ways authors use words to make their points.

As you go through the first unit, remember to rely on your own common sense and what you have learned from experience. If you read carefully, you will find that many of the skills come easily. Even if an area gives you trouble, don't worry. The classical literature unit will give you more opportunities for practice.

LESSON 1 Comprehension Skills: Identifying the Main Idea

When you identify the main idea, you understand the most important point an author is trying to make. The main idea can be stated at the beginning, middle, or end of a paragraph.

In many paragraphs the **main idea** is clearly stated in a single sentence. This sentence often is at the beginning or at the end of the paragraph. If it is at the beginning, then the rest of the paragraph adds details that support or explain the main idea. If it is at the end, then the details are given first and then summed up. Usually the sentence containing the main idea is more general than the other sentences. Sometimes the first and last sentences in a paragraph may seem to be details. In this case, the main idea may appear in the middle of a paragraph. When you think you have identified the main idea, see if the details in the rest of the paragraph help to support that idea.

For example, suppose that the main idea of a passage is that a divorced woman wishes she had worked harder to save her marriage. One of the supporting details might be that she now misses her husband. This detail would support the idea that she wishes her marriage were not over.

Fiction

In this lesson you will be reading from works of **fiction**. Fiction is a form of writing that tells a story. The most common works of fiction are short stories and novels. Fiction may be about any subject: romance, sports, mystery, science, history.

When you read fiction, as well as other forms of literature, you must be able to identify the main idea. As you read, ask yourself, "What is this paragraph all about?" Passages and stories also have main ideas; the best place to start to recognize them is in a paragraph.

☞ *See Also: GED Exercise Book Literature and the Arts, pages 4–9*

Practicing Comprehension, Application, and Analysis Skills

Read the following passage by Louis Auchincloss.

WHAT DOES THE FUTURE HOLD FOR MADGE?

Madge Dyett felt that the year 1937, which had marked for so many of her friends a turning point in the Great Depression, seemed only to confirm its permanent doom for herself and her parents. They continued to live in the shabby, four-story, red brick house on
(5) East Thirty-fourth Street, but only because they could not sell it, and the top floor was rented to an uncle and aunt. Her father was out of work and prattled all day, with a self-confidence that nothing could justify, of his financial prospects and plans. Madge had had to give up college and take a job teaching at Miss Fairfax's School, of
(10) which she and her mother were alumnae. Her only future seemed to be to stay there until she was old enough to retire.

Source: *Narcissa and Other Fables*.

Questions 1 and 2 refer to the passage. Circle the best answer for each question.

1. Which of the following sentences best states the main idea of the paragraph?

   (1) Madge had to help support her family by teaching.
   (2) The Great Depression forced people to sell their homes.
   (3) Madge and her parents seemed permanently doomed by the Great Depression.
   (4) Many people during the Great Depression had to live in shabby houses.
   (5) The year 1937 was a turning point in Madge's life.

2. Which of the following details does not support the main idea?

   (1) Madge and her mother had graduated from Miss Fairfax's school.
   (2) The family was unable to sell the house.
   (3) Madge had to quit college.
   (4) Mr. Dyett was out of work.
   (5) Mr. Dyett had no reason to be confident about his finances.

To check your answers, turn to page 44.

Read the following passage by Carolyn Keene.

WHAT IS THERE FOR NANCY TO WORRY ABOUT?

Hannah Gruen, coming into the dining room, knew from Nancy's expression that something was wrong.

"What is it?" she cried, "Not bad news, I hope."

Nancy showed her the warning note. "I can't imagine who could
(5) have sent it," she said, "unless it was the pickpocket."

"Oh, Nancy, I'm so worried!" the housekeeper exclaimed after she had read the anonymous message. "It must have something to do with the case you're working on. Please give up trying to help Mrs. Struthers!"

(10) "I can't let a little note like this frighten me," said Nancy. "Anyway, I think the person who sent it merely means he wants me to stay away from Wrightville."

"Then promise me you will," begged Hannah Gruen.

"All right," Nancy laughed, giving the housekeeper an affection-
(15) ate hug. "By the way, any telephone calls for me while I was in the shower?"

"One from the yacht club. A friend of yours said she was to let you know about picking up some clothes over there."

"Oh, yes," Nancy said absently. "I got a new locker and left some
(20) things in the old one. Well, I'll run out and get them now."

"Do be careful," Mrs. Gruen urged, as Nancy went out the door.

"I'll be all right," Nancy called cheerily, as she hopped into her car.

Source: *The Clue in the Old Album.*

Questions 3 and 4 refer to the passage. Circle the best answer for each question.

3. Which of the following statements best describes the main idea of the passage?

(1) Nancy never listens to what Hannah says.
(2) Hannah is worried about something that does not seem to bother Nancy.
(3) Nancy had forgotten to pick up the clothes she had left in a locker.
(4) Nancy has been frightened by a person who picked her pocket.
(5) Nancy is always cheerful and friendly.

4. Based on the information in the passage, which of the following is Nancy most likely to do?

(1) follow the instructions in the note
(2) stay at home to avoid trouble
(3) stop helping Mrs. Struthers
(4) continue to help Mrs. Struthers
(5) stop reading her mail

To check your answers, turn to page 44.

Read the following passage by Larry McMurtry.

WHY DID THE WIFE EAT IN THE LOFT?

She seldom did eat with them. It bothered July a good deal, though he made no complaint. Since their little table was almost under the loft he could look up and see Elmira's bare legs as he ate. It didn't seem normal to him. His mother had died when he was six,
(5) yet he could remember that she always ate with the family; she would never have sat with her legs dangling practically over her husband's head. He had been at supper in many cabins in his life, but in none of them had the wife sat in the loft while the meal was eaten. It was a thing out of the ordinary, and July didn't like for
(10) things to be out of the ordinary in his life. It seemed to him it was better to do as other people did—if society at large did things a certain way, it had to be for a good reason, and he looked upon common practices as rules that should be obeyed. After all, his job was to see that common practices were honored—that citizens
(15) weren't shot, or banks robbed.

Joe didn't share July's discomfort with the fact that his mother seldom came to the table. When she did come it was usually to scold him, and he got scolded enough as it was—besides, he liked eating with July. So far as he was concerned, marrying July was the best
(20) thing his mother had ever done. She scolded July as freely as she scolded him, which didn't seem right to Joe. But then July accepted it and never scolded back, so perhaps that was the way of the world.

Source: *Lonesome Dove.*

Questions 5 and 6 refer to the passage. Circle the best answer for each question.

5. Which statement best reflects the main idea of the first paragraph?

(1) July believes that common practices should be followed.
(2) Children have no right to complain about their parents.
(3) A wife should eat with her family.
(4) Bank robbers should be caught.
(5) Elmira should wear stockings during meals.

6. Which of the following details does not support the main idea in the first paragraph?

(1) July's mother had always eaten with the family.
(2) Elmira sat in the loft while her husband ate dinner.
(3) July's mother died when he was six.
(4) Most wives did not sit in the loft during a meal.
(5) July's job was to see that customs were honored.

To check your answers, turn to page 44.

GED Mini-Test

Directions: Choose the best answer to each item.

Items 1 to 6 refer to the following excerpt by John Knowles.

WHY DOES THE WAR STILL LIVE FOR THE AUTHOR?

Everyone has a moment in history which belongs particularly to him. It is the moment when his emotions achieve their most powerful sway over him, and afterward when you say to this person "the world today" or "life" or "reality" he will assume that you mean
(5) this moment, even if it is fifty years past. The world, through his unleased emotions, imprinted itself upon him, and he carries the stamp of that passing moment forever.

For me, this moment—four years is a moment in history—was the war. The war was and is reality for me. I still instinctively live
(10) and think in its atmosphere. These are some of its characteristics: Franklin Delano Roosevelt is the President of the United States, and he always has been. The other two eternal world leaders are Winston Churchill and Josef Stalin. America is not, never has been, and never will be what the songs and poems call it, a land of plenty.
(15) Nylon, meat, gasoline, and steel are rare. There are too many jobs and not enough workers. Money is very easy to earn but rather hard to spend, because there isn't very much to buy. Trains are always late and always crowded with "servicemen." The war will always be fought very far from America, and it will never end.
(20) Nothing in America stands still for very long, including the people who are always either leaving or on leave. People in America cry often. Sixteen is the key and crucial and natural age for a human being to be, and people of all other ages are ranged in an orderly manner ahead of and behind you as a harmonious setting for the
(25) sixteen-year-olds of the world. When you are sixteen, adults are slightly impressed and almost intimidated by you. This is a puzzle finally solved by the realization that they foresee your military future, fighting for them. You do not foresee it. To waste anything in America is immoral. String and tinfoil are treasures. Newspapers
(30) are always crowded with strange maps and names of towns, and every few months the earth seems to lurch from its path when you see something in the newspapers, such as the time Mussolini, who almost seemed one of the eternal leaders, is photographed hanging upside down on a meathook.

Source: *A Separate Peace*.

1. Which statement best describes the main idea of the first paragraph?

   (1) History is made by emotional people.
   (2) People should not dwell on the past.
   (3) People should be more interested in history.
   (4) Yesterday is more real than today.
   (5) Every person's life has a special moment.

2. According to the author, the war was

   (1) only four years ago
   (2) a dim memory
   (3) an immoral waste
   (4) proof that America is a land of plenty
   (5) a time that shaped his reality

3. The passage suggests that the war years affected the author as they did because

   (1) he was young and impressionable
   (2) he admired Roosevelt's policies
   (3) money was easy to get
   (4) everyone was very sad
   (5) people left America to fight

4. The main idea of the second paragraph is best described as

   (1) much different than the main idea in the first paragraph
   (2) more general than the main idea in the first paragraph
   (3) the same as the main idea in the first paragraph
   (4) unrelated to the main idea of the first paragraph
   (5) an example of the main idea in the first paragraph

5. The author helps the reader understand how he feels about the war by

   (1) explaining how the world imprints itself on people
   (2) talking about the war as if it were happening now
   (3) referring to well-known world leaders
   (4) specifically stating his emotions
   (5) making it sound romantic

6. Which of the following statements would this author be most likely to agree with?

   (1) Politics makes strange bedfellows.
   (2) There is no time like the present.
   (3) Time is something we will never understand.
   (4) Every person sees the world from a personal point of view.
   (5) Time stands still for no one.

To check your answers, turn to page 45.

Answers and Explanations

Practicing Comprehension, Application, and Analysis Skills (pages 39–41)

1. (Literal Comprehension) **(3) Madge and her parents seemed permanently doomed by the Great Depression.** This idea is stated in the first sentence. Option (1) may be true, but it is a detail, not the main idea. Options (2) and (4) may have been true, but they are not supported by the paragraph. Option (5) is untrue.

2. (Inferential Comprehension) **(1) Madge and her mother had graduated from Miss Fairfax's School.** This detail is about the school where Madge was teaching. Options (2), (3), (4), and (5) help to explain why the family seemed doomed.

3. (Literal Comprehension) **(2) Hannah is worried about something that does not seem to bother Nancy.** It is stated that Hannah is worried (line 6) and wants Nancy to be careful. Nancy is laughing and says she is not frightened (line 10), so option (4) is wrong. Option (1) is not supported by the passage. Option (3) is a detail of the story. Option (5) may be true, but it is not the main idea.

4. (Application) **(4) continue to help Mrs. Struthers** Nancy says that the note does not frighten her, so she will probably find some way to help Mrs. Struthers and solve the case. Therefore, options (1), (2), and (3) are wrong. There is no support for option (5).

5. (Literal Comprehension) **(1) July believes that common practices should be followed.** This general statement is supported by such details as those in options (3), (4), and (5). Option (2) is not supported in the passage.

6. (Literal Comprehension) **(3) July's mother died when he was six.** Options (1), (2), and (4) refer to people following social rules or people breaking them. July's job, option (5), affected his belief, which is the main idea.

1. (Literal Comprehension) **(5) Every person's life has a special moment.** This is stated in the first sentence. There is no evidence for options (1) and (4). Options (2) and (3) may be true but are not suggested in the paragraph.

2. (Literal Comprehension) **(5) a time that shaped his reality** This is stated in the second sentence of paragraph two. Options (1), (2), and (4) are contradicted in the passage. Option (3) is not suggested in the passage.

3. (Inferential Comprehension) **(1) he was young and impressionable** He seems to have seen the events from a youthful point of view; sixteen is an age when emotions are easily influenced. Options (2) and (4) may be true but are not supported. Options (3) and (5) are mentioned, but they were not the cause of the author's feelings.

4. (Literal Comprehension) **(5) an example of the main idea in the first paragraph** The phrasing of the first sentence in paragraph two points out that it is an example. Because the ideas are similar, options (1) and (4) are wrong. The second main idea is more specific, so options (2) and (3) are wrong.

5. (Analysis) **(2) talking about the war as if it were happening now** The present tense makes the war seem more immediate, as close as it seems to the author. Options (1) and (3) are mentioned but do not help to explain the author's feelings. Options (4) and (5) are false.

6. (Application) **(4) Every person sees the world from a personal point of view.** This statement is similar to the author's belief that a person is affected by certain events in life. Because people's experiences are different, their understanding of how the world works will be different. Option (1) is not suggested by the passage. Option (2) suggests the present is more important than the past, but the author is talking about the importance of the past. Option (3) is too general, and option (5) has nothing to do with what the author is saying.

LESSON 2 Comprehension Skills: Identifying an Unstated Main Idea

This skill helps you understand the most important point an author is trying to make. An unstated main idea is hinted at. We say that it is implied.

As you learned in the last lesson, most paragraphs have a main idea. However, the main idea is not always clearly stated. Sometimes there is no single key sentence that sums up the paragraph. The author wants you to grasp the idea yourself. You must figure out what the author is trying to say.

Before you look for an unstated, or implied, main idea, first make sure that the passage does not have a clearly stated main idea—a key sentence that sums up the paragraph. If not, you will need to look for an **implied main idea**—one that is suggested or hinted at without being actually stated. To do this, you must read all the information. You must infer what the author's main idea is. To **infer** means to guess based on available information.

To infer the main idea of a paragraph:

1. Decide what the paragraph is about (the topic).
2. Decide what points the details make about the topic.
3. Combine the topic with the point the details make about it.

Even when a main idea is not stated, it is still the central idea of the paragraph. It gives the paragraph a purpose because all the ideas are related to it in some way. To find an unstated main idea, look for words or phrases that seem to relate to a common topic.

You will have to think about all the details, not just one or two. Just as in an arithmetic problem, all of the statements add up to a sum. Imagine that you are trying to tell someone what you have read. Instead of repeating the minor points, you will probably sum up all the ideas in one statement. Or imagine that you have to give the paragraph a title. The title should give a clear idea of the main idea.

Practicing Comprehension, Application, and Analysis Skills

Read the following passage by Rex Stout.

WHAT HAPPENED WHEN THE DOORBELL RANG?

When the doorbell rang that Tuesday evening in September and I stepped to the hall for a look and through the one-way glass saw Inspector Cramer on the stoop, bearing a fair-sized carton, I proceeded to the door, intending to open it a couple of inches and
(5) say through the crack, "Deliveries in the rear." He was uninvited and unexpected, we had no case and no client, and we owed him nothing, so why pretend he was welcome?

But by the time I reached the door I had changed my mind. Not because of him. He looked perfectly normal—big and burly,
(10) round red face with bushy gray eyebrows, broad heavy shoulders straining the sleeve seams of his coat. It was the carton. It was a used one, the right size, the cord around it was the kind McLeod used, and the NERO WOLFE on it in blue crayon was McLeod's style of printing. Having switched the stoop light on, I could observe
(15) those details as I approached, so I swung the door open and asked politely, "Where did you get the corn?"

Source: "Murder Is Corny," from *Trio for Blunt Instruments*.

Questions 1 and 2 refer to the passage. Circle the best answer for each question.

1. Which of the following best states the main idea of the first paragraph?

   (1) Deliveries should go to the rear door.
   (2) The speaker did not want to let the man in.
   (3) The speaker is probably a private detective.
   (4) Policemen are always unwelcome visitors.
   (5) One-way glass is the best way to avoid unwelcome visitors.

2. Which of the following is the best reason why the speaker changed his mind?

   (1) He realized his first idea was very rude.
   (2) The inspector looked normal enough.
   (3) McLeod's packages were always welcome.
   (4) He was curious about the carton.
   (5) He decided to pretend the inspector was welcome.

To check your answers, turn to page 52.

Read the following passage by Diane Dwayne.

WHO IS THIS CREATURE?

One of the creatures in the front circle shook itself all over and, still shaking, moved very, very slowly toward Spock. He didn't move a muscle. The creature put out a long slender pseudopod, gleaming in the sunshine like suddenly blown glass, and poked Spock's boot

(5) with it. Then it made the scratchy sound again, more laughter, and said a word:

"Gotcha!"

It jumped back to its place. All the other creatures began to echo the scratch-laughter. Spock looked around him with mild

(10) bemusement. "Captain," he said, "I suspect we have found a kindergarten at recess, or something similar."

Source: *Star Trek: Doctor's Orders.*

Question 3 to 6 refer to the passage. Circle the best answer for each question.

3. The creature's actions suggest that it

   (1) is angry
   (2) has a sense of humor
   (3) has trouble communicating
   (4) is afraid
   (5) has a low level of intelligence

4. Which of the following would be the best title for this selection?

   (1) Self-Control
   (2) Curiosity
   (3) The Proper Care of Children
   (4) Shaking All Over
   (5) The Alien of Glass

5. Which of the following best describes the situation in the passage?

   (1) an old friendship
   (2) a terrifying encounter
   (3) a first meeting
   (4) a prearranged conference
   (5) part of a school day

6. The author uses the word "kindergarten" (line 11) to suggest that

   (1) Spock is a teacher
   (2) the Captain has been looking for a school
   (3) Spock is confused about the creatures
   (4) the creatures seem childlike to Spock
   (5) only children have scratchy laughter

To check your answers, turn to page 52.

Read the following passage by Olive Ann Burns.

WHAT DID GRANDPA BLAKESLEE'S WILL SAY?

"Now I want my burying to remind folks that death aint always awful. God invented death. Its in God's plan for it to happen. So when my time comes I do not want no trip to Birdsong's Emporium or any other. Dressing somebody up to look alive don't make it so. . . .

(5)   "I don't want no casket. Its a waste of money. What I would really like is to be wrapped up in two or three feed sacks and laid right in the ground. But that would bother you all, so use the pine box upstairs at the store that Miss Mattie Lou's coffin come in. I been saving it. . . ."

Source: *Cold Sassy Tree*.

Questions 7 to 10 refer to the passage. Circle the best answer for each question.

7. Which of the following best expresses the main idea of the selection?

  (1) The speaker does not want a fuss made at his funeral.
  (2) Death eventually happens to everyone.
  (3) Birdsong's Emporium is too expensive.
  (4) Funerals should be simple and dignified.
  (5) The speaker does not want to be dressed up after he dies.

8. Which of the following best supports Grandpa's idea of saving money?

  (1) using the box a coffin came in
  (2) storing things upstairs
  (3) going to a cheap funeral home
  (4) making clothes out of feed sacks
  (5) having an unmarked grave

9. The main idea in the second paragraph

  (1) is very different from the main idea in the first paragraph
  (2) explains why dressing up a dead person is wrong
  (3) is a good example of common sense
  (4) gives an example of the main idea of the passage
  (5) explains the reason for the man's belief

10. Grandpa Blakeslee is probably

  (1) conventional
  (2) very vain
  (3) mindful of others' expectations
  (4) not concerned about what society thinks
  (5) in the funeral business

To check your answers, turn to page 52–53.

GED Mini-Test

Directions: Choose the best answer to each item.

Items 1 to 6 refer to the following passage by Louis Auchincloss.

WHAT DO PEOPLE DO ON A CRUISE?

The Foxens, like most of the passengers, lived in the past. But it was not, Betty noted, necessarily the real past. It was rather a past that was being constantly edited, smoothed, brightened, touched up. It was a past studded with the little victories of the
(5) person who was in the process of creating it. Ned Foxen loved to relate to her how cleverly he had dealt with this or that ornery customer of his Buick agency in Rochester and how he had steered a bill to passage in the Albany assembly by playing both sides against the middle. And Roseanne enjoyed telling her how often she
(10) had been right in warning her married children not to do the things that they had then done and later regretted. The past had been purged of thorns and bitterness; it was now an unending source of complacency.

And the future? Well, of course, there was not so very much of
(15) that to look forward to. It was better to divide one's time between a semifictional past and an artificial present. The world of the cruise was a world that had abolished all the bogies of old people: the difficulty of cooking and cleaning without servants, the problem of how to use leisure time, the ache of loneliness. On board the *Stella*
(20) *Maris*, obsequious Italian stewards administered to their every need; their working hours were filled with a gentle round of cocktail parties, card parties, lectures, movies and deck games; and there was no end of ears in which to plant their reminiscences, no end of tongues to offer them those of others. It was a world in which the
(25) only imaginable task was that of mixing the drinks oneself if one entertained in one's cabin. Even death, if it came on the cruise, was easy. There were several fine coffins, inlaid with satin, ready for emergency, in the hold.

Source: *Narcissa and Other Fables*.

1. Which statement best describes the main idea of the first paragraph?

   (1) The Foxens lived in the past.
   (2) The past got better with time.
   (3) Ned Foxen loved to tell stories.
   (4) Ned Foxen was a clever man.
   (5) The Foxens were retired.

2. Why does Roseanne enjoy talking about her children's problems?

   (1) She is a mean person.
   (2) She just likes to talk.
   (3) It is her way of editing the past.
   (4) She does not have anything else to talk about.
   (5) Her children do not have good sense.

3. Which statement best describes the main idea of the second paragraph?

   (1) There is not much to do on a cruise.
   (2) Cruises are set up to fill the empty lives of old people.
   (3) Cruises are a lot of fun for young people.
   (4) Old people have many bogies.
   (5) Life on a cruise is easy.

4. Which of the following ideas would you expect the Foxens to be most likely to agree with?

   (1) Their childhoods were simple and pleasant.
   (2) Children should not go on cruises.
   (3) Drinking will lead to an easy death.
   (4) Older people tend to get lonely.
   (5) The past will always come back to haunt you.

5. Why do the people on the cruise not like to think about their future?

   (1) They are too busy having fun.
   (2) It is hard to cope without servants.
   (3) They are entertaining in their cabins.
   (4) Death will soon overtake them.
   (5) They are worried about the problems of their children.

6. Which statement does not support the main idea of the passage?

   (1) On the cruise there were stewards who administered to every need.
   (2) Mixing drinks was the only task that anyone on the cruise would ever have to do without help.
   (3) Even death was made easy for the passengers on the ship.
   (4) There was always another passenger to listen to reminiscences.
   (5) The cruise ship was named the *Stella Maris*.

To check your answers, turn to page 53.

Answers and Explanations

Practicing Comprehension, Application, and Analysis Skills (pages 47–49)

1. (Inferential Comprehension) **(2) The speaker did not want to let the man in.** The details add up to this idea. Option (1) refers to a detail, not to the main idea. Although option (3) is probably true, it is not what the paragraph is about. Options (4) and (5) cannot be inferred from the information given.

2. (Literal Comprehension) **(4) He was curious about the carton.** This is indicated by the first, second, and fourth sentences in paragraph two. Options (1) and (5) are not suggested. Option (2) is true but is not the reason the speaker opened the door. There is no evidence for option (3).

3. (Inferential Comprehension) **(2) has a sense of humor** The laughter and the speech that accompany the poke suggest that the creature is playing. The action is not threatening, so option (1) is wrong. Option (3) is wrong because speech and laughter indicate communication. There is no evidence of fear, so option (4) is wrong. Option (5) has no support.

4. (Inferential Comprehension) **(2) Curiosity** The creatures appear to be cautiously curious about Spock, and Spock appears to be curious about them. Option (1) refers only to the moment when Spock stands quite still. Option (3) does not fit the situation described. Options (4) and (5) refer only to the movement and appearance of the creature.

5. (Literal Comprehension) **(3) a first meeting** In addition to the suggestion of exploration by each group, the idea of a first meeting is supported by Spock's statement that they have "found" this group. Option (1) is wrong because the two groups are not familiar with each other. The attitudes appear friendly, so option (2) is wrong. The meeting seems unexpected, so option (4) is wrong. Option (5) refers to Spock's remark about the creatures, not to the actual situation.

6. (Analysis) **(4) the creatures seem childlike to Spock** The description creates an image of youthful play, not of adult behavior. There is no support for options (1) and (2). Option (3) is wrong because the word does not suggest confusion. Option (5) is wrong because scratchy laughter has nothing to do with kindergarten.

7. (Inferential Comprehension) **(1) The speaker does not want a fuss made at his funeral.** All the details are about avoiding anything fancy at burial. Options (2), (3), and (5) are details that help to suggest that idea. The speaker may believe funerals should be simple but does not care about dignity, so option (4) is wrong.

8. (Literal Comprehension) **(1) using the box a coffin came in** The box would cost the family nothing. Option (2) is too general. Options (3), (4), and (5) are not supported by the passage.

9. (Analysis) **(4) gives an example of the main idea of the passage** The problem of wasting money is a specific example of making too much fuss. Option (1) suggests the main ideas are opposite, which is wrong. Option (2) is not related to the idea of money. The idea in the paragraph is not really practical, so option (3) is wrong. At best, the main idea is only a partial reason for the man's belief, so option (5) is wrong.

10. (Application) **(4) not concerned about what society thinks** Option (1) is wrong because his plans are hardly conventional. Option (2) is wrong because his plans for his funeral are not at all vain. Option (3) is unlikely because Grandpa is so unconventional. Option (5) is contradicted by his opposition to conventional funerals.

GED Mini-Test (pages 50–51)

1. (Literal Comprehension) **(2) The past got better with time.** Option (1) is close to the main idea, but an understanding of the irony in the passage leads to option (2) as the correct answer. Options (3) and (4) are true statements from the passage, but both are merely details that support the main idea. Option (5) is a reasonable inference from the information in the passage but is also merely a detail.

2. (Inferential Comprehension) **(3) It is her way of editing the past.** There is no indication in the passage that Roseanne is a mean person, option (1). Options (2) and (4) are reasonable inferences, but option (3) relates more closely to the main idea. Option (5) is also a possible inference, but it is not as close to the main idea as option (3).

3. (Literal Comprehension) **(2) Cruises are set up to fill the empty lives of old people.** Option (1) is contradicted in the passage. Option (3) may be true, but there is no reference to young people; the whole focus of the passage is on the elderly and their problems. Options (4) and (5) are both true; however, these details support the main idea and are not the main idea itself.

4. (Application) **(1) Their childhoods were simple and pleasant.** The Foxens would have forgotten any unpleasantness. There is no support for options (2) and (3). Although option (4) may be true, the Foxens have gone on a cruise in part to avoid loneliness and seem to be succeeding in doing so. Option (5) is not supported in the passage.

5. (Inferential Comprehension) **(4) Death will soon overtake them.** Option (1) is an overstatement not supported by the passage. Option (2) is not relevant for the people on the cruise because they do have servants. Option (3) is not supported by the passage. Option (5) may be true, but it has little to do with their future.

6. (Literal Comprehension) **(5) The cruise ship was named the *Stella Maris*.** Keeping in mind that the main idea of the passage deals with the empty lives of some old people, it is clear that only option (5) has no relationship to the concerns of the elderly and is thus the correct answer. Options (1), (2), (3), and (4) are related to the concerns of old people on a cruise.

LESSON 3 Comprehension Skills: Restating Information

This skill helps you identify the main idea and supporting details in order to present information in another way. It can often help you to understand something you are reading or studying.

Often an author will say the same thing in a number of ways. It may not be clear that the same thing is being said; the author may use a variety of examples, each with different details but all making the same point.

This is often true about feelings. Instead of just saying how a character felt, the author will tell you things the character did. The character may not even understand why these acts are important, but these actions are the details that support the main idea. When you read these details and examples, you will find that they make the main point clearer to you. If you look for the way the author restates a major idea by the use of supporting details, it will help you understand the passage.

Remember that an author may restate his or her main idea by giving contrasting details, as well as by giving multiple examples of details that directly support the main idea.

In fiction, the author uses facts and details to make the main idea seem exciting. If the main idea were simply stated directly, the reader would probably not be as interested.

Sometimes you will be asked to find or restate facts or details from an excerpt. Often these will be facts or details that support the main idea or explain a change or contrast. When you read a passage looking for the main idea, you should also note the details that support it.

Remember that restating something means simply saying an idea in a different way. As you read, think of different ways you might say what the author means.

Practicing Comprehension, Application, and Analysis Skills

Read the following passage by Nadine Gordimer.

WHAT IS BEHIND THE CHAIN AND THE CURTAIN?

When I got home that same evening, the fellow wasn't there. He'd gone. Not a word, not a note; nothing. Every time I heard the lift [elevator] rattling I thought, here he is. But he didn't come. When I was home on Saturday afternoon I couldn't stand it any
(5) longer and I went up to the Versfelds and asked the old lady if I couldn't sleep there a few days, I said my flat [apartment] was being painted and the smell turned my stomach. I thought, if he comes to the garage, there are people around, at least there are the boys. I was smoking nearly as much as *he* used to and I couldn't
(10) sleep. I had to ask Mr. Levine to give me something. The slightest sound and I was in a cold sweat. At the end of the week I had to go back to the flat, and I bought a chain for the door and made a heavy curtain so's you couldn't see anyone standing there. I didn't go out, once I'd got in from work—not even to the early flicks [movies]—so
(15) I wouldn't have to come back into the building at night. You know how it is when you're nervous, the funniest things comfort you: I'd just tell myself, well, if I shouldn't turn up to work in the morning, the boy'd send someone to see.

Then slowly I was beginning to forget about it. I kept the
(20) curtain and the chain and I stayed at home. . . .

Source: *Something Out There.*

Questions 1 and 2 refer to the passage. Circle the best answer for each question.

1. Which sentence below best restates the main idea of the passage?

   (1) The lady in the passage is allergic to paint.

   (2) The lady in the passage does not like her apartment any longer.

   (3) The lady in the passage has really let herself go.

   (4) The lady is afraid of someone she knows.

   (5) The lady is very careful to maintain a secure apartment.

2. Which sentence below does <u>not</u> in some way support the main idea of the passage?

   (1) The lady was smoking too much and could not sleep.

   (2) The slightest noise caused her to break into a cold sweat.

   (3) She did not want to come back into the building at night.

   (4) She worked at a garage with some boys.

   (5) She made a heavy curtain so no one could see into her apartment.

To check your answers, turn to page 60.

Read the following paragraph by Garrison Keillor.

HOW DO LAKE WOBEGONIANS CHOOSE THEIR CARS?

In Lake Wobegon, car ownership is a matter of faith. Lutherans drive Fords, bought from Bunsen Motors, the Lutheran car dealer, and Catholics drive Chevies from Main Garage, owned by the Kruegers, except for Hjalmar Ingqvist, who has a Lincoln. (5) Years ago, John Tollerud was tempted by Chevyship until (then) Pastor Tommerdahl took John aside after church and told him it was his (Pastor Tommerdahl's) responsibility to point out that Fords get better gas mileage and have a better trade-in value. And he knew for a fact that the Kruegers spent a share of the Chevy (10) profits to purchase Asian babies and make them Catholics. So John got a new Ford Falcon. It turned out to be a dud. The transmission went out after ten thousand miles and the car tended to pull to the left. In a town where car ownership is by faith, however, a person doesn't complain about these things, and John figured there must (15) be a good reason for his car trouble, which perhaps he would understand more fully someday.

Source: *Lake Wobegon Days.*

Questions 3 to 6 refer to the paragraph. Circle the best answer for each question.

3. When the author says "perhaps he would understand more fully" (lines 15–16), which idea is he supporting?

   (1) Pastor Tommerdahl felt responsible.
   (2) The car's transmission failed.
   (3) The Kruegers spent their profits to convert their adopted Asian babies.
   (4) Car ownership is a matter of faith.
   (5) Religious people should not buy Fords.

4. According to this excerpt, Hjalmar Ingqvist is probably

   (1) Lutheran
   (2) Catholic
   (3) Methodist
   (4) tempted by Chevies
   (5) a friend of the pastor

5. Which of the following words best describes the car John finally bought?

   (1) Chevy
   (2) lemon
   (3) bargain
   (4) trade-in
   (5) blessing

6. Why does the author tell the story about John Tollerud?

   (1) He tells the story to show how people make choices based on religion.
   (2) He wants to point out that Fords get good gas mileage.
   (3) He wants to show how religion taught John not to complain.
   (4) He wants to show that Fords have bad transmissions.
   (5) He wants to show how John was punished for wanting a Chevy.

To check your answers, turn to page 60.

Read the following passage by Rita Mae Brown.

WHAT INFECTED RICHMOND?

     A carnival of hope infected Richmond. McClellan stayed at
Harrison's Landing. He plopped there like a frog full of buckshot.
He moved neither forward nor backward, but seemed imprisoned by
his own weight. Richmond was saved. Churches offered up services,
(5) people shouted, "Gloria in Excelsis," and Lee, instead of being the
goat, was now the hero.
     While Lutie, like everyone around her, offered up prayers of
thanksgiving to Almighty God, she thought of the weeks of battles
as the slaughterhouse of heroes. The death lists were appalling.
(10) The best families of the South lost their husbands, sons, and
brothers. Hardly anyone was untouched, especially since the upper
classes led the regiments, brigades, and divisions. The leaders, the
wealthy and the gifted, were cut down by the scythe of war no less
than the small farmer, the shopkeeper, even the vagrant seeking to
(15) redeem himself by military service. They died alike, and Death, as
always, impartially selected his victims. She used to think of Death
as a personal force, the god of the underworld, Hades or Pluto. Odd,
too, that Pluto was the god of riches. Each day you bargained with
this god, but in the end he got the better of the deal. She put aside
(20) that embroidered, mythical notion. Death these days was a
threshing machine. Someone started the blades whirling, and it
wouldn't cut off.

Source: *High Hearts*.

Questions 7 to 9 refer to the passage. Circle the best answer for each question.

7. Most of the details in the second
paragraph are restatements of

   (1) the saving of Richmond
   (2) Lutie's prayer
   (3) Lee's heroism
   (4) the appalling death lists
   (5) the decline of the South

8. If Lutie's final image of Death were to
be modernized, which of the following
might she have chosen?

   (1) a Wall Street success
   (2) a bulldozer
   (3) a lawn mower
   (4) a computer game
   (5) a wealthy politician

9. What does the author mean when she
says "Death, as always, impartially
selected his victims" (lines 15–16)?

   (1) She is showing that Death is
final.
   (2) She is showing that rich men as
well as poor men were killed.
   (3) She is showing that Death is
generous and brings its victims
peace.
   (4) She is showing how awful Death
is.
   (5) She is showing that Death is a
threshing machine or a sweeping
scythe.

To check your answers, turn to pages 60–61.

GED Mini-Test

Directions: Choose the best answer to each item.

Items 1 to 6 refer to the following passage by Olive Ann Burns.

WHAT WAS GRANDPA TWEEDY LIKE?

Then there was Grandpa Tweedy, my daddy's daddy out in Banks County. He talked hard times morning, noon, and night. Called himself a farmer, but you never saw him behind a plow or driving a team. Lazy, great goodness. Like the lilies of the field in
(5) the Bible, he toiled not, neither did he spend his own money. He was always asking Papa to help him out. All he ever did was sit on the porch and swat flies, and like I said, even had him a pet hen to peck them up.

When Papa left the farm at sixteen to go work for Grandpa
(10) Blakeslee, he made twenty dollars a month and had to send half of it home to pay the field hand who took his place. That was the custom. But even after Papa married at nineteen, making forty dollars a month, he still had to send Grandpa Tweedy ten of it, till the day he was twenty-one. My mother never said she didn't like
(15) her father-in-law, but I could tell she didn't, and that may of been why.

What started me hating him, he wouldn't let me fish on Sunday. Said it was a sin. I remember I put out some set hooks late one Saturday, thinking if I caught a fish, it wouldn't be a sin to take him off
(20) the hook next morning. End his suffering, you know. Early Sunday I ran down to the river and one of the lines was just a-jiggling! But when I ran up the hill and asked Grandpa's permission to get my fish off the hook, he said, "Hit'll still be thar t'morrer, Lord willin'. The Lord ain't willin', it'll be gone. Now git in the house and study
(25) yore catechism till time to leave for preachin'."

Of course the fish was gone Monday morning. But I got back at Grandpa Tweedy. I'd noticed a big hornet's nest in the privy, just under the tin roof, so I bided my time behind a tree till I saw him go in there. Giving him just long enough to get settled good, I let fly
(30) with a rock and it hit that tin roof like a gunshot. . . .

Source: *Cold Sassy Tree*.

1. The statement "All he ever did was sit on the porch and swat flies" (lines 6–7) is a restatement of

    (1) "he toiled not"
    (2) "he talked hard times"
    (3) "called himself a farmer"
    (4) "neither did he spend his own money"
    (5) "even had him a pet hen to peck them up"

2. Which of the following actions would you expect Grandpa Tweedy to take?

    (1) He would be the first man to fix anything that needed fixing.
    (2) He would tend his lilies night and day just like in the Bible.
    (3) He would talk for hours on end about his incredible good fortune.
    (4) He would be glad to lend a helping hand to any of his children.
    (5) He would let a fence fall down before he would repair it.

3. Which statement reflects the most likely reason that Papa sent money home to Grandpa Tweedy?

    (1) Papa was paying back his father for money loaned to him for school.
    (2) Children have a moral obligation to support parents who cannot support themselves.
    (3) Papa felt guilty for having left the farm.
    (4) Papa felt guilty for not having brought his wife back to the farm to live.
    (5) Grandpa Tweedy did not like to spend his own money, so he asked Papa to help out.

4. What happened when the speaker told Grandpa Tweedy about the fish?

    (1) Grandpa said it was a gift from God.
    (2) Grandpa refused permission to take the fish off the hook.
    (3) Grandpa gave his permission to get the fish.
    (4) Grandpa said to wait until after the preaching.
    (5) Grandpa got angry at the speaker.

5. Which of the following is the best summary of what happened in lines 26–30?

    (1) The speaker started hating Grandpa Tweedy.
    (2) Grandpa threw a rock at the privy.
    (3) The fish got away from the hook.
    (4) The speaker stirred up the hornets while Grandpa was in the outhouse.
    (5) The speaker set a trap for Grandpa by hiding a hornet's nest in a tree.

6. How did the speaker justify taking the fish off the hook?

    (1) The speaker planned to ask Grandpa's permission to get the fish off the hook.
    (2) The speaker said that if it were done on Saturday, it would not be a sin.
    (3) The speaker thought that it would be almost a good deed.
    (4) The speaker told Grandpa that it was less work that way.
    (5) The speaker planned to study the catechism as soon as the fish was off the hook.

To check your answers, turn to page 61.

Answers and Explanations

Practicing Comprehension, Application, and Analysis Skills (pages 55–57)

1. (Inferential Comprehension) **(4) The lady is afraid of someone she knows.** Option (1) is incorrect; there is no suggestion that the woman is really allergic to paint. There is no evidence for option (2). Options (3) and (5) are supported in the passage, but they do not restate the main idea.

2. (Literal Comprehension) **(4) She worked at a garage with some boys.** Options (1), (2), (3), and (5) all are details that support the main idea of the passage—that she was worried and afraid. Although option (4) is true, it has nothing to do with the main idea of the passage.

3. (Literal Comprehension) **(4) Car ownership is a matter of faith.** Faith refers not only to religion but also to accepting things without a complete explanation. There is no connection between the quotation and options (1) and (3). Option (2) is wrong because although John may not understand why his car failed, the quotation refers to the reason he does not question it. Option (5) is an opinion not supported by the passage.

4. (Inferential Comprehension) **(2) Catholic** Ingqvist is linked to the Catholics by being referred to as an exception. This makes option (1) wrong. Option (3) is not mentioned. Ingqvist owns a Lincoln, not a Chevrolet, so option (4) is wrong. There is no evidence for option (5).

5. (Application) **(2) lemon** This is another term for a car that does not work well. Option (1) is contradicted in the paragraph. Options (3) and (5) do not apply to a car that does not run well. There is no evidence that John traded the car, option (4).

6. (Analysis) **(1) He tells the story to show how people make choices based on religion.** There is support in the passage for options (2) and (4), but these details do not support the main idea of the paragraph. There is no support in the passage for options (3) and (5).

7. (Literal Comprehension) **(4) the appalling death lists** The details talk about the men who have died. Options (1) and (3) are not related to the details. Option (2) is a result of the temporary end of the dying. There is no suggestion of option (5).

8. (Application) **(2) a bulldozer** Lutie's final image is of a large destructive machine. Options (1) and (5) are not related to Lutie's final image. Option (3) is close but is on too small a scale. Option (4) is modern but has nothing to do with death.

9. (Analysis) **(2) She is showing that rich men as well as poor men were killed.** Although option (1) is a true statement about death, it is not what the author means. Option (3), like option (2), treats death as a person; however, the characteristics in option (3) are not the ones the author intends. Option (4) is wrong; the author is trying to show how death is impartial, not awful. Option (5) has support later in the passage, but it has nothing to do with this statement.

GED Mini-Test (pages 58–59)

1. (Literal Comprehension) **(1) "he toiled not"** Grandpa Tweedy never worked, so what he did was just sit around. Options (2) and (3) suggest that he worked. Option (4) is a different idea. Option (5) is a detail that describes his sitting on the porch.

2. (Application) **(5) He would let a fence fall down before he would repair it.** Since laziness seems to be one of Grandpa's basic qualities, option (1) is unlikely. There is no support for option (2). Options (3) and (4) are wrong; the passage indicates the opposite.

3. (Inferential Comprehension) **(5) Grandpa Tweedy did not like to spend his own money, so he asked Papa to help out.** This is suggested by information in the first paragraph. Option (1) is wrong because there is no indication that Grandpa loaned anyone money. Option (2) is wrong because the passage does not indicate that Grandpa could not support himself. Options (3) and (4) might be true, but Grandpa's feelings about money make option (5) the most likely reason.

4. (Literal Comprehension) **(2) Grandpa refused permission to take the fish off the hook.** Grandpa's long-winded speech boils down to this. Options (1) and (4) are not what Grandpa said. Option (3) is contradicted in the passage. There is no evidence for option (5).

5. (Literal Comprehension) **(4) The speaker stirred up the hornets while Grandpa was in the outhouse.** The thrown rock stirred up the hornets. Option (1) refers to the previous paragraph. Options (2) and (5) are misreadings of the paragraph. Option (3) simply gives a reason for the speaker's actions.

6. (Inferential Comprehension) **(3) The speaker thought that it would be almost a good deed.** Preventing the suffering of an animal could be thought of as a good deed. Options (1) and (2) would not give a good excuse but do form the basis of option (3). There is no evidence for options (4) and (5).

LESSON 4 Comprehension Skills: Getting Meaning From Context

This skill shows you how to use the words and phrases around a new word to find clues to the new word's meaning. These words and phrases may be in the same sentence or in a group of nearby sentences.

If you are faced with a word you do not know, look for clues in the words around it to help you figure out what the word means. Sometimes the nearby words or **context** will **define** a word. Look for key words that help define: *because, that is, means, such as, is called*. Sometimes the context will compare a new word to a known word. Or the context may provide a contrast to a new word to give a clue to its meaning. Here are some key words that show **contrast**: *however, yet, still, nevertheless, but, instead of, while*.

The context may even give the meaning of a word or words by using examples. Again, an author may use the context to repeat the meaning of a word, using words or phrases that are more familiar. Sometimes you will find that the context includes details that give clues to the word's meaning.

Even if you cannot figure out the exact meaning of a word or group of words, clues from the context will help you to make a good guess. The context in writing is simply the whole situation that is being talked about. When you think about a single word in its context, you are looking at that word against its background. If you understand the background, you can often figure out the meaning of an unknown word. If you saw an unfamiliar item in a store, you would probably look around at the other things on the shelf. If the surrounding things—the context—were pots and pans, you probably would be right in guessing that the unfamiliar item had something to do with cooking.

Practicing Comprehension, Application, and Analysis Skills

Read the following passage by Gore Vidal.

HOW DO THE REPUBLICANS AND FEDERALISTS DIFFER?

During the last session of the Third Congress I led the battle in the Senate against ratification of Jay's treaty with England. The treaty was clumsily drawn and to our disadvantage. It actually contained a clause forbidding us to export cotton in *American* ships.
(5) In effect, the treaty made us a colony again. It also revealed for the first time the deep and irreconcilable division between the Republican and Federalist parties—and they were now actual political parties, no longer simply factions. One was pro-French; the other pro-British. One wanted a loose confederation of states, the
(10) other a strong central administration; one was made up of independent farmers in alliance with city workers; the other was devoted to trade and manufacturing. One was Jefferson; the other was Hamilton.

Source: *Burr: A Novel*.

Questions 1 and 2 refer to the passage. Circle the best answer for each question.

1. Which of the following is the probable meaning of "ratification" (line 2) as it is used in the context of this paragraph?

    (1) advantage
    (2) approval
    (3) forbidding
    (4) disapproval
    (5) colonization

2. You can figure out that the phrase "in alliance with" (line 11) means "joined up with" by seeing that the pair of words "farmers" and "city workers" (line 11) is linked together in the paragraph in the same way as

    (1) the treaty and the clause
    (2) pro-French and pro-British
    (3) Jefferson and Hamilton
    (4) trade and manufacturing
    (5) parties and factions

To check your answers, turn to page 68.

WHAT WISDOM CAN TWO BITS BUY?

And in this book, which cost me just twenty-five cents, I found everything I needed to set my mind at rest. Reincarnation is the only belief I hold, Mr. Morgan. I explain my genius this way—some of us have just lived more times than others. So you see, what you
(5) have spent on scholars and traveled around the world to find, I already knew. And I'll tell you something, in thanks for the eats, I'm going to lend that book to you. Why, you don't have to fuss with all these Latiny things, he said waving his arm, you don't have to pick the garbage pails of Europe and build steamboats to sail the
(10) Nile just to find out something you can get in the mail order for two bits!

Source: *Ragtime.*

Questions 3 to 6 refer to the passage. Circle the best answer for each question.

3. The author helps the reader to understand the meaning of "reincarnation" (line 2) by

(1) calling it a belief
(2) saying "lived more times"
(3) referring to traveling
(4) specifically explaining the term
(5) saying it set his mind at rest

4. The phrase "Latiny things" (line 8) probably refers to which of the following things?

(1) garbage pails
(2) steamboats
(3) scholarly books
(4) the eats
(5) mail order catalogs

5. In which of the following ways does the author provide a clue to the meaning of the term "two bits"?

(1) by putting it in the last sentence
(2) by referring to mail order
(3) by contrasting the book to one of Mr. Morgan's
(4) by comparing it to the cost of steamboats
(5) by saying the book cost twenty-five cents

6. The speaker probably also believes that getting a college degree in philosophy

(1) improves one's mind
(2) involves examining garbage
(3) would be a waste of time
(4) leads to having enough to eat
(5) leads to reincarnation

To check your answers, turn to page 68.

Read the following passage by Kate Wilhelm.

HOW DO IDENTICAL TWINS BEHAVE?

"Anyhow, years ago Huysman got interested in the study of monozygotic twins. Identical twins. He did some important work, good research. There are anomalies in twin behavior that have yet to be understood completely. If they are separated at birth and
(5) raised separately, there are often similarities in their lives that are hard to understand. For instance, say Carol and Karen are born in New York and Karen is taken a few months later to grow up in California. They both marry a man named George on a June day in the same year at the same time. They both have two sons born at
(10) the same time. They have the same illnesses and the same accidents. And so on. This is repeated over and over. They don't know about each other, don't know they are twins. In fact, when twins are raised together this pattern is less likely to occur."

Drew felt at a loss. "There must be some reason. I mean, it
(15) isn't just Carol and Karen. It's also the Georges and the people driving the other cars involved with their accidents. Or not clearing snow off their sidewalks, whatever the accidents are. In fact, it's like an infinite regression of what ifs. You know, the what if I hadn't been on that corner at the time you came out, we'd never have met.
(20) And so on, back through their entire lives."

Source: *Huysman's Pets*.

Questions 7 and 8 refer to the passage. Circle the best answer for each question.

7. The best meaning for the word "anomalies" (line 3) as it is used in this context is

(1) irregularities
(2) discoveries
(3) illnesses
(4) accidents
(5) monozygotic

8. The author helps the reader to understand the meaning of the word "pattern" (line 13) by doing which of the following things?

(1) The author defines the word in the next paragraph.
(2) The author gives examples of twins raised together before using the word.
(3) The author gives examples of identical twins who are raised apart but repeatedly act alike.
(4) The author says that twins can be raised apart.
(5) The author never gives any examples before using the word.

To check your answers, turn to page 69.

GED Mini-Test

Directions: Choose the best answer to each item.

Items 1 to 6 refer to the following passage by Carl Sagan.

WHAT IS THE STORY OF ADNIX?

Years before, he had invented a module that, when a television commercial appeared, automatically muted the sound. It wasn't at first a context-recognition device. Instead, it simply monitored the amplitude of the carrier wave. TV advertisers had taken to running

(5) their ads louder and with less audio clutter than the programs that were their nominal vehicles. News of Hadden's module spread by word of mouth. People reported a sense of relief, the lifting of a great burden, even a feeling of joy at being freed from the advertising barrage for the six to eight hours out of every day that the average

(10) American spent in front of the television set. Before there could be any coordinated response from the television advertising industry, Adnix had become wildly popular. It forced advertisers and networks into new choices of carrier-wave strategy, each of which Hadden countered with a new invention. Sometimes he invented circuits to

(15) defeat strategies which the agencies and the networks had not yet hit upon. He would say that he was saving them the trouble of making inventions, at great cost to their shareholders, which were at any rate doomed to failure. As his sales volume increased, he kept cutting prices. It was a kind of electronic warfare. And he was

(20) winning.

They tried to sue him—something about a conspiracy in restraint of trade. They had sufficient political muscle that his motion for summary dismissal was denied, but insufficient influence to actually win the case. The trial had forced Hadden to investigate

(25) the relevant legal codes. Soon after, he applied, through a well-known Madison Avenue agency in which he was now a major silent partner, to advertise his own product on commercial television. After a few weeks of controversy his commercials were refused. He sued all three networks and in *this* trial was able to prove conspir-

(30) acy in restraint of trade. He received a huge settlement, that was, at the time, a record for cases of this sort, and which contributed in its modest way to the demise of the original networks.

Source: *Contact.*

1. Which of the following words in the passage is the best clue for figuring out the meaning of "amplitude" (line 4)?

    (1) automatically
    (2) monitored
    (3) louder
    (4) context-recognition
    (5) module

2. Which of the following is the most probable meaning of the word "strategies" (line 15) as it is used in this paragraph?

    (1) plans
    (2) advertisements
    (3) inventions
    (4) burdens
    (5) responses

3. Which of the following best helps you to understand the meaning of "insufficient" (line 23)?

    (1) There were relevant legal codes.
    (2) The advertisers' influence was not enough to win the case.
    (3) Hadden investigated legal codes.
    (4) There was a conspiracy.
    (5) Hadden received a settlement.

4. Which of the following would be the best title for this excerpt?

    (1) Success in Advertising
    (2) Consumer Laws
    (3) A History of Inventions
    (4) A Lot of Noise About Noise
    (5) Madison Avenue

5. What happened in the lawsuit filed by the advertisers against Hadden?

    (1) They used their political muscle to destroy his product.
    (2) They won their case because Hadden had insufficient evidence.
    (3) Hadden won by filing a motion for summary dismissal.
    (4) Hadden investigated all the relevant legal codes.
    (5) Hadden won because the advertisers failed to prove their case.

6. What happened in the lawsuit filed by Hadden against the networks?

    (1) Hadden proved a conspiracy and won a huge settlement.
    (2) Hadden became the owner of all three networks.
    (3) Hadden lost the case.
    (4) Hadden entered the advertising business.
    (5) Hadden's motion for dismissal was denied.

To check your answers, turn to page 69.

Answers and Explanations

Practicing Comprehension, Application, and Analysis Skills (pages 63–65)

1. (Inferential Comprehension) **(2) approval** Options (1) and (5) do not make sense in the sentence; they are just words from the details. The rest of the paragraph shows that the author clearly does not like the treaty that is apparently being considered by the Senate; therefore, options (3) and (4) are wrong.

2. (Literal Comprehension) **(4) trade and manufacturing** The parallel structure the writer uses is part of the clue. One party was made up of people in trade and people in manufacturing; the other party was made up of people who farmed and people who worked in the city. Restating the idea helps you see the meaning. Option (1) is wrong because the clause is part of the treaty, not an additional thing. The pairs of words in options (2), (3), and (5) are opposites, not things linked together.

3. (Analysis) **(2) saying "lived more times"** This comes in the next sentence and so hints at its meaning. Option (1) is not a direct definition. Option (3) does not help give the meaning. The author does not explain the term, option (4). Option (5) refers to a book, not the word.

4. (Inferential Comprehension) **(3) scholarly books** This is an implied contrast of the speaker's book to what Mr. Morgan probably reads. Options (1) and (2) are mentioned in addition to "Latiny things." Option (4) is something the speaker appreciated. There is no evidence for option (5).

5. (Literal Comprehension) **(5) by saying the book cost twenty-five cents** This information is in the first sentence. Option (1) does not give any clues. Option (2) gives only information about how the book was acquired. Options (3) and (4) refer to things that are not specifically mentioned.

6. (Application) **(3) would be a waste of time** The speaker states that all one needs to know can be found in his book, so he probably does not think much of a degree of any sort. The speaker shows little respect for scholarly activity in general, so option (1) is wrong. Option (2) refers to a joking insult, not a real belief. There is no support for either option (4) or (5).

7. (Inferential Comprehension) **(1) irregularities** The text goes on to explain odd things about twins. Option (2) is wrong because a discovery would probably be fairly well understood. Options (3) and (4) refer to specific details that help to explain what is unusual in twins' lives. Option (5) has already been defined as meaning identical.

8. (Analysis) **(3) The author gives examples of identical twins who are raised apart but repeatedly act alike.** The word follows this series of examples and so probably refers to the way the twins act. Options (1), (2), and (5) are not true. Option (4) does not help to explain the meaning of the word.

GED Mini-Test (pages 66–67)

1. (Literal Comprehension) **(3) louder** This is one of the several words that refer to sound. Options (1) and (2) refer to how the device worked, not what it affected. Option (4) does not help because it needs definition itself. Option (5) is the device itself.

2. (Inferential Comprehension) **(1) plans** This is suggested by surrounding information describing the actions of the advertisers and networks. Options (2) and (3) refer to the things each party is protecting. Options (4) and (5) would not make sense in the sentence.

3. (Inferential Comprehension) **(2) The advertisers' influence was not enough to win the case.** The first clue is in the contrast with "sufficient"; the second clue is that the advertisers failed. Options (1), (3), and (5) do not provide information about the advertisers. The charge that there was a conspiracy, option (4), does not help to explain "insufficient."

4. (Application) **(4) A Lot of Noise About Noise** There was arguing back and forth about the noise levels of TV ads. Options (1), (2), (3), and (5) all are too general.

5. (Literal Comprehension) **(5) Hadden won because the advertisers failed to prove their case.** Options (1), (2), and (3) are all specifically contradicted in the passage. Option (4) is true, but it is plain that this answer relates to something that happened as a result of the trial's outcome. Option (5) summarizes what did happen in the case.

6. (Literal Comprehension) **(1) Hadden proved a conspiracy and won a huge settlement.** There is no support in the passage for option (2). Option (3) is clearly wrong. Option (4) is true, but it did not happen in the lawsuit filed by Hadden. Option (5) occurred during the advertisers' suit against Hadden.

LESSON 5 Comprehension Skills: Drawing A Conclusion

This skill helps you to make decisions about facts that have been given to you. When you sort out the information given and put it together with what you already know, you are drawing a conclusion.

Now that you have mastered the skills of determining the main idea, restating information, and figuring out meaning from context, you can use these skills to come to a **conclusion**. Remember that a conclusion is an ending—that is, the place you want to reach. So in addition to using the other skills, you will be interpreting the given information as well as understanding it.

Here is an example:

You know that if you dial a phone number, you will hear a ringing noise.
You dial a friend's number.
Conclusion: You expect to hear a ringing noise.

This may seem simple, but it describes the reasoning process that people use to come to a conclusion—a decision that can be arrived at based on the facts given.

Nonfiction

In **nonfiction**, the author is writing about the world or the people in it as they actually are. The reading skill of drawing conclusions based on the information in a passage is important in both fiction and nonfiction.

What you will read in this lesson is nonfiction. The excerpts are from biographies or autobiographies. The authors are not trying to create a world from imagination; they are describing the real world. Selections from other types of nonfiction will be covered in a later lesson.

Remember when you read nonfiction that although the author is describing people and events that are real, the author may color a description with his or her own feelings.

☞ *See Also: GED Exercise Book Literature and the Arts, pages 10-14*

Practicing Comprehension, Application, and Analysis Skills

Read the following passage by James Huntington and Lawrence Elliott.

WHERE IS THE EDGE OF NOWHERE?

"My mother was Athabascan, born around 1875 in a little village at the mouth of the Hogatza River, a long day's walk north of the Arctic Circle. The country was wild enough—blizzards and sixty-below cold all the winter months, and floods when the ice tore
(5) loose in spring, swamping the tundra with spongy muskegs so that a man might travel down the rivers, but could never make a summer portage of more than a mile or so between them.

And the people matched the land. From the earliest time in Alaska, there had been bad feeling between Indian and Eskimo,
(10) and here the two lived close together, forever stirring each other to anger and violence. If an Indian lost his bearings and tracked the caribou past the divide that separated the two hunting grounds, his people would soon be preparing a potlatch in his memory, for he was almost sure to be shot or ground-sluiced, and his broken body
(15) left for the buzzards. Naturally this worked both ways. Then, in the 1890's, prospectors found gold to the west, on the Seward Peninsula, and the white man came tearing through. Mostly he was mean as a wounded grizzly. He never thought twice about cheating or stealing from the native people, or even killing a whole family if
(20) he needed their dog team—anything to get to Nome and the gold on those beaches.

Source: *On the Edge of Nowhere*.

Questions 1 and 2 refer to the passage. Circle the best answer for each question.

1. Which of the following is the best conclusion to draw about spring coming to Alaska?

   (1) Women are able to make long journeys to see their families.

   (2) It is the best time for prospecting.

   (3) Travel is still difficult, but not quite as hard as in winter.

   (4) The weather becomes pleasant and makes travel easy.

   (5) The Indians and Eskimos begin fighting.

2. What conclusion can you draw from the author's statement "And the people matched the land" (line 8)?

   (1) The white man never thought twice about cheating or stealing.

   (2) Even skilled hunters got lost.

   (3) A man killed by an enemy was often left unburied.

   (4) People's acts were as violent and uncontrollable as the weather.

   (5) The people endured cold winters and wet springs.

To check your answers, turn to page 76.

Read the following passage from an article by Maurice Herzog.

WHAT MAKES THIS EXPERIENCE SPECIAL?

My own awakening to the magical spirit of adventure came in my university days. In Paris, I was a student, dividing my time between law and speculation in the pure sciences. Then, one February, I had the chance to go to the Alps. I came to a village peacefully
(5) hibernating among snow-covered mountains. I started at sunrise and climbed the lower mountain slopes until I came to a small forest. Far from any inhabited place, I had only myself to count on. The solitude suddenly made me feel extremely vulnerable. I had the sensation that my life was in danger. I was venturing alone up immense
(10) snow slopes. Avalanches were a constant threat.

I was part of nature, like an animal among other animals—white hares, marmots, chamois, jackdaws, foxes. I felt my muscles acting as muscles naturally should. I was steeped in brilliant sunshine, although I fought against the piercing cold. Finally, worn and
(15) hungry, I reached the crest. I had striven against nature like a primitive man to gain that goal, and suddenly I experienced a vast exultancy.

Source: "Adventure—The Unending Challenge," from *Man Against Nature*.

Questions 3 to 5 refer to the passage. Circle the best answer for each question.

3. It can be concluded from this passage that the author thinks adventure consists of

(1) being in Paris
(2) studying law and science
(3) finding a peaceful village in the Alps
(4) facing the dangers of nature
(5) being hungry

4. Which of the following is the best conclusion to draw about the Alps?

(1) Many students go there.
(2) They are snowy, isolated mountains.
(3) Climbers often die in avalanches.
(4) The Alps are quite near Paris.
(5) Primitive men live there.

5. Why might the author be interested in an opportunity to sail down the Mississippi River on a raft?

(1) He likes to be alone.
(2) It would be a change from the mountains where he lives.
(3) There would not be any animals to watch out for.
(4) It would be a challenge.
(5) There would be a lot of sunshine and fresh air.

To check your answers, turn to page 76.

Read the following passage from an article by Ira A. J. Baden as told to Robert H. Parham.

WHAT IS HAPPENING AT THE ROOSEVELT HOTEL?

By seven o-clock I was dead tired and soaked with rain and perspiration. I walked to the Roosevelt, hoping to get a room for a brief rest. Instead of taking guests, however, the hotel was busy evacuating them. There were no lights, and the threat of explosion

(5) from escaping gas had increased throughout the demolished area. Another warning of the possibility of a second tornado had been issued. Fearful persons jammed the lobby in silent wait for the next blow.

The Roosevelt switchboard had one telephone circuit in

(10) operation. The operator called the Raleigh Hotel up the street and reserved rooms for Roy Miller and me, although I did not know Roy's whereabouts at the time. Next time I saw him he said he had driven to Hillsboro, about thirty-five miles away, to telephone his wife and reassure her of his safety. He was fuming.

(15) "I drive seventy miles to call my wife," he said; "I says, 'Honey, I'm all right. I'm safe. You don't need to worry any longer.' And what do I get? She says, 'Who's worried? You always have been all right. Why do you have to call me long distance to tell me so? Roy Miller,' she says, 'what have you been up to?'" Mrs. Miller had not

(20) heard of the storm.

Source: "Forty-five Seconds Inside a Tornado," from *Man Against Nature*.

Questions 6 and 7 refer to the passage. Circle the best answer for each question.

6. Which of the following is the most accurate conclusion to draw about the general situation in this passage?

(1) Men worry about what their wives will think.
(2) The Raleigh Hotel's business improved during the storm.
(3) People were reacting to the effects of a tornado.
(4) The tornado had shut down phone service within seventy miles of the town.
(5) Tornadoes can cause gas leaks.

7. You can conclude from the information given that the speaker would have rented a room at the Roosevelt if

(1) it had not been damaged by the tornado
(2) Roy Miller had not needed a room too
(3) he had not been so tired
(4) rooms had not been available at the Raleigh Hotel
(5) he had known where Roy Miller was

To check your answers, turn to page 76.

GED Mini-Test

Directions: Choose the <u>best answer</u> to each item.

<u>Items 1 to 6</u> refer to the following paragraph by Max Jones and John Chilton.

WHAT HAPPENED BEFORE THE SHOW COULD START?

Here was this man, Louis Armstrong, just before the show was due to start, waiting silently. He was smartly dressed, in dinner jacket, and holding his Selmer trumpet. The band was ready—there had been no rehearsal—and he was about to perform. Then
(5) Collins suddenly said, "Where's the dough? If I don't get the dough, Louis don't play." The promoter had a huge crowd and there was no problem. He offered a cheque but Collins was adamant—no cash, no Louis. It must have been humiliating for Louis, though he showed no sign of it. He just looked at the floor and went on swinging his
(10) trumpet in his hand until such time as matters were settled. He seemed utterly detached as this pasty-faced man with the cigar in his mouth demanded the money there and then, or no show. I estimate they had some two thousand people in there, and the promoter went to his box office and came back with several bags of half-crowns,
(15) of silver anyway, and put them down in front of Collins. "There's your money," he told Collins, and I remember thinking: he doesn't know how to count it.

Source: *Louis Armstrong Story 1900–1971.*

1. Which of the following can be concluded from this passage about the relationship between Louis Armstrong and Collins?

   (1) Collins is the promoter of Armstrong's show.
   (2) Armstrong and Collins often argue publicly.
   (3) Collins handles Armstrong's money.
   (4) Collins is one of Armstrong's biggest fans.
   (5) Armstrong admires the way Collins acts.

2. It can be concluded from the scene in this passage that musicians

   (1) sometimes were not paid after their performances
   (2) get nervous in front of large crowds
   (3) always rehearse before a show
   (4) demand large sums of money for performing
   (5) are easily embarrassed

3. What is the best conclusion about the person who is telling this story?

   (1) He thought Collins did the right thing.
   (2) He was embarrassed by Armstrong's behavior.
   (3) He was a member of Armstrong's band.
   (4) Armstrong was thinking of hiring him as a manager.
   (5) He thought Armstrong behaved better than Collins.

4. Which of the following best describes how Armstrong probably acted on most occasions?

   (1) impatiently
   (2) calmly
   (3) aggressively
   (4) awkwardly
   (5) rudely

5. Which of the following is the best meaning for the word "adamant" (line 7) as it is used in this paragraph?

   (1) noisy
   (2) firm
   (3) confused
   (4) polite
   (5) pleased

6. Which of the following would be the best title for this paragraph?

   (1) No Cash, No Show
   (2) The Silent Man
   (3) A Promoter's Troubles
   (4) They Came to See Louis
   (5) Several Bags of Silver

To check your answers, turn to page 77.

Answers and Explanations

Practicing Comprehension, Application, and Analysis Skills (pages 71–73)

1. (Inferential Comprehension) **(3) Travel is still difficult, but not quite as hard as in winter.** River travel is possible, but the tundra (the land) is swampy. Options (1), (2), and (5) are wrong because they describe events that have no connection with spring. Option (4) is not suggested in the passage.

2. (Inferential Comprehension) **(4) People's acts were as violent and uncontrollable as the weather.** This is suggested by the details. Options (1) and (3) have nothing to do with the land. Options (2) and (5) are true but do not answer the question.

3. (Inferential Comprehension) **(4) facing the dangers of nature** He felt that he was testing his own abilities through the challenge of climbing a mountain. Options (1) and (2) refer to what he was doing before he found adventure. Option (3) is a detail about the adventure. Option (5) is a detail of the result.

4. (Inferential Comprehension) **(2) They are snowy, isolated mountains.** The details of the passage add up to this. Option (1) is not supported by any reference to other students. There is no evidence for options (3) and (5). Option (4) is wrong because there is no suggestion of distance.

5. (Application) **(4) It would be a challenge.** The author enjoyed the struggle against a natural obstacle. Options (1) and (5) might be true, but they are only partial reasons for his enjoyment. Option (2) is wrong because there is no evidence that he lives in the mountains. Option (3) has no support.

6. (Inferential Comprehension) **(3) People were reacting to the effects of a tornado.** This covers the actions of all the people in the passage. Options (1), (2), (4), and (5) refer to details in the passage, not to the general situation.

7. (Inferential Comprehension) **(1) it had not been damaged by the tornado** He wanted to rent a room there, but the hotel lacked light and was even sending its guests elsewhere. Options (2) and (5) have no connection with his renting a room. Option (3) did not affect his decision. Option (4) is wrong because he eventually went to get a room at the Raleigh, since rooms were not available at the Roosevelt.

1. (Inferential Comprehension) **(3) Collins handles Armstrong's money.** Both Armstrong and the promoter accept Collins's right to demand payment, so it is probably his usual job. Option (1) is not true because Collins is talking to the promoter. Because Armstrong ignores Collins's action, there is no support for options (2) and (5). There is no mention of Collins's opinion of Armstrong, so option (4) is wrong.

2. (Inferential Comprehension) **(1) sometimes were not paid after their performances** Collins would not have felt the need to demand payment before the show if the money were guaranteed. Options (2) and (5) are not supported by the passage. Line 4 mentions there was no rehearsal, so option (3) is incorrect. Option (4) is wrong because here it is the manager, not the musician, who is concerned with money; also, no amount is mentioned.

3. (Inferential Comprehension) **(5) He thought Armstrong behaved better than Collins.** He describes Armstrong in positive terms but refers to Collins negatively. There is no support for options (1), (3), and (4). Option (2) is wrong because he seems to admire Armstrong's patience.

4. (Application) **(2) calmly** Armstrong remains cool through an embarrassing moment, which suggests he is usually calm. Therefore, options (1) and (4) are wrong. There is no evidence for options (3) and (5); those qualities describe how Collins acted.

5. (Literal Comprehension) **(2) firm** Collins won't take no for an answer and won't accept anything but what he asked for. There is no evidence for option (1). Options (3), (4), and (5) do not describe Collins's attitude.

6. (Application) **(1) No Cash, No Show** The focus of the paragraph is on Collins's demand. Options (2) and (4) are wrong because they suggest a focus on Armstrong or his audience. Option (3) is wrong because this is only one problem a promoter might have; besides, the promoter himself is not the focus either. Option (5) refers only to a detail of the solution.

LESSON 6 Analysis Skills: Identifying Elements of Style and Structure

This skill shows you how to identify the characteristic ways that an author uses language and organizes his or her material.

Nonfiction Essay

Another form of nonfiction writing is the **essay**. An essay usually gives information about a subject the reader knows little about. Some essays are for readers who already know about the subject but want to learn more about it from an expert in the field. Because writers do not have much space in an essay to develop an idea, they depend on style and structure to help the reader understand the attitude and points they want to express.

Style is the term for the way writers choose and use words. A formal style uses general, standard English and complete sentences. Formal style is usually serious. This book is an example of formal writing. An informal style is more relaxed than a formal style and often sounds like casual speech. Slang words and sentence fragments are acceptable in an informal essay. Humorous essays are often written in an informal style. Writers choose the style that best makes clear to the reader the way they feel about the subject. Pay attention to the words a writer uses, and think about why those words were chosen.

Structure is the way writers organize their ideas. In fiction, the story being told has its own structure. Writers of nonfiction, on the other hand, have to decide how to put together all the information they want the reader to understand. One method of structuring is by time, writing about something in the order that it happened. Another way is by comparison, dividing the subject into parts to compare or contrast them. A third method of structuring is by definition, dividing the subject into different types and giving examples to illustrate. Still another way of organizing is by describing where things are located, such as "to the left" and "to the right."

One structural element is **apposition**—a parallel, or repetitive, structure that restates or tells you something additional about the subject. An appositive is a word or phrase that gives more information. Several phrases may be used in sequence. Writers use appositives to convey a lot of information in a small space. Commas or dashes may be clues to the use of this technique.

Practicing Comprehension, Application, and Analysis Skills

Read the following passage by Jacci Cole.

WHO ARE THE WHALE WATCHERS?

The song of the humpback has captured the intense interest of many biologists. Why do they sing these songs, and do they sing them all the time? Do the songs carry messages to other whales, or are they just for fun?

(5) Jacques Cousteau says both the male and female humpback sing. He states that they sing their song "day and night during their long migration to and from the warm southern waters."

Dr. Roger Payne disagrees. For several months during 1971, Payne and his colleague, Scott McVay, recorded humpbacks off the (10) coast of Bermuda. They found that all the humpbacks in one area sing the same underwater song. However, they also found that the whales sing only in their winter breeding ground and not while traveling.

Later, Payne's wife Katy, also a whale watcher and researcher, (15) found that not only are humpback whales "singers" but also "composers, constantly tinkering with their song so that it changes completely in only a few years." As individual whales make minor changes in the song, others learn those changes and pass them on. The Paynes theorized that the changes take place as the breeding (20) season progresses and not between seasons.

Source: *Animal Communication: Opposing Viewpoints,* from the series *Great Mysteries.*

Questions 1 and 2 refer to the passage. Circle the best answer for each question.

1. Which of the following is the best explanation of why the author included the detail "also a whale watcher and researcher" (line 14)?

(1) to fill up space
(2) to show that Katy is an expert in her own right
(3) to explain why Katy disagrees with her husband
(4) to explain why whales sing
(5) to catch the reader's attention

2. The best way to describe the overall organization in this passage is

(1) one thing follows another
(2) definition
(3) location
(4) contrast
(5) apposition

To check your answers, turn to page 84.

Read the following passage from an article by Donald McCraig.

WHAT'S THERE TO SEE AT THE COUNTY FAIR?

The crafts judges form a sorority of expert peers, most from out of county. Several have been to the judging school at the Augusta Presbyterian Church, with cards to prove it. Unwary novice judges are assigned to cookies, jellies, and jams. Hundreds of sweet things
(5) are entered: platters of brownies, cakes, jams, and jellies. You'd think it would be fun tasting them, until you thought twice. The jelly judges did stay for lunch afterwards (thanks to the Highland Girl Scouts), but they hardly ate a thing.

Sewing judges sit at a table while assistants bring them
(10) garments to inspect for fabric grain lines, stitching, suitable thread, smooth darts, pleats, tucks, gathers, and facings. One lady holds up a black-and-white checked child's jumper. "Oh, look, she's covered the buttons."

The second judge turns a sundress pocket inside out to inspect
(15) the stitching. "What do you do when they're both nice?"

The senior judge says, "You get to nitpicking," and she awards first prize to the jumper. I don't know how it is other places, but in Highland County, covered buttons are *it*."

Many skills and crafts shown here are traditional, but not all
(20) of them. Kids' art is pretty much the same as kids' art anywhere; a few more sheep and cows, a few less McDonald's arches. Mrs. Leo Schwartz has prepared a Japanese exhibit...because an exchange student from Japan stayed with her family this summer. And Rafe Levien, a computer whiz, has an exhibit of computer art.

(25) The canned vegetable judges look for a perfect seal and a nice-looking ring and label. The liquid should be free of sediment and bubbles. The color should be natural, pieces must be uniform and of good quality. Mildred Detamore holds a jar of stewed tomatoes up to the light and sighs, "The tomatoes are so much seedier this year.
(30) It's because of the drought."

Source: "The Best Four Days in Highland County," *Country Journal.*

Questions 3 and 4 refer to the passage. Circle the best answer for each question.

3. Which of the following words is the best example of informal use of words?

(1) peers
(2) garments
(3) traditional
(4) kids
(5) seedier

To check your answers, turn to page 84.

4. The author uses the word "sighs" (line 29) to suggest that

(1) the judge is tired
(2) judging is hard work
(3) the jar is too heavy
(4) the judge is sorry about the problem
(5) the judge will not get paid

Read the following passage from an article by Jack Agueros.

WHERE DID THIS BOY GROW UP?

My mother kept an immaculate household. Bedspreads
(chenille seemed to be very in) and lace curtains, washed at home
like everything else, were hung up on huge racks with rows of tight
nails. The racks were assembled in the living room, and the
(5) moisture from the wet bedspreads would fill the apartment. In a
sense, that seems to be the lasting image of that period of my life.
The house was clean. The neighbors were clean. The streets, with
few cars, were clean. The buildings were clean and uncluttered with
people on the stoops. The park was clean. The visitors to my house
(10) were clean, and the relationships that my family had with other
Puerto Rican families, and the Italian families that my father had
met through baseball and my mother through the garment center,
were clean. Second Avenue was clean and most of the apartment
windows had awnings. There was always music, there seemed to be
(15) no rain, and snow did not become slush. School was fun, we wrote
essays about how grand America was, we put up hunchbacked cats
at Halloween, we believed Santa Claus visited everyone. I believed
everyone was Catholic. I grew up with dogs, nightingales, my
godmother's guitar, rocking chair, cat, guppies, my father's
(20) occasional roosters, kept in a cage on the fire escape. Laundry
delivered and collected by horse and wagon, fruits and vegetables
sold the same way, windowsill refrigeration in winter, iceman and
box in summer. The police my friends, likewise the teachers.

Source: "Observations: Looking at Ourselves," from *Ourselves Among Others*.

Questions 5 and 6 refer to the passage. Circle the best answer for each question.

5. The author suggests the meaning of the word "immaculate" (line 1) by

(1) describing his mother
(2) talking about school
(3) referring to religion
(4) using an appositive
(5) giving examples of how clean the house was

6. Which of the following is the best reason for the author to repeat the word "clean" so many times?

(1) It sets up a contrast to how he lives now.
(2) It emphasizes the lasting image he has of the time.
(3) It shows how much his mother's habits influenced him.
(4) It adds more detail.
(5) It gets rid of the need for more explanation.

To check your answers, turn to page 84.

GED Mini-Test

Directions: Choose the <u>best answer</u> to each item.

<u>Items 1 to 6</u> refer to the following passage by Bruce Hutchinson.

WHAT HAPPENED TO THE WIDE, OPEN SPACES?

Cities were built, new provinces. Legislatures and governments were created with all the trappings and gold braid of an ancient system on this empty land. Innumerable wooden towns sprang up beside the railways and the red wooden grain elevators stood
(5) everywhere, with square shoulders against the sky.

Presently Regina, a Royal Northwest Mounted Police post, where Riel had been hanged in the jail yard, found itself the capital of Saskatchewan with a domed parliament building beside a slough, dammed to form an ornamental lake. Trees, shrubs, and flowers grew
(10) around it where the buffalo had grazed a few years before. Saskatoon to the north expanded out of the river bank like a mushroom.

To the edge of the Rockies the plow turned up the land, turned up the old grasses and "prairie wool" that had fed the buffalo and then the cattle—for which nature would take a terrible revenge later
(15) on in dust storm and erosion. In the foothills, in sight of the mountains, they built the rollicking ten-gallon, hair-pant, and joyous town of Calgary, where business men wore cowboy hats and high-heeled boots, and R. B. Bennett, living at the Palliser, wore cutaway coats and striped gray trousers, on his sure way to the premiership
(20) of Canada and the British House of Lords. North again, almost at the edge of the tundra, they laid out Edmonton, with Jasper Avenue running, paved, for miles into the prairies; and then built another parliament building for another province until at night its lights twinkled on the river like a Rhine castle.

Source: *The Unknown Country*.

1. Which of the following phrases from the passage does not help to show how this excerpt is organized?

   (1) beside the railroads
   (2) where the buffalo had grazed
   (3) to the edge of the Rockies
   (4) in the jail yard
   (5) miles into the prairies

2. Which of the following phrases from the passage does not suggest that the development of the land was quite sudden?

   (1) were built
   (2) sprang up
   (3) found itself the capital
   (4) like a mushroom
   (5) a few years before

3. According to the context of this passage, a "slough" (line 8) is probably

   (1) grassland
   (2) a grove of trees
   (3) an ancient system
   (4) a waterway
   (5) an ornamental lake

4. If the author had been talking about similar growth in the United States, he might have used the example of

   (1) a small Vermont town that is losing its young people to New York
   (2) ghost towns in the West
   (3) the 1860s gold rush that brought thousands of people to the Black Hills of South Dakota
   (4) the legalization of the lottery in Illinois
   (5) the closing of automotive parts factories in Muncie, Indiana

5. The people who built these towns and plowed the grasses up probably wanted to

   (1) live quiet country lives
   (2) get rich quickly
   (3) go back where they came from
   (4) get rid of the Mounted Police
   (5) take revenge on nature

6. For which of the following would the style of this piece be most suitable?

   (1) a book of love poetry
   (2) a mystery novel
   (3) a comic Broadway play
   (4) a popular history book
   (5) a science textbook

To check your answers, turn to page 85.

Answers and Explanations

Practicing Comprehension, Application, and Analysis Skills (pages 79–81)

1. (Analysis) **(2) to show that Katy is an expert in her own right** This is an appositive that gives important information about Katy Payne. Option (1) has no support. Option (3) is wrong because she agrees with her husband. Option (4) is wrong because her qualifications have nothing to do with why whales sing. Option (5) wrong because it is only a minor detail.

2. (Analysis) **(4) contrast** The main point is the disagreement between Cousteau and Payne, so option (2) is wrong. There is no real support for options (1) and (3). Option (5) is wrong because there are no general parallel structures used here.

3. (Analysis) **(4) kids** "Kid" is slang for child. Options (1) and (2) are standard English words but hint at formal use. Options (3) and (5) could occur in either formal or informal use.

4. (Analysis) **(4) the judge is sorry about the problem** A sigh can show sympathy or regret. Option (1) may be true but has no support in the passage. There is no evidence for options (2) and (3). Option (5) may be true, but the passage indicates that the judge is not sighing about not being paid.

5. (Inferential Comprehension) **(5) giving examples of how clean the house was** The word refers to the house. Options (1), (2), and (3) are wrong because they do not help the reader understand what the house looks like. Option (4) is wrong because no appositive is used near the word.

6. (Analysis) **(2) It emphasizes the lasting image he has of the time.** Options (1) and (3) are wrong because we have no information about what he is like now. Option (4) is wrong because repetition of a word is not adding detail. Option (5) is wrong because more explanation is given.

GED Mini-Test (pages 82–83)

1. (Analysis) **(4) in the jail yard** Although it talks about location, this phrase refers to an event that happened to a single person. Options (1), (2), (3), and (5) refer to the expansion of settlements into what had been unclaimed land.

2. (Analysis) **(1) were built** Building is a commonplace activity and can take place at any speed. Options (2), (3), (4), and (5) imply surprise and speed.

3. (Literal Comprehension) **(4) a waterway** A slough is an inlet or a swamp. The clue here is that it was dammed to form a lake. Options (1), (2), and (3) cannot be dammed. Since the slough was dammed to form the lake, it could not have been the lake to begin with, option (5).

4. (Application) **(3) the 1860s gold rush that brought thousands of people to the Black Hills of South Dakota** The main idea is the rapid development of an uninhabited area. Until the gold rush, whites were forbidden by treaty to settle there. Options (1), (2), and (5) are about the loss of population, not its increase. Option (4) might have pleased people in Illinois but would not have much effect on the growth of population there.

5. (Inferential Comprehension) **(2) get rich quickly** The speed of the building and farming suggests that the motive was to make money, so option (1) is wrong. The permanence of the building suggests they intended to stay, so option (3) is wrong. There is no support for options (4) and (5).

6. (Application) **(4) a popular history book** The author seems interested in how a country developed, but interested less in dates than in fascinating facts. The style is not romantic, so option (1) is wrong. There is no support for options (2) and (5). The style is straightforward, not witty, so option (3) is wrong.

LESSON 7 Analysis Skills: Identifying Techniques (Figurative Language)

This skill will help you learn how to recognize figurative language and understand the effect it creates. Good figurative language is forceful and brief, and it has a sense of freshness about it.

All writers look for ways to make their ideas more lively. To do this, many authors use **figurative language**. A figure of speech happens when words are used in a fresh, new way instead of in a literal way—that is, instead of the way they are normally used. Although figurative language is used most often in fiction, poetry, and drama, authors of nonfiction sometime use it to make a point or create an image.

Most figurative language is based on comparison of things that are not really alike. Direct comparisons, or **similes**, say that one thing is like another—for example, "His hair looked like a worn-out whiskbroom" (meaning his hair was a mess) or "Her nails were as bright as a stoplight" (meaning her nail polish was very red). Indirect comparisons, or **metaphors**, simply state that one thing *is* another—for example, "My sister is an accident waiting to happen" (meaning she is clumsy). Indirect and direct comparisons make descriptions more clear and interesting.

Another use of figurative language is to build up, or exaggerate, in order to make a point. Exaggerating is not the same as lying but is used to add emphasis. If you come in from the rain and say, "I nearly drowned out there!" you really mean that you got very wet. An opposite effect comes from **understatement**—saying less than you mean. If you say, "I suppose I could use a bite to eat" when the person to whom you are talking knows that you are very hungry, you are using understatement for effect, probably to make the person laugh.

A fourth type of figurative language gives human qualities, such as feelings and physical features, to nonhuman things—for example, "The night has a thousand eyes."

Whatever figure of speech is used, the author wants to create an effect. For example, in describing a character the author could say "He had white hair and was seven feet tall." How much more interesting it is if the author instead says "He was a skyscraper capped by a fluffy white cloud." As you read the passages in this lesson, ask yourself what the authors mean by their use of figurative language and what effect they are trying to create.

Practicing Comprehension, Application, and Analysis Skills

Read the following passage from an article by Thomas Griffith.

WHAT'S SO SPECIAL ABOUT NEWS MAGAZINES?

Beyond the bottom line, Wall Street doesn't much care about editorial quality; journalists do and others should. Not because journalism is perfect, but because it isn't.

(5) News magazines come at the end of the food chain of journalism. First radio reports the news hourly, then the evening television news repeats it and adds pictures. Newspapers fill out the story in greater detail. Finally the news magazine comes along to summarize and analyze it. By that time the reader may be suffering an acute case of information glut. It takes wit, reflection,

(10) a gift for compression, some fresh reporting or consultation with experts, and an original turn of mind to add something new. The real job of the news magazine is to help the reader to make sense out of his times. Those who can do this, the best of them, form a shaggy group of contentious minds.

Source: "What's So Special About News Magazines?" *Newsweek.*

Questions 1 and 2 refer to the passage. Circle the best answer for each question.

1. What point about news reporting is the author making by saying news magazines are "at the end of the food chain of journalism" (lines 4–5)?

   (1) As each news medium reports news that has already been reported, reporting in an interesting way gets harder.

   (2) News magazines have smaller lunch expense accounts than newspapers or television stations.

   (3) News magazines are given less detailed information and fewer pictures.

   (4) The quality of the food served gets better as a reporter moves up through the ranks.

   (5) Because Wall Street does not care about quality, journalism has become a dog-eat-dog world.

2. What is the effect of saying "suffering an acute case of information glut" (line 9)?

   (1) It describes how the reader makes sense of his world.

   (2) It suggests that there is too much news on TV.

   (3) It reminds the reader of having an upset stomach from overeating.

   (4) It suggests that readers need to find new sources of information.

   (5) It implies that magazine readers should stop watching television news programs.

To check your answers, turn to page 92.

Read the following passage from an article by Vera Schurer.

WHERE CAN A WINDMILL BE FOUND?

Only in the Far West have windmills remained indispensable. On the open range, windmills serve as guideposts and landmarks, as familiar as neighbors. A windmill tower has pointed the way home to many a lost cowboy.

(5) The windmill is usually what a cowboy sees first in the distance when riding in from a cattle drive. He begins thinking about a cool drink and a hot meal while the cattle mother-up in the corrals.

For the ranch woman, the windmill is often used as a lookout tower which she can climb and look off to spot the return of her cow-

(10) boy. When she sees a tide of red dust where the trails come together, she knows he's safe and it's time to put the biscuits in the oven.

The purr of the windmill is often the ranch woman's only company all day. She knows its pitch and tone, like the voice of a beloved friend, and will likely remember it until the day she dies.

(15) Windmills speak to those who listen. Spring is seldom silent. The blades thrash and churn and chatter as the southwest wind batters the winter-worn plains. As spring storms violate the land, an old windmill turns its cheek to the anger of the storm and stands firm.

Source: "Windmills," *Country*.

Questions 3 to 5 refer to the passage. Circle the best answer for each question.

3. Which of the following is <u>not</u> used as a figurative verb in the passage?

    (1) pointed
    (2) speak
    (3) listen
    (4) chatter
    (5) stands

4. What is probably meant by "turns its cheek to the anger of the storm" (line 18)?

    (1) fights back
    (2) hides
    (3) endures the weather
    (4) works more efficiently
    (5) is bent by the winds

5. Which of the following is the author most likely doing when she describes windmills as being "familiar as neighbors" (line 3) and the windmill's sound as being "like the voice of a beloved friend" (lines 13–14)?

    (1) explaining that windmills are very noisy
    (2) suggesting how important the windmills are to people
    (3) saying that westerners think windmills are alive
    (4) referring to the friendliness of western folk
    (5) suggesting that cowboys do not have a good sense of direction

To check your answers, turn to page 92.

Read the following passage from an article by Steve Rushin.

WHAT CAN WILLIE DO WITH A POOL CUE?

The old man with the custom cue knocks the balls off the table
as if he were a schoolboy with a slingshot and the stripes and solids
were so many crows perched on a telephone wire. *Click click click*.
When the pool table has been cleared, 74-year-old Willie Mosconi

(5) shrugs and says, "Nothin' to this game." He's playing in front of the
Sears store at the Northridge shopping mall in Milwaukee; the pool
legend is making another exhibition appearance.

"I could arrange it so she doesn't make a ball," Mosconi tells
the audience while setting up a trick shot for a young woman he

(10) has selected from the crowd. Almost 200 people are watching, if you
count shopping-weary passersby and ascending escalator riders. It
turns out the woman *can't* make a ball, even though Mosconi has
arranged it so that a simple shot should pocket six at once. After
three failed attempts and as many tedious setups, the Showman

(15) grows impatient and the Shark in Mosconi surfaces.

"Ever play this game before?" he asks her. (By his tone he is
clearly saying, "You *have* played this game before, *haven't* you?)

"No," the woman says.

The Shark takes—yanks, really—the cue form her hand and

(20) the woman slinks back into the crowd, disappearing behind a potted
palm. Then Mosconi the Salesman catches himself and remembers
that he's here to pitch pool tables and make friends for Sears.

"Thank you," he says to the potted palm. "Uh, let's hear it for
the young lady."

Source: "In Pool, the Shark Still Leaves a Wide Wake," *Sports
Illustrated*.

Questions 6 and 7 refer to the passage. Circle the best answer for each question.

6. The phrase "a schoolboy with a
slingshot" (line 2) gives you the
impression that

(1) playing pool is easy
(2) Mosconi is having fun
(3) Mosconi was young when he
    started playing pool
(4) pool players can be careless
(5) crows can be hit with pool balls

7. The best way to describe Willie
Mosconi is a(n)

(1) old man
(2) Sears salesman
(3) entertainer
(4) expert pool player
(5) magician

To check your answers, turn to page 92.

GED Mini-Test

Directions: Choose the best answer to each item.

Items 1 to 6 refer to the following passage by Frank W. Aitken and Edward Hilton.

WHAT DID THE TITANS DO TO THE EARTH?

Toward midnight the cafés and restaurants began to fill. Parties dropped in for those quiet little suppers that were a part of the city's fame. The rattle of dishes and clink of glasses, a merry laugh or a happy chuckle, a snatch of a stage joke or a bit of
(5) repartee—this for an hour or two; then all was still.

The city slept. A lone policeman on his rounds, the clanging bell of some owl car anxious to be off the street, the tread of a man hurrying home, the uncertain antics of some befuddled fellow— scarcely more than this anywhere. The city slept, unconscious of
(10) the manner of its awakening.

Slowly dawn crept over the hills; some sleepy folk were getting their wares out for the early buyers. A sudden rumbling hurried closer and closer. The houses of the sleeping city shook as if seized with a sudden ague. At first came a sharp but gentle swaying
(15) motion that grew less and less; then a heavy jolting sidewise—then another, heaviest of all. Finally a grinding round of everything, irregularly tumultuous, spasmodic, jerky. It was as if some Titans, laying hold of the edge of the world, were trying to wrest it from each other by sudden wrenchings.

(20) Plaster showered from the walls; nails creaked in their sockets and pulled and tried to free themselves. Crockery and glassware smashed upon the floor. Doors flew open—swung round—jerked off their hinges. Furniture toppled. Pianos rattled their keys in untimed janglings. Chimneys snapped and fell. Houses groaned and
(25) twisted and reeled on their foundations. Outside, streets were seized with writhings. Hillsides slid. The city shook itself like a dog coming out of the water.

Source: "Earthquake at San Francisco," from *Man Against Nature.*

1. Which of the following best states the main idea of this passage?

   (1) The peace of the city is being disturbed.
   (2) A terrible fight happened after midnight.
   (3) An earthquake began in the early morning.
   (4) City folk are not prepared for disaster.
   (5) Sleep is the best preparation for a crisis.

2. The author uses the figurative "slept" (line 6) not only to suggest that the city was quiet at night, but also

   (1) to imply that the policeman was tired
   (2) to point out the importance of remaining alert
   (3) to prepare the reader for what happened next
   (4) as a dramatic contrast to how the city woke up
   (5) as an explanation of the word "still"

3. The word "crept" (line 11) helps to emphasize

   (1) the slow, sleepy pace of early awakening
   (2) how unwilling the sun is to begin its day
   (3) how slow people were to realize what was happening
   (4) the excitement of the parties the night before
   (5) the slow way the fight began

4. The author used descriptions of nails freeing themselves, pianos rattling their keys, and houses groaning to add to the horror of the situation because

   (1) these are ordinary and familiar actions
   (2) it can be frightening to imagine objects acting on their own
   (3) plaster falling is not dramatic enough
   (4) they illustrate how the hillsides slid
   (5) they explain why the streets were filled with writhings

5. Which of the following best explains the effectiveness of the sentence "The city shook itself like a dog coming out of the water" (lines 26–27)?

   (1) There were a number of animals running wildly in the streets.
   (2) Dogs often break household objects by their roughness.
   (3) Objects were acting like the spray flying off a dog's back.
   (4) People were terrified by the violence of what was happening.
   (5) Dogs do not like being in water.

6. Which of the following would be the best title for this passage?

   (1) The Day the Earth Stood Still
   (2) The Calm Before the Storm
   (3) An Awful Surprise
   (4) When the Earth Shrugged Its Shoulders
   (5) How to React to an Earthquake

To check your answers, turn to page 93.

Answers and Explanations

Practicing Comprehension, Application, and Analysis Skills (pages 87–89)

1. (Analysis) **(1) As each news medium reports news that has already been reported, reporting in an interesting way gets harder.** Options (2) and (4) refer to food literally, so both are wrong. Option (3) is not true according to the passage. There is no support for option (5).

2. (Analysis) **(3) It reminds the reader of having an upset stomach from overeating.** The figurative suggestion in "acute case of . . . glut" is parallel to feeling uncomfortable because of hearing the same thing over and over. More information, option (4), would only add to the problem. Option (1) has no support. Option (2) might be true in general, but other media besides television are a part of the problem discussed. Option (5) is not suggested.

3. (Analysis) **(3) listen** People do the listening—literally. But a windmill cannot really point or speak or chatter, so options (1), (2), and (4) are used figuratively. Option (5) is figurative because it suggests an act of willpower.

4. (Analysis) **(3) endures the weather** This figure of speech refers to a biblical passage that advises not resisting one who harms you instead of struggling; therefore, option (1) is wrong. The cheek is turned to face the storm, not away from it, so options (2) and (5) are wrong. There is no evidence for option (4).

5. (Analysis) **(2) suggesting how important the windmills are to people** These comparisons refer to people we think of as close and essential in our lives. Options (1) and (5) are not supported by the passage. Option (3) is not true; the words are figurative, not literal. Option (4) misses the point of the comparison.

6. (Analysis) **(2) Mosconi is having fun** The simile refers to a child at play. Hitting something with a slingshot is difficult, so option (1) is wrong. Options (3) and (4) have no support in the passage. Option (5) confuses the figurative with the literal.

7. (Literal Comprehension) **(4) expert pool player** This is demonstrated throughout the passage. Even though he is old, option (1), and is working as a salesman and entertainer, options (2) and (3), he is best known for his great pool playing. Mosconi uses skill, not magic, so option (5) is wrong.

1. (Inferential Comprehension) **(3) An earthquake began in the early morning.** The descriptions in the last two paragraphs imply the results of the earth shaking; the time is stated. Option (1) is true but much too general. Option (2) refers to a figurative image, not a literal one. There is not enough evidence for option (4). Option (5) may be true but is not suggested here.

2. (Analysis) **(4) as a dramatic contrast to how the city woke up** Option (1) is wrong because the word does not refer to the policeman. Option (2) has no support. The word "sleep" suggests peacefulness, but what happened next was the opposite; therefore, option (3) is wrong. The literal meaning of "still" would explain "slept," not the other way around, so option (5) is incorrect.

3. (Analysis) **(1) the slow, sleepy pace of early awakening** The word suggests slowness and is followed by the example of people beginning their day. Option (2) is wrong because the sun has no feelings. The word describes the sun, not people's awareness, so option (3) is wrong. The dawn has no connection to the parties, so option (4) is wrong. Option (5) is not supported.

4. (Analysis) **(2) it can be frightening to imagine objects acting on their own** By giving objects human actions, the author creates the atmosphere of unreality and horror. Option (1) is wrong because objects do not usually do this. Option (3) is partially true but is not enough to explain why these images were used. Options (4) and (5) are wrong because what happened inside the houses does not illustrate or explain what happened outside.

5. (Analysis) **(3) Objects were acting like the spray flying off a dog's back.** The familiar image of the dog is usually amusing, but in this context it is scary. People and their possessions are being treated as impersonally as water drops. There is no evidence for option (1). Options (2) and (4) may be true but have nothing to do with the question. Option (5) is not true and also does not explain why the comparison works.

6. (Application) **(4) When the Earth Shrugged Its Shoulders** This title not only suggests an earthquake but also uses the same type of figurative language found in the passage. Option (1) is wrong because the earth moved. Option (2) refers only to the first two paragraphs. Option (3) is much too general. Proper reactions are not mentioned, so option (5) is wrong.

LESSON 8 Comprehension Skills: Identifying Figurative Language

With this skill, you will learn how to recognize figurative language in poetry and to understand the effect it creates. In poetry, figurative language is usually forceful and brief and is intended to make the reader think.

Poetry often seems difficult to understand. The reason is that poetry has a language of its own—that is, poetry uses ordinary words in a way different from prose. The language of poetry is something like shorthand: it condenses ideas into a few words or phrases. One powerful phrase can suggest an idea that might otherwise need a long and detailed explanation. However, the power of poetry is not the result of the shortness of the piece (some poems are longer than a short story). The effect of poetry comes from the way language is used.

Because poets want to make their readers look at the world in a new way, they appeal to the senses, to the emotions, and to the imagination. They do this by choosing words that will make the reader experience the ideas and feelings, not just understand them. The same kind of figurative language that you have seen in fiction and nonfiction is used in poetry as one method to get the most from the possible meanings of a word.

Remember that a poet is not trying to confuse the reader with unusual word usage. Figurative language in a poem helps to make a stronger point than might have been the case if ordinary prose were used. As you read, ask yourself if the poet is using words literally or figuratively. It will help to look for a stated main idea or an unstated main idea and to use context clues to figure out a phrase that at first may seem hard to understand.

Practicing Comprehension, Application, and Analysis Skills

Read the following poem by Joyce Carol Oates.

WHAT HAPPENED WHEN THE WIND WENT CRAZY?

Where the Wind Went Crazy

the tops of the palm trees are smashed
palm leaves hang down, shredded
limp and light as threads
the trunks like concrete
(5) that never lived

mammoth towers
uninhabited

I feel the two of us grown to
mammoth towers
(10) our heads dizzied by the height
time is piled beneath us
blocks pushing us up
there is motion of nerves between us
strung between us like wires

(15) lovers, we need no hurricane
to make war upon each other
and each cell of our living tissue
is at peace

Source: *Nightside.*

Questions 1 and 2 refer to the poem. Circle the best answer for each question.

1. Why does the poet describe palm trees?

   (1) She likes palm trees.

   (2) She is comparing palm trees and telephone poles.

   (3) She is comparing lovers to palm trees torn up by a hurricane.

   (4) She is comparing palm trees to a hurricane.

   (5) She is comparing palm trees to empty apartment buildings.

2. Which statement below best describes what the poet means in lines 13–14?

   (1) She feels like a palm tree.

   (2) There is a sense of tension, like electricity, between the lovers.

   (3) The hurricane makes her nervous.

   (4) She feels like a tower.

   (5) She is insane.

To check your answers, turn to page 100.

Read the following poem by Langston Hughes.

WHAT IS A RAISIN IN THE SUN?

Harlem

What happens to a dream deferred?

Does it dry up
like a raisin in the sun?
Or fester like a sore—
(5)   and then run?
Does it stink like rotten meat?
Or crust and sugar over
like a syrupy sweet?
Maybe it just sags
(10)   like a heavy load.

Or does it explode?

Source: *The Panther and the Lash: Poems of Our Times.*

Questions 3 to 6 refer to the poem. Circle the best answer for each question.

3. What is the main idea of this poem?

   (1) Lots of dreams smell bad.
   (2) There is a graveyard of dreams like the graveyard of the elephants.
   (3) People suffer when dreams are deferred.
   (4) Dreams get better when they are deferred.
   (5) You do not have to pay for your dreams right away.

4. Which of the following is the best restatement of "dream deferred" (line 1)?

   (1) a nightmare remembered
   (2) a desire postponed
   (3) a wish fulfilled
   (4) a dream come to life
   (5) a request granted

5. What does "dry up / like a raisin in the sun" (lines 2–3) suggest about a dream that is deferred?

   (1) It loses its freshness.
   (2) It is easily forgotten.
   (3) It becomes hard to understand.
   (4) It becomes more valuable.
   (5) It starts to seem silly.

6. Which is the most important line in the poem?

   (1) "like a raisin in the sun"
   (2) "What happens to a dream deferred?"
   (3) "like a syrupy sweet"
   (4) "Does it stink like rotten meat?"
   (5) "Maybe it just sags"

To check your answers, turn to page 100.

Read the following poem by Wendell Berry.

WHERE CAN YOU GO WITHOUT LEAVING HOME?

Traveling at Home

Even in a country you know by heart
it's hard to go the same way twice.
The life of the going changes.
The chances change and make a new way.
(5) Any tree or stone or bird
Can be the bud of a new direction. The
natural connection is to make intent
of accident. To get back before dark
is the art of going.

Source: *A Part*.

Questions 7 to 10 refer to the poem. Circle the best answer for each question.

7. What does the poet mean by "Any tree or stone or bird / Can be the bud of a new direction" (lines 5–6)?

  (1) Small things can change the direction of a person's life.
  (2) Stones, trees, and birds are good guideposts.
  (3) Stones, trees, and birds are unfriendly to travelers on life's road.
  (4) A person can read hidden meaning in the world of nature.
  (5) Like trees and birds, stones are alive.

8. Which of the following is the most likely reason for the poet's choice of the word "accident" (line 8)?

  (1) as a warning to be careful
  (2) to explain the art of going
  (3) to explain where new directions lead
  (4) to emphasize the idea of chance
  (5) to explain the word "intent"

9. What is the best restatement of "a country you know by heart" (line 1)?

  (1) a loving home
  (2) a distant land
  (3) a familiar place
  (4) a boring place
  (5) a memorized path

10. Which statement below best reflects the main idea of this poem?

  (1) People who travel should always take maps to avoid getting lost.
  (2) Even the most experienced traveler will not be able to go exactly the same way every time.
  (3) The art of living involves shaping chance happenings to your own purposes.
  (4) People should be prepared not to reach their destinations before dark.
  (5) Travelers risk having motor vehicle accidents.

To check your answers, turn to pages 100–101.

GED Mini-Test

Directions: Choose the best answer to each item.

Items 1 and 2 refer to the following poem by Marge Piercy.

WHO WANTS TO BE OF USE?

To be of use

The people I love the best
jump into work head first
without dallying in the shallows
and swim off with sure strokes almost out of sight.
(5) They seem to become natives of that element,
and black sleek heads of seals
bouncing like half-submerged balls.

I love people who harness themselves, an ox to a heavy cart,
who pull like water buffalo, with massive patience,
(10) who strain in the mud and the muck to move things forward,
who do what has to be done, again and again.

I want to be with people who submerge
in the task, who go into the fields to harvest
and work in a row and pass the bags along,
(15) who are not parlor generals and field deserters
but move in a common rhythm
when the food must come in or the fire be put out.

The work of the world is common as mud.
Botched, it smears the hands, crumbles to dust.
(20) But the thing worth doing well done
has a shape that satisfies, clean and evident.
Greek amphoras for wine or oil,
Hopi vases that held corn, are put in museums
but you know they were made to be used.
(25) The pitcher cries for water to carry
and the person for work that is real.

Source: *Circles on the Water*.

1. Why does the speaker in the poem say that people "jump into work head first / without dallying in the shallows" (lines 1–3)?

    (1) to lead into the rest of the water image
    (2) as a contrast to their becoming natives of that element
    (3) because people like to swim
    (4) as a contrast to people who are like water buffalo
    (5) as an example of how people play like seals

2. What is meant by the phrase "Botched, it smears the hands, crumbles to dust" (line 19)?

    (1) People should not be afraid to get their hands dirty.
    (2) People should not use cheap materials that will not stand the test of time.
    (3) People should wear gloves when they work to cut down on messy hands.
    (4) Work poorly done hurts the worker and does not last.
    (5) Work is a burden we all have to bear.

Items 3 and 4 refer to the following poem by Karl Shapiro.

WHAT IS MAN'S SHELL?

Man on Wheels

Cars are wicked, poets think.
Wrong as usual. Cars are part of man.
Cars are biological.
A man without a car is like a clam without a shell.
(5) Granted, machinery is hell,
But carless man is careless and defenseless.
Ford is skin of present animal.
Automobile is shell.
You get yourself a shell or else.

Source: *Collected Poems 1940–1978*.

---

3. What is meant by the phrase "Ford is skin of present animal" (line 7)?

    (1) There is a new animal living today called a Ford.
    (2) Cars are as much a part of people's lives today as their own skin.
    (3) People should buy Fords, not GM cars.
    (4) Modern life is too full of machinery.
    (5) If you cannot have a skin, you need a shell.

4. What is the poet's basic attitude toward cars?

    (1) Cars are wicked.
    (2) Cars and other machines are hell.
    (3) Cars are a necessary part of modern life.
    (4) Clams should drive cars.
    (5) A man without a car does not have a care in the world.

To check your answers, turn to page 101.

Answers and Explanations

Practicing Comprehension, Application, and Analysis Skills (pages 95–97)

1. (Analysis) **(3) She is comparing lovers to palm trees torn up by a hurricane.** The first half of the poem describes the palms, and the second half the lovers; the last four lines draw the connection. Option (1) may be true, but it is clearly not the reason the poet is using the image of palm trees. Option (2) is wrong because the poem as a whole is focused on the palm trees and the lovers. Option (4) is false. Option (5) is not as good an answer as option (3), which focuses on the lovers.

2. (Analysis) **(2) There is a sense of tension, like electricity, between the lovers.** The wires suggest electricity, and the tension is suggested by nerves. Options (1) and (4) both are ideas supported by the poem but not by lines 13–14. There is no support for option (5). Option (3) is a possible inference from the word "nerves," but not a very strong one.

3. (Inferential Comprehension) **(3) People suffer when dreams are deferred.** The series of questions points to unpleasant consequences. Option (1) would be true only if the poet were speaking literally, and in any case, his concern is not with dreams themselves but with the deferral of dreams. There is no support for option (2), although it is a possible inference. Option (4) is not supported by the context of the poem; the results seem to get worse, not better. There is no support for option (5); the poet is not talking about deferred payment.

4. (Inferential Comprehension) **(2) a desire postponed** The dream is not the kind one has while sleeping. In the context of this poem, the comparisons suggest that something negative has happened to the dream or hope. Option (1) refers to a literal dream and would not make sense in the context. Options (3), (4), and (5) all refer to something positive.

5. (Analysis) **(1) It loses its freshness.** A raisin in the sun loses its juice, shrinks, and becomes hard and tasteless. Options (2), (3), and (5) have no connection to what happens to a raisin. Option (4) is the opposite of what happens.

6. (Analysis) **(2) "What happens to a dream deferred?"** The poem makes sense only if you focus on this line. The poet focuses on it by making it the first line and placing it to the left of all the other lines. Options (1), (3), (4), and (5) are descriptions of what may happen to a dream deferred; they are all answers to the poet's question. But in this poem none of these lines is as important as the first line.

7. (Analysis) **(1) Small things can change the direction of a person's life.** Here "bud" means a new beginning, influenced by what might appear to be unimportant things. Option (2) is a good choice, but the poem focuses on the accidental changes and making adjustments to them, not on finding a way by reading signs. There is no support for options (3) and (5). Option (4) is wrong because there is no suggestion of hidden meanings.

8. (Analysis) **(4) to emphasize the idea of chance** This repeats the idea that unexpected things happen. Option (1) refers to another meaning of "accident." There is no support for options (2), (3), and (5).

9. (Literal Comprehension) **(3) a familiar place** "By heart" means committed to memory. Option (1) refers to another idea suggested by the word "heart." Options (2) and (4) misinterpret the phrase. Option (5) is wrong because a country is not a path.

10. (Inferential Comprehension) **(3) The art of living involves shaping chance happenings to your own purposes.** There is only one option that is focused on chance, or accidental occurrences. Options (1) and (5) are wrong because they are general observations about traveling, but not the sort of travel the poet means. Option (2) is a true statement but is in support of the main idea. Option (4) is wrong because it is literal and because it is not what the poet says.

GED Mini-Test (pages 98–99)

1. (Analysis) **(1) to lead into the rest of the water image** This beginning allows the poet to say figuratively that people submerge themselves in work, just as they would be submerged in deep water. Option (2) is wrong because the one idea is a result of the other, not a contrast. Option (3) is a misreading of the literal meaning. Option (4) is wrong because the two ideas are alike, not opposite. Option (5) is not supported by the poem.

2. (Inferential Comprehension) **(4) Work poorly done hurts the worker and does not last.** This line is in contrast to the following lines. Options (1) and (3) are inferences that are too literal; also they do not address the key word "botched." The focus of the poem is on work that is botched, not work in general. Option (2) is closer to the meaning, since the test of time as a measure of good work is mentioned; however, option (2) does not focus on botching work. Option (5) is a general statement that may be true, but it does not answer this question.

3. (Analysis) **(2) Cars are as much a part of people's lives today as their own skin.** This is supported by the previous lines. Ford here stands for all cars, and the "present animal" is man. Option (1) is false; the poet is not talking about a new animal but about people. Option (3) is wrong because it takes the language literally, and the poet is speaking figuratively. Option (4) may be true, but it is not the meaning of the line. Option (5) uses words from the poem but is not what is meant.

4. (Inferential Comprehension) **(3) Cars are a necessary part of modern life.** The last five lines of the poem explain what it is like to be without a car. Options (1) and (2) are wrong because the focus is on coping and not really on machines being evil. Although the poem mentions both clams and cars, it does not say that clams should drive, so option (4) is wrong. Option (5) is false; the poem says the opposite.

LESSON 9 Analysis Skills: Identifying Techniques (Symbols and Images)

With this skill you will learn to identify the poetic symbols and images that can help you understand the meaning of a poem.

A **symbol** is a word or phrase that means more than its literal meaning. It stands for an important idea the poet is talking about. A fork in a road can literally be the place where the road splits in two, while figuratively it can stand for the choices a person has to make in life. A symbol often is difficult to recognize by itself. You need to look at the context of the poem before trying to find any symbols. Poets do not simply make up symbolic meanings. They use ideas that most people are familiar with or that can be figured out from the literal meaning of the word. A rosebud used in a poem about young people could be a literal flower and also be recognized as a symbol for youth, because we all know that a rosebud is the first stage in the life of a rose. Be careful not to see symbols where only the literal meaning is being used. Most poets are not trying to trick you with "hidden meanings." They want you to understand their work.

An **image** can be either figurative or literal. Images appeal to the reader's senses. They recreate sensations of sight, taste, touch, smell, and hearing. A poet will create an image by using words that readers can associate with their own experiences. An image does not need to use the types of figurative language you have read about. It can be a simple but striking description. The word "grime" should remind a reader of the sticky dirt that feels awful to the touch and is difficult to clean. But figurative language is often helpful in creating an image. "The freight train pawed and snorted" should remind readers of the pace of a train's wheels and of the sound the engine makes, while also bringing to mind the image of a bull.

Images and symbols are used to make the point more clear. They also help to suggest the mood, or emotion, that dominates the poem.

Practicing Comprehension, Application, and Analysis Skills

Read the following poem by Roderick Jellema.

WHO ARE THE MIGRANTS?

Migrants

Birds obeying migration maps etched in their brains
Never revised their Interstate routes.
Some of them still stop off in Washington, D.C.

This autumn evening as the lights of the Pentagon
(5) Come on like the glare of urgent trouble through surgery
    skylights,
Come on like a far-off hope of control,

I watch a peaceful V-sign of Canada Geese
Lower their landing gear, slip to rest on the slicky Potomac,
(10) Break rank and huddle with the bobbing power boats.

Wings of jets beating the air, taking turns for the landing—
Pterodactyls circling the filled-in swamps under National Airport.
There is a great wild honking

Of traffic on the bridges—
(15) The daily homing of migrants with headlights dimmed
Who loop and bank by instinct along broken white lines.

Source: *Something Tugging the Line.*

Questions 1 and 2 refer to the poem. Circle the best answer for each question.

1. Which statement best describes what the poet is doing in the poem?

(1) He is comparing spring and fall.
(2) He is comparing the river and the airport.
(3) He is contrasting boats and jets.
(4) He is contrasting the geese and the Interstate highway.
(5) He is comparing the commuters and the geese.

2. What is the poet suggesting about commuters when he uses the image of the birds following a migration map?

(1) They have maps etched on their brains.
(2) They follow habits, like the geese.
(3) He does not like them at all.
(4) They want to fly away, like the geese.
(5) They are confused, like the geese.

To check your answers, turn to page 108.

Read the following poem by Wendell Berry.

FOR WHOM DOES THE WHEEL TURN?

The Wheel

At the first strokes of the fiddle bow
the dancers rise from their seats.
The dance begins to shape itself
in the crowd, as couples join,
(5) and couples join couples, their movement
together lightening their feet.
They move in the ancient circle
of the dance. The dance and the song
call each other into being. Soon
(10) they are one—rapt in a single
rapture, so that even the night
has its clarity, and time
is the wheel that brings it round.

In this rapture the dead return.
(15) Sorrow is gone from them.
They are light. They step
into the steps of the living
and turn with them in the dance
in the sweet enclosure
(20) of the song, and timeless
is the wheel that brings it round.

Source: *The Wheel*.

Questions 3 to 5 refer to the poem. Circle the best answer for each question.

3. On the simplest level, what is the poet describing in this poem?

  (1) a Ferris wheel at a county fair
  (2) a church choir at a country church
  (3) a square dance or some similar sort of dance
  (4) the milky way
  (5) a funeral procession

To check your answers, turn to page 108.

4. What is the mood of this poem?

  (1) sarcastic
  (2) joking
  (3) thoughtful
  (4) despairing
  (5) angry

5. Which of the following is the best symbolic meaning of the dance?

  (1) the cycle of life and death
  (2) a joyous occasion
  (3) the end of life
  (4) an ancient ritual
  (5) the day-to-day routine

Read the following poem by Karl Shapiro.

WHY IS THE POET CALLING THE CHILD?

Calling the Child

From the third floor I beckon to the child
Flying over the grass. As if by chance
My signal catches her and stops her dance
Under the lilac tree;
(5) And I have flung my net at something wild
And brought it down in all its loveliness.
She lifts her eyes to mine reluctantly,
Measuring in my look our twin distress.

Then from the garden she considers me
(10) And gathering joy, breaks from the closing net
And races off like one who would forget
That there are nets and snares.
But she returns and stands beneath the tree
With great solemnity, with legs apart,
(15) And wags her head at last and makes a start
And starts her humorous marching up the stairs.

Source: *Collected Poems 1940–1978*.

Questions 6 to 8 refer to the poem. Circle the best answer for each question.

6. What is suggested by the child's "flying over the grass" (line 2)?

(1) The child can actually fly.
(2) The little girl has a lot of energy.
(3) The speaker is imagining things.
(4) The girl thinks she can fly.
(5) The girl is trying to get to the safety of the sidewalk.

7. The little girl returns because

(1) she likes being by the tree
(2) she is tired of racing
(3) she realizes it is time to go inside
(4) it is getting dark
(5) the garden is too solemn a place to play in

8. What is the effect of the image of the net in the poem?

(1) It emphasizes the child's wild, free nature.
(2) It shows that the speaker is a skilled hunter.
(3) It shows that parents trap their children.
(4) It shows that the speaker is heartless.
(5) It shows that movement adds meaning to the poem.

To check your answers, turn to page 108.

GED Mini-Test

Directions: Choose the best answer to each item.

Items 1 to 6 refer to the following poem by Randall Jarrell.

WHAT GOES ON AT THE ZOO?

The Woman at the Washington Zoo

The saris go by me from the embassies.

Cloth from the moon. Cloth from another planet.
They look back at the leopard like the leopard.

And I. . . .
(5) This print of mine, that has kept its color.
Alive through so many cleanings; this dull null
Navy I wear to work, and wear from work, and so
To my bed, so to my grave, with no
Complaints, no comment: neither from my chief,
(10) The Deputy Chief Assistant, nor his chief—
Only I complain . . . this serviceable
Body that no sunlight dyes, no hand suffuses
But, dome-shadowed, withering among columns,
Wavy beneath fountains—small, far-off, shining
(15) In the eyes of animals, these beings trapped
As I am trapped but not, themselves, the trap,
Aging, but without knowledge of their age,
Kept safe here, knowing not of death, for death—
Oh, bars of my own body, open, open!

(20) The world goes by my cage and never sees me.
And there come not to me, as come to these,
The wild beasts, sparrows pecking the llamas' grain,
Pigeons settling on the bears' bread, buzzards
Tearing the meat the flies have clouded. . . .
(25)   Vulture,
When you come for the white rat that the foxes left,
Take off the red helmet of your head, the black
Wings that have shadowed me, and step to me as man:
The wild brother at whose feet the white wolves fawn;
(30) To whose hand of power the great lioness
Stalks, purring. . . .
                    You know what I was,
You see what I am: change me, change me!

Source: *The Woman at the Washington Zoo.*

1. What does the poem suggest about the speaker's job?

   (1) The speaker is a bureaucrat in Washington, D.C.
   (2) The speaker is an animal keeper at the Washington Zoo.
   (3) The poem does not suggest anything.
   (4) The speaker is retired.
   (5) The speaker works at an embassy.

2. Which of the following statements best describes the main idea of the poem?

   (1) The speaker is happy with her lot in life.
   (2) The speaker believes in the rights of animals.
   (3) The speaker feels that she is trapped like the animals in the zoo.
   (4) The speaker is sad because she does not have much money for bright clothes.
   (5) The speaker wants to be changed into a lion.

3. What does the speaker mean by "these beings trapped/As I am trapped but not, themselves, the trap" (lines 15–16)?

   (1) She knows she is insane and all the animals are insane, too.
   (2) She lives in a prison next door to the zoo.
   (3) She was once caught in an animal trap by accident.
   (4) The animals have been put behind bars, while she is trapped within herself.
   (5) She is as dangerous as an animal trap.

4. What is the most likely meaning of "And there come not to me, as come to these / The wild beasts" (lines 21–22)?

   (1) She does not have the ability to talk to wild animals.
   (2) Wild animals are afraid of her.
   (3) Many wild animals break into the zoo.
   (4) She throws bread to the pigeons but they will not get too close to her.
   (5) There is no variety or adventure in her life.

5. From the context, it is reasonable to assume that "saris" (line 1) are

   (1) moonrocks
   (2) worthless people
   (3) leopard trainers
   (4) some sort of clothing
   (5) foreign cars used by embassies

6. "The wild brother at whose feet the white wolves fawn" (line 29) probably means

   (1) the woman's brother
   (2) the Deputy Chief Assistant
   (3) the great lioness
   (4) untamed man
   (5) an Eskimo

To check your answers, turn to page 109.

Answers and Explanations

Practicing Comprehension, Application, and Analysis Skills (pages 103–105)

1. (Inferential Comprehension) **(5) He is comparing the commuters and the geese.** Options (1), (2), and (3) have no support; the birds are a major part of the poem but are not mentioned in these options. Option (4) refers to one complete image, in which there is no element of contrast.

2. (Analysis) **(2) They follow habits, like the geese.** The idea of habit is suggested by the words "obeying," "never revised," and "still stop off" (lines 1–3). Option (1) is wrong; it is the geese who have the maps in their brains. There is no support for option (3). Options (4) and (5) are wrong because the geese are not confused and do not want to fly away.

3. (Literal Comprehension) **(3) a square dance or some similar sort of dance** The real focus of the poem is dancing, and option (3) is the only option that mentions a dance. Options (1), (2), (4), and (5) are not supported in the poem.

4. (Analysis) **(3) thoughtful** Most of the poem is literal and straightforward; the poet shifts from that only to comment in a way clearly designed to make the reader reflect on what has been said. The poet is not sarcastic, joking, or angry in this poem, so options (1), (2), and (5) are incorrect. Although the poem talks of death, it is not despairing; therefore, option (4) is also incorrect.

5. (Analysis) **(1) the cycle of life and death** Both the living and the dead participate in the dance; one clue is in the phrase "ancient circle." Option (2) ignores the solemn nature of the poem. Option (3) refers only to a portion of the dance. Option (4) is too literal a meaning. Option (5) has no support.

6. (Analysis) **(2) The little girl has a lot of energy.** The word "flying" suggests that the girl is running and leaping. Options (1), (3), and (4) assume the word is meant literally. Option (5) is wrong because it suggests that the girl was afraid of the grass; however, she was having fun.

7. (Inferential Comprehension) **(3) she realizes it is time to go inside** The speaker signals that it is time to come in, but even though children want to play just a little longer, the girl knows what the signal means. Options (1), (2), and (4) have no support in the details. Option (5) is wrong because the child is obviously happy playing in the garden.

8. (Analysis) **(1) It emphasizes the child's wild, free nature.** A net is usually used to trap wild animals. Options (2) and (4) would be right only if you take the image literally, but it is figurative language. Option (3) is clearly not what is meant. Option (5) has nothing to do with the image of the net.

1. (Inferential Comprehension) **(1) The speaker is a bureaucrat in Washington, D.C.** Option (2) is a possible answer, but there is more support for option (1) in the context. Option (3) is false; there is substantial information in the poem about the speaker's job and her dissatisfaction with it. There is no support for option (4); it is contradicted by "I wear to work." Option (5) is wrong, it is not the speaker who has any connection with an embassy but the people who wear the saris.

2. (Literal Comprehension) **(3) The speaker feels that she is trapped like the animals in the zoo.** This is partially stated in line 16. Options (1) and (2) are not supported in the poem. There is some support for option (4); however, the poet is using clothes as a detail and not as the main idea. Option (5) is a possible inference from figurative language, but it does not fit the rest of the poem as well as option (3).

3. (Analysis) **(4) The animals have been put behind bars, while she is trapped within herself.** Her own life is the trap, not something done to her by someone else. There is no support for option (1), although it is a possible inference. Neither is there any evidence for option (2). There is no support for options (3) and (5); the poem has nothing to do with animal traps.

4. (Analysis) **(5) There is no variety or adventure in her life.** Nothing at all different happens to her. This is figurative language that you can assume to be related to the main idea. Options (1), (2), (3), and (4) do not seem to be related to the main idea, and none of them has direct support in the poem.

5. (Inferential Comprehension) **(4) some sort of clothing** The clue here is "Cloth" (line 2). Option (1) is wrong; the speaker is talking about exotic cloth, not rock from the moon. There is no support for options (2) or (3). Option (5) is a possible guess, but the clue about cloth makes option (4) a better answer from the context.

6. (Analysis) **(4) untamed man** The phrase is introduced by a colon following the word "man"; therefore, it may be a restatement. The woman is looking for something as uncivilized as the wild beasts in the zoo. Option (1) might be true only if this language were literal, and even then there is no support for it. There is no support for options (2) and (5) in the poem. Option (3) is also wrong; it is plain from the context that the great lioness is different from the wild brother.

LESSON 10 Analysis Skills: Identifying Techniques (Characterization)

With this skill you will learn to recognize the ways we find out about characters and draw conclusions about them.

There are several ways to find out about people, or characters, in literature. First, you can learn from what the characters themselves say. You may find out how they feel or why they are doing something. Second, you can learn from what they do. Sometimes their actions will not match their words. Third, what other characters say about them will also give you more information. Just as in real life, you will have to judge whether the person you are listening to is honest and reliable, whether the speaker is being fair or unfair, and whether the person's judgment is good. Finally, you can learn from what the author, or narrator, has to say about a character.

In drama, the main way to understand **characterization**, or the way a character is represented, is through what the characters say. Plays are written in lines of speech, or dialogue. Dialogue can also tell you how people are related to each other—for example, if they are friends or enemies. The stage directions (the words in parentheses) may give you some information about where people are, what they have, what they are doing, or how they feel. Sometimes a play has a narrator who acts as the voice of the playwright and tells you about the characters.

In a play, a story is being told through dialogue and action. You are rarely told directly why people are doing what they are doing. To figure out what they intend or what they want, you have to pay attention to their words. As you read the following passages from plays, ask yourself why a character says certain things and what the character wants. The reason for the character's words and actions is called motivation. You will understand more about the story and purpose of a play when you understand the motivations of the characters in it.

☞ *See Also: GED Exercise Book Literature and the Arts, pages 20–24*

Practicing Comprehension, Application, and Analysis Skills

Read the following passage from Charles Aidman's stage version of Edgar Lee Masters's *Spoon River Anthology*.

WHAT DOES THIS JUDGE LOOK FORWARD TO?

JUDGE SELAH LIVELY: Suppose you stood just five feet two,
And had worked your way as a grocery clerk,
Studying law by candlelight
Until you became an attorney at law?
(5) And then suppose through your diligence,
And regular church attendance,
You became attorney for Thomas Rhodes,
Collecting notes and mortgages,
And representing all the widows
(10) In the Probate Court? And through it all
They jeered at your size, and laughed at your clothes
And your polished boots? And then suppose
You became the County Judge?
And Jefferson Howard and Kinsey Keene,
(15) And Harmon Whitney, and all the giants
Who had sneered at you, were forced to stand
Before the bar and say "Your Honor"—
Well, don't you think it was natural
That I made it hard for them?

Source: *Spoon River Anthology.*

Questions 1 and 2 refer to the passage. Circle the best answer for each question.

1. You can infer from the speech that the judge basically wanted to

   (1) be a good lawyer
   (2) get revenge on people who laughed at him
   (3) stop representing widows
   (4) give up his judgeship
   (5) put Jefferson Howard and all his friends in jail

2. You can infer that the townspeople laughed at the judge mainly because of

   (1) his poor skill as a lawyer
   (2) his job as a grocery clerk
   (3) his church attendance
   (4) his size
   (5) his choice of law school

To check your answers, turn to page 116.

Read the following passage by Jane Martin.

WHY DOES THE SPEAKER'S MOTHER BEHAVE THIS WAY?

LAURIE: The day my mother found out she was dying she asked me
to go out and buy her these clear glass marbles. Dad and I
hadn't even known she was ill which was nothing new.
Whenever you asked my mother if she was ill she would throw

(5) things at you, sesame buns, the editorial page, a handful of hair
ribbons. "Do not," she would say, "suggest things to suggestible
people." Anyway, I brought her the marbles and she counted
ninety of them out and put them in this old cut-glass bowl
which had been the sum total of great Aunt Helena's estate.

(10) Apparently, the doctor had given her three months and she set
great store by doctors. She said she always believed them
because they were the nearest thing to the Old Testament we
had. "I wouldn't give you two bits for these young smiley guys,"
she'd say, "I go for a good, stern-furrowed physician." She

(15) wouldn't even have her teeth cleaned by a dentist under fifty. So
she counted out ninety clear glass marbles and set them in the
bowl on her bedside table. Then she went out and spent twelve
hundred dollars on nightgowns. She said, "In my family you are
only dying when you take to your bed, and that, my darlings, is

(20) where I am going." And she did.

Source: *Talking With . . .*

Questions 3 and 4 refer to the passage. Circle the best answer for each question.

3. Which of the following can be inferred about Laurie's mother?

(1) She enjoyed being ill.
(2) She had a mind of her own.
(3) She did not accept the idea of death.
(4) She did not trust the doctor's opinion.
(5) She had no idea of how to prepare for death.

4. Which of the following is the most likely thing that Laurie's mother did with the marbles?

(1) used them to count the days until she died
(2) played childhood games with them
(3) threw them at people who asked how she was
(4) willed them to Aunt Helena
(5) gave them to her doctor

To check your answers, turn to page 116.

Read the following passage by William Gibson.

HOW CAN ANNIE AND HELEN WORK TOGETHER?

ANNIE: It's hopeless here. I can't teach a child who runs away.

KELLER: (*nonplussed*) Then—do I understand you—propose—

ANNIE: Well, if we all agree it's hopeless, the next question is what—

(5) KATE: Miss Annie. I am not agreed. I think perhaps you—underestimate Helen.

ANNIE: I think everybody else here does.

KATE: She did fold her napkin. She learns, she learns, do you know she began talking when she was six months old? She could say
(10) "water." Not really—"wahwah." "Wahwah," but she meant water, she knew what it meant, and only six months old, I never saw a child so—bright, or outgoing—It's still in her, somewhere, isn't it? You should have seen her before her illness, such a good-tempered child—

(15) ANNIE: (*agreeably*) She's changed.

KATE: Miss Annie, put up with it. And with us.

KELLER: Us!

KATE: Please? Like the lost lamb in the parable, I love her all the more.

(20) ANNIE: Mrs. Keller, I don't think Helen's worst handicap is deafness or blindness. I think it's your love. And pity.

KELLER: Now what does that mean?

ANNIE: All of you here are so sorry for her you've kept her—like a pet, why, even a dog you housebreak. No wonder she won't let
(25) me come near her. It's useless for me to try to teach her language or anything else here. I might as well—

KATE: (*cuts in*) Miss Annie, before you came we spoke of putting her in an asylum.

Source: *The Miracle Worker.*

Questions 5 and 6 refer to the passage. Circle the best answer for each question.

5. Which of the following best explains why Kate says what she does?

(1) She is jealous of Helen.
(2) She believes Annie can help.
(3) She does not want to take care of Helen anymore.
(4) She is angry at Mr. Keller.
(5) She feels like a lost lamb.

6. With which of these statements about children with handicaps would Annie agree?

(1) They cannot be taught language.
(2) They should be given everything they want.
(3) They must be taught, not pitied.
(4) They are better off in an asylum.
(5) They should be treated like pets.

To check your answers, turn to page 116.

GED Mini-Test

Directions: Choose the best answer to each item.

Items 1 and 2 refer to the following passage by James Baldwin.

WHAT DO DAVID AND LUKE HAVE IN COMMON?

LUKE: You play piano like I dreamed you would.

DAVID: I been finding out lately you was pretty good. Mama never
    let us keep a phonograph. I just didn't never hear any of your
    records—until here lately. You was right up there with the best,
(5)   Jellyroll Morton and Louis Armstrong and cats like that. . . .
      You never come to look for us. Why?

LUKE: I started to. I wanted to. I thought of it lots of times.

DAVID: Why didn't you never do it? Did you think it was good
    riddance we was gone?

(10) LUKE: I was hoping you wouldn't never think that, never.

DAVID: I wonder what you expected me to think. I remembered you,
    but couldn't never talk about you. I use to hear about you
    sometime, but I couldn't never say, That's my daddy. I was too
    ashamed. I remembered how you used to play for me sometimes.
(15)   That was why I started playing the piano. I used to go to sleep
    dreaming about the way we'd play together one day, me with my
    piano and you with your trombone.

LUKE: David. David.

DAVID: You never come. You never come when you could do us some
(20)   good. You come now, now when you can't do nobody any good.
    Every time I think about it, think about *you*, I want to break
    down and cry like a baby. You make me—ah! You make me feel
    so bad.

LUKE: Son—don't try to get away from the things that hurt you.
(25)   The things that hurt you—sometimes that's all you got. You got
    to learn to live with those things—and—use them.

Source: *Blues for Mister Charlie.*

---

1. David mainly wants to

  (1) be a musician and leave his family
  (2) forget about his father for good
  (3) be a better musician than his father
  (4) find out what his father thinks of him
  (5) understand why his father has been gone

2. According to this passage, Luke mainly wants to

  (1) show David that he can live with pain
  (2) brag about his musical success
  (3) pretend David's pain does not exist
  (4) encourage David to leave home
  (5) tell David what a good pianist he is

WHAT DOES SHIRLEY DO TO ENTERTAIN HERSELF?

JOHN: You better watch that one. She's gettin' a little big for her pants, ain't you? How old are you now? How old are you?

JUNE: You wouldn't know, of course.

SHIRLEY: Age is the most irrelevant judge of character or maturity
(5) that—

JOHN: Yeah, yeah, how old are you?

JUNE: She's thirteen.

SHIRLEY: I am nineteen and I will be twenty next month.

JUNE: She's thirteen.

(10) SHIRLEY: I am eighteen years old, and it is none of your business. . . .

JUNE: She's thirteen.

SHIRLEY: I'm seventeen. If you must know.

JUNE. You are not seventeen, you cretin.

SHIRLEY: I am fifteen years old!

(15) JUNE: She's fourteen. (JOHN *picks* SHIRLEY *up and carries her over his shoulder to the porch and slams the door on her. All through this, she is screaming: "Put me down, put me down, Rhett Butler, put me down")*

JOHN: (*Smiles, turns back to the bedroom*) Yeah? You better watch
(20) that one. (*Exits to his bedroom*)

SHIRLEY: (*Comes back in, follows him to steps*) I happen to, am going to be an artist, and an artist has no age. . . .

Source: *Talley's Folley.*

---

3. You can infer that which of the following is true?

(1) Shirley is pleased that June keeps insisting that she is thirteen.
(2) Shirley is an artist.
(3) John and Shirley are used to fighting.
(4) June does not like to tease Shirley.
(5) Shirley does not like to argue.

4. Shirley acts the way she does in order to

(1) antagonize everyone
(2) get experience to use in her art
(3) dramatize herself and get attention
(4) force others to keep track of her birthday
(5) make people see that age is not important

To check your answers, turn to page 117.

Answers and Explanations

Practicing Comprehension, Application, and Analysis Skills (pages 111–113)

1. (Analysis) **(2) get revenge on people who laughed at him** The last line especially suggests this attitude, and the entire speech supports option (2). Options (1) and (3) are wrong because he obviously had already done these things. Options (4) and (5) are not supported by the passage.

2. (Inferential Comprehension) **(4) his size** The judge several times mentioned being ridiculed for his size. Option (1) is contradicted by his becoming judge. Option (2) is something he may feel ashamed of, but it is not a cause for laughter. Options (3) and (5) are not supported by the passage.

3. (Inferential Comprehension) **(2) She had a mind of her own.** The character of Laurie's mother might be described as stubborn and decisive. She definitely does not want other people to tell her what to do. Options (1) and (4) are the opposite of what is stated in the text. She is not denying that she will die, so option (3) is wrong. The entire passage is about her preparations, so option (5) is wrong.

4. (Application) **(1) used them to count the days until she died** The ninety marbles represent the days in three months. There is no support for options (2) and (5). As she now realizes she is ill, the act in option (3) probably would not happen. Option (4) is wrong because the aunt is dead.

5. (Analysis) **(2) She believes Annie can help.** Kate is trying to get Annie to stay. Kate loves Helen and sees the good in her, so option (1) is wrong. Option (3) is wrong because there is no evidence that Kate took care of Helen. There is no support for option (4). Helen is the lost lamb, not Kate, so option (5) is wrong.

6. (Application) **(3) They must be taught, not pitied.** Annie says pity stands in the way of teaching Helen. Option (1) is untrue, or she would not be a teacher of a blind and deaf child. Options (2) and (5) are the opposite of what she has said she believes in the passage. Option (4) is obviously something they are all trying to avoid.

1. (Analysis) **(5) understand why his father has been gone** Option (5) is correct because of David's frequent questions along these lines. Option (1) is not supported. Option (2) could be true because his father has caused him pain, but it is also not supported. Option (3) may be true, but there is no evidence for it. Option (4) is true but only supports David's main motivation.

2. (Analysis) **(1) show David that he can live with pain** This is correct because he has learned this himself and hopes to pass it on, which rules out option (3). Option (2) is not supported by the passage. Option (4), from what he says, is not a choice Luke would make for David. Option (5) is true but does not tell Luke's major motivation.

3. (Inferential Comprehension) **(3) John and Shirley are used to fighting.** The fight is conducted good-naturedly, and Shirley's protest when John carries her off is slightly humorous. This suggests they have fought often on a friendly level. Option (1) is obviously not true, because Shirley is annoyed with June. There is not enough evidence to support option (2). Options (4) and (5) are the opposite of what is shown throughout this scene.

4. (Analysis) **(3) dramatize herself and get attention** Shirley's actions are those of someone seeking attention. Option (1) is too strong. Though she may become an artist, her concerns are really with the present moment, ruling out option (2). Option (4) is not supported. Option (5) is wrong because she shows in the passage that age—that is, being older—is important to her.

LESSON 11 Analysis Skills: Identifying Elements of Style and Structure (Theme)

This skill helps you learn to recognize the general subject or topic that a writer is talking about.

The subject of a work of literature is not the same as its plot. The plot is what happens, how the subject is worked out. The central idea in literature is called the **theme**. A theme cannot be identified as something so general as love, war, or sacrifice. A theme says something specific about a topic—for example, "Love is based on understanding." The theme of a play is rarely stated directly, so it is up to the reader to decide what it is. To discover a theme, you must use all the skills you have learned so far to find out what the author means. As you read the passages, ask yourself, "What does this mean? What does this say about human nature? What does this say about how people behave and why they behave that way?" Be careful not to sum up the plot or refer to any specific character or action.

There are two main kinds of popular drama. A **comedy** is a play in which the playwright communicates his or her ideas mainly by making you, the audience, laugh. A **drama**, on the other hand, is a play in which the playwright communicates his or her ideas mostly by making you think deeply or feel strongly about something.

As you may have guessed from your own reading and television watching, comedies and dramas may use the same themes. They differ in approach. One play may present an argument between children and parents in a comic way. Another play may let you see the sadness in such a conflict.

The line between comedy and drama is often blurred, especially today. Many comedies are about serious subjects, and many dramas contain funny characters or comic scenes.

Practicing Comprehension, Application, and Analysis Skills

Read the following passage from a comedy by Woody Allen.

WHAT IS MADE FUN OF IN THIS SCENE?

AMBASSADOR: . . . Axel, most fathers start their sons in the mail room and let them work their way up. I started you on top and you worked your way to the mail room. This Embassy is a clean start for you. If it's not run letter perfect, I'll fire you and if your
(5) own father fires you—it's the end of the line. Goodbye. (*Exits.*)

MAGEE: Have a good flight, Dad. (*Crosses to door and calls.*) Mr. Kilroy!

KILROY: (*Entering.*) You called?

MAGEE: For the next two weeks I am in charge of this Embassy.
(10) Business will go on as usual and it would mean a great deal to me to have your full cooperation.

KILROY: Your father should have known better than to leave in charge a man who was asked to leave Africa.

MAGEE: That's not fair. Some of the best men in the foreign service
(15) have at one time or another been recalled from a country.

KILROY: Africa is a continent. You've been recalled from an entire continent. And what about Japan, you never mention that, or the Soviet Union—you managed to cover that up, too.

MAGEE: You know I've had some bad breaks careerwise.
(20) KILROY: (*Accusatory.*) And you were hung in effigy in Panama!

MAGEE: I admitted I was!

KILROY: Yes, but you didn't say it was by our own Embassy!
(*Phone rings.* KILROY *lets* MAGEE *get it.*)

MAGEE: (*Into phone.*) Yes? Yes, this is the American Embassy. . . .

Source: *Don't Drink the Water*.

Questions 1 and 2 refer to the passage. Circle the best answer for each question.

1. The theme of this scene is

(1) the conflict between Magee and Kilroy
(2) U.S. embassy etiquette
(3) the differences among countries
(4) the inefficiency of the U.S. foreign service
(5) the efficiency of the U.S. foreign service

2. The element most likely to cause laughter in this scene is

(1) the ambassador's and Kilroy's comments on Magee's career
(2) the phone call
(3) the character of Magee
(4) the character of the ambassador
(5) the possibility of Magee's being hanged in effigy

To check your answers, turn to page 124.

Read the following passage by Paddy Chayefsky.

WHAT KIND OF LIVES DO MARTY AND ANGIE LEAD?

ANGIE: Well, what do you feel like doing tonight?

MARTY: I don't know. What do you feel like doing?

ANGIE: Well, we're back to that, huh? I say to you: "What do you feel
like doing tonight?" And you say to me: "I don't know, what do
(5) you feel like doing?" And then we wind up sitting around the
house with a couple of cans of beer, watching Sid Caesar on
television. Well, I tell you what I feel like doing. I feel like
calling up Mary Feeney. She likes you. (MARTY *looks up quickly
at this*.)

(10) MARTY: What makes you say that?

ANGIE: I could see she likes you.

MARTY: Yeah, sure.

ANGIE: (*Half rising in his seat*) I'll call her up.

MARTY: You call her up for yourself, Angie. I don't feel like calling
(15) her up. (ANGIE *sits down again. They both return to reading the
paper for a moment. Then* ANGIE *looks up again.*)

ANGIE: Boy, you're getting to be a real drag, you know that?

MARTY: Angie, I'm thirty-six years old. I been looking for a girl
every Saturday night of my life. I'm a little, short, fat fellow, and
(20) girls don't go for me, that's all. I'm not like you. I mean, you joke
around, and they laugh at you, and you get along fine. I just
stand around like a bug. What's the sense of kidding myself?
Everybody's always telling me to get married. Get married. Get
married. Don't you think I wanna get married? I wanna get
(25) married. They drive me crazy. Now, I don't wanna wreck your
Saturday night for you, Angie. You wanna go somewhere, you go
ahead. I don't wanna go.

ANGIE: Boy, they drive me crazy too. My old lady, every word outta
her mouth, when you gonna get married?

Source: *Television Plays.*

Questions 3 and 4 refer to the passage. Circle the best answer for each question.

3. Which of the following best states the theme in this passage?

(1) Marriage is a natural state.
(2) Saturday nights can be boring.
(3) Marty is missing opportunities.
(4) Two people cannot decide what to do on Saturday night.
(5) Lonely people often stop being socially active.

To check your answers, turn to page 124.

4. The things Marty and Angie say imply that they both

(1) spend a lot of evenings calling up women for dates
(2) want to get married
(3) spend a lot of evenings sitting around
(4) are under pressure from each other to get married
(5) believe they will be married soon

Read the following passage by Elizabeth Diggs.

WHAT PROBLEM DOES THIS FAMILY NEED TO FACE?

JOSEPHINE: Good morning, dear. (EVELYN *turns on stove to heat coffee,* THAYER *takes a large mixing bowl and pours cornflakes in it, then adds milk and sugar*) What do you think I did? I overslept! Haven't slept past six-thirty in I don't know how long.

(5) EVELYN: You were up late.

JOSEPHINE: Oh, I usually am. I go to bed with a good book and I can't stop for hours. Funny, isn't it? Puts most people to sleep. Your grandfather couldn't turn two pages before his eyes would close. But not me. I get wide awake with excitement—even

(10) books I've read before—isn't that the limit?

EVELYN: Did you see any shooting stars?

JOSEPHINE: Don't recall any. (THAYER *exits to porch with his bowl of cornflakes*)

EVELYN: I saw four or five on the way up here Friday night. I

(15) stopped to look.

JOSEPHINE: My, that's a lot of wishes! I guess I'm too old for wishes. I haven't looked for a shooting star in many years.

EVELYN: You did last night.

JOSEPHINE: Oh no. (*shakes her head as if the idea is absurd*)

(20) EVELYN: (*puzzled, can't really believe that* JOSEPHINE *doesn't remember*) We all stayed in here talking, and you went outside. You said you were looking for shooting stars.

JOSEPHINE: (*confused*) Is that right?

EVELYN: You don't remember, do you?

(25) JOSEPHINE: You know, I don't.

EVELYN: You were telling us about how Grandfather used to rehearse his arguments and everybody'd get in on it. (JOSEPHINE *chuckles*) You remember that, don't you?

Source: *Close Ties.*

Questions 5 and 6 refer to the passage. Circle the best answer for each question.

5. You can infer from the passage that

(1) Evelyn is fond of Josephine
(2) Evelyn is tired of Josephine's stories
(3) Thayer is Josephine's son
(4) Josephine usually sleeps late
(5) Josephine is worried about something

6. Which of the following best states the theme in this passage?

(1) Old people don't sleep much.
(2) Josephine misses her husband.
(3) Wishes can be made on shooting stars
(4) The failings of old age are puzzling to the young.
(5) Memories of the past are best forgotten.

To check your answers, turn to page 124.

GED Mini-Test

Directions: Choose the best answer to each item.

Items 1 to 6 refer to the following passage by Michael Wilson.

WHAT IS ESPERANZA SEARCHING FOR?

ESPERANZA: . . . Ramón, we're not getting weaker. We're stronger than ever before. (*He snorts with disgust.*) *They're* getting weaker. They thought they could break our picket line. And they failed. And now they can't win unless they pull off something
(5)   big, and pull it off fast.

RAMÓN: Like what?

ESPERANZA: I don't know. But I can feel it coming. It's like . . . like a lull before the storm. Charley Vidal says . . .

RAMÓN: (*exploding*) Charley Vidal says! Don't throw Charley Vidal
(10)   up to me!

ESPERANZA: Charley's my friend. I need friends. (*She looks at him strangely.*) Why are you afraid to have me as your friend?

RAMÓN: I don't know what you're talking about.

ESPERANZA: No, you don't. Have you learned nothing from this strike?
(15)   Why are you afraid to have me at your side? Do you still think you can have dignity only if I have none?

RAMÓN: You talk of dignity? After what you've been doing?

ESPERANZA: Yes. I talk of dignity. The Anglo bosses look down on you, and you hate them for it. "Stay in your place, you dirty Mexican"—
(20)   that's what they tell you. But why must you say to me "Stay in *your* place"? Do you feel better having someone lower than you?

RAMÓN: Shut up, you're talking crazy.

(*But* ESPERANZA *moves right up to him, speaking now with great passion.*)

(25) ESPERANZA: Whose neck shall I stand on, to make me feel superior? And what will I get out of it? I don't want anything lower than I am. I'm low enough already. I want to rise. And push everything up with me as I go. . . .

RAMÓN: (*fiercely*) Will you be still?

(30) ESPERANZA (*shouting*) And if you can't understand this you're a fool—because you can't win this strike without me! You can't win *anything* without me!

(*He seizes her shoulder with one hand, half raises the other to slap her.* ESPERANZA's *body goes rigid. She stares straight at him,*
(35)   *defiant and unflinching.* RAMÓN *drops his hand.*)

ESPERANZA: That would be the old way. Never try it on me again— never.

Source: *Salt of the Earth.*

1. The theme of this passage is

   (1) human dignity is something worth standing up for
   (2) people should try to avoid going to war
   (3) strikes should be handled in a certain way
   (4) winning can seem like the most important thing
   (5) Ramón and Esperanza disagree on fundamental issues

2. Esperanza compares the way Ramón has been treating her to the way

   (1) adults treat children
   (2) the workers treat the bosses
   (3) the Anglos treat the Mexicans
   (4) humans treat animals
   (5) the Mexicans treat the Anglos

3. You can infer form this passage that Ramón believes that

   (1) no one should go on strike
   (2) workers and bosses are allies
   (3) friendship is not possible between men and women
   (4) women should be allowed to express themselves
   (5) men and women together will win the strike

4. With which of the following statements would Esperanza most likely agree?

   (1) It is important to succeed no matter whom you hurt.
   (2) It is important to grow without pushing anyone else down.
   (3) It is important for one person in a marriage to be stronger than the other.
   (4) It is important to stay in your place and avoid conflict.
   (5) It is important to struggle alone and without friends.

5. You can infer that Esperanza believes that dignity means

   (1) having friends
   (2) walking a picket line
   (3) having self-respect
   (4) being independent
   (5) being more powerful than others

6. In lines 34–35 Esperanza makes the decision that she will

   (1) leave Ramón soon
   (2) not be involved in the strike
   (3) urge the strikers to end the strike
   (4) not allow Ramón to hit her again
   (5) become Ramón's friend

To check you answers, turn to page 125.

Answers and Explanations

Practicing Comprehension, Application, and Analysis Skills (pages 119–121)

1. (Analysis) **(4) the inefficiency of the U.S. foreign service** Option (4) is correct because most of the content treats Magee's obvious lack of competence. Option (1) describes a relationship between characters, which is too specific for a theme. Option (2) is not supported. Option (3) is a minor point mentioned by Kilroy; it is not a theme. Option (5) is the opposite of what is shown in the scene.

2. (Analysis) **(1) the ambassador's and Kilroy's comments on Magee's career** According to them, Magee's behavior has been the opposite of that of a good foreign diplomat. Option (1) does not involve comic material. You do not learn enough about either Magee or the ambassador to justify options (3) or (4). Option (5) is incorrect because it states something that has already taken place.

3. (Analysis) **(5) Lonely people often stop being socially active.** Even though they are together in this scene, Marty and Angie are clearly lonely and have stopped trying to do much about it. Option (1) is wrong because the focus is not on marriage itself. Option (2) is not the main issue here. Options (3) and (4) refer to a specific person and a specific plot line; therefore, they do not express a theme.

4. (Inferential Comprehension) **(3) spend a lot of evenings sitting around** Option (3) can be inferred from Angie's second speech, which also rules out option (1). Option (2) is incorrect because only Marty says he wants to get married. Option (4) is not supported by the passage. Option (5) is unlikely in their present situation.

5. (Inferential Comprehension) **(1) Evelyn is fond of Josephine** Evelyn's concern about Josephine's forgetfulness and her willingness to listen to Josephine's stories support this conclusion. Therefore, option (2) is wrong. There is no support for option (3). Option (4) is the opposite of what is stated in the text. Option (5) is wrong because Josephine does not seem bothered by much at all.

6. (Analysis) **(4) The failings of old age are puzzling to the young.** Evelyn's confusion illustrates this idea. Option (1) may be true, but it is not the central idea of this passage. Option (2) is wrong because it refers to a specific person. Option (3) refers to a detail, not to the theme of the passage. Option (5) is not suggested in this passage.

1. (Analysis) **(1) human dignity is something worth standing up for** In the strike and in her relationship with Ramón, Esperanza is searching for dignity. Option (2) is not supported by the passage. Option (3) is too specific for a theme. Option (4) is a theme statement but is not correct here. Because it refers to specific charaters, option (5) is not a theme statement.

2. (Literal Comprehension) **(3) the Anglos treat the Mexicans** Option (3) is correct because of Esperanza's words in lines 19–21, which would also rule out option (5). Options (1) and (4) are possible comparisons, but they are not Esperanza's. Since in this case the Anglos are the bosses and the Mexicans the workers, option (2) must also be ruled out.

3. (Inferential Comprehension) **(3) friendship is not possible between men and women** Ramón resists Esperanza's wish that he be her friend. Option (1) can be ruled out since he obviously is on strike. Option (2) also is clearly incorrect. Options (4) and (5) must be ruled out because of Ramón's current views of women and of the strike.

4. (Application) **(2) It is important to grow without pushing anyone else down.** This is correct because of her words in lines 25–28, which also rule out option (1). Option (3) is incorrect because of her obvious wish for equality. Options (4) and (5) are not supported by her statements in the passage.

5. (Inferential Comprehension) **(3) having self-respect** Everything Esperanza says indicates a wish to think well of herself and others. Option (1) is important to her, but it does not mean the same as "dignity." Option (2) is something Esperanza would do to *gain* self-respect. From her words, she clearly does not wish to be independent, option (4), or more powerful than others, option (5).

6. (Literal Comprehension) **(4) not allow Ramón to hit her again** The stage directions indicate that he begins to strike her and then stops. Her lines reinforce that decision. Option (1) is clearly not the case; she wants them to struggle together. Options (2) and (3) are not supported by the passage. Option (5) is incorrect because she already *is* Ramón's friend, although he does not believe it.

Review: Popular Literature

In the preceding lessons, you have learned strategies for reading fiction and nonfiction, poetry and drama. You have read and analyzed passages from popular literature. What you have studied is similar to the passages and questions that appear on the GED exam. By doing the Practices and the GED Mini-Tests, you have shown yourself that you can perform well on this part of the GED exam.

The following is a final review of all the skills you have studied. The questions that follow each passage may test whether you have understood what you have read, or they may test whether you can apply what you have learned in another context. You may also be asked questions about the techniques the authors use and what the effects of those techniques are.

As you do this review, keep in mind one basic point: authors—whether poets, dramatists, or writers of fiction or nonfiction—are writing because they want to communicate with you. First, last, and always, your goal should be to understand what the author is trying to say.

Directions: Choose the best answer to each item.

Items 1 to 3 refer to the following passage by James Michener.

WHAT DID THE GIANT RATTLESNAKE DO?

The Quimpers were less lucky with another event caused by the flood, and this too would be remembered. The excessive waters disturbed many animals, causing them to venture into new areas and adopt new habits, and one of those most seriously displaced
(5) was a huge rattlesnake eight feet three inches long from the tip of his rattle and as big around as a small tree. He was really a monstrous creature, with a head as big as a soup plate and fangs so huge and powerful, they could discharge a dreadful injection. Veteran of many struggles, master of the sudden ambush, he had sub-
(10) dued baby pigs and fawns and rabbits and a multitude of rats and mice. His traditional home had been sixteen miles up the Brazos in a rocky ledge that gave him excellent protection and a steady supply of victims, but the floods had dislodged him and sent him tumbling down the river along with deer and alligators and javelinas. During
(15) the height of the flood each animal was so preoccupied with its own salvation that it ignored friends and enemies alike, but as the waters receded, each resumed its habits, and the snake found itself far

downstream, lodged in unfamiliar rocks and with a most uncertain food supply. . . .

(20) This great beast at Quimper's ferry, longer than any hitherto seen along the Brazos, did not seek contact with human beings; it did its best to avoid them, but if any threatened the quiet of its domain, it could strike with terrifying force. It would not have come into contact with the Quimpers had not Yancey gone probing along (25) the farther bank, not doing any serious work or accomplishing much, but merely poking into holes with a stick to see what might be happening. As he approached where the snake lay hidden, he heard but did not recognize the warning rattle. Thinking it to be a bird or some noisy insect, he probed further, and found himself staring at the (30) huge coiled snake not ten feet away.

"Mom!" he screamed, and Mattie, working at the ferry, grabbed the gun she kept aboard for protection against wandering Karankawa, and ran to help, but when she reached Yancey she found him immobilized, pointing at the coiled snake whose rattles echoed. "Do (35) something!" he pleaded.

Infuriated by his craven behavior and terrified of the snake, she pushed her son aside, and with her heart beating at a rate which must soon cause her to faint, she raised the gun. Not firing blindly, because she knew she had only one chance, she took aim as the (40) snake prepared for its deadly thrust, and pulled the trigger. She felt the shock against her shoulder; she felt the snake brush against her knee; and she fainted.

Source: *Space.*

---

1. From the context it can be inferred that the Brazos is

(1) a river
(2) a county
(3) a ferryboat
(4) a snake farm
(5) a homestead

2. The author restates the mother's terror by saying which of the following?

(1) infuriated by his craven behavior
(2) with her heart beating at a rate . . .
(3) she had only one chance
(4) prepared for its deadly thrust
(5) felt the shock

3. Which of the following statements describes an action Yancey Quimper would probably take?

(1) He would keep his head under fire.
(2) He would work from dawn to dusk.
(3) He would go far in the world on true grit and character.
(4) He would be unable to act in a time of crisis.
(5) He would make his living as a traveling salesman.

Items 4 and 5 refer to the following passage by Cleveland Amory.

WHAT IS THIS CAT'S ROUTINE?

Cats do, however, like routine—in fact, they love it. And, in the days—and nights—which followed the rescue my cat and I worked out many routines. Or rather he worked them out, and I, as dutifully as I could, worked at following them.

(5) Some of these routines necessarily involved compromises. My cat, for example, liked to get up early—in fact he liked to get up at 3 A.M. That was, of course, all right with me. His hours, it had been one of our understandings, were his own. The trouble was that, at 3 A.M., he liked a midnight snack of Tender Vittles. Again, seemingly,

(10) no problem. Simply leave out a bowl of Vittles before he went to bed.

But unfortunately there was a problem. I could not just leave out a bowl of Vittles before I went to bed. He would eat them before he went to bed. He did not have, when you came right down to it, either any good old-fashioned Boston discipline—as I would have

(15) thought he would have at least begun to learn from me—or, for that matter, my good sound sensible Boston foresight. No matter how large a bowl I filled of Vittles before he retired, the bowl was empty before he retired.

His hours in this routine thus became my hours. And so we

(20) compromised. Before going to bed each night, I put out an empty dish on the floor by the bed and a package of Tender Vittles on my bedside table. At 3 A.M.—and he was extraordinarily accurate about this—he would wake up, roll over, and wake me up. At 3:01 I would roll over, put some Vittles in his dish, or at least reasonably

(25) near it, and go back, or at least attempt to go back, to sleep.

Source: *The Cat Who Came to Christmas.*

---

4. Which of the following is a conclusion that can be drawn from this passage?

   (1) Cats are harder to please than dogs are.
   (2) The author has trouble getting his cat to eat.
   (3) The author is fond of his cat.
   (4) Boston cats are old-fashioned.
   (5) Cats can be trained to tell time.

5. The main idea of this passage is that

   (1) the cat finally agreed to the man's schedule
   (2) the man had to figure out an easy way to feed the cat in the middle of the night
   (3) the man had to figure out a way to get his cat to go on a diet
   (4) cats will eat any time they find food in front of them
   (5) establishing routines often means making compromises

IS THIS PERSON A GOOD PATIENT?

Obviously this is not the moment to be talking about operations when here we all are—in the very bloom of health. But these are troubled times, and there are people in St. Vincent's Hospital today who, as recently as yesterday, didn't know they had a spinal disk.

(5) The thing to do, I say, is be prepared, bone up, get the facts so that your stay in the hospital will be the jolly, satisfying interlude it ought to be.

I don't know whether or not I am speaking for convalescents everywhere, but I can tell you that *my* big mistake when I go to the (10) hospital is being too cheerful. I arrive the day before the operation and, while it would be stretching things to suggest that on this occasion I feel fit, I at least feel human. So I try to be agreeable. Agreeable nothing; I'm adorable to a point just short of nausea. With my gay sayings and my air of quiet self-deprecation, I creep into the (15) heart of one and all.

"Yes," I murmur to the night nurse, "I did ring for you an hour ago, but that's *perfectly* all right." And I reassure the orderly who forgot to bring my dinner tray with a blithe "Don't worry about it, I'm not the least bit hungry and besides I have these delicious cherry (20) cough drops."

Source: *How I Got to Be Perfect*.

---

6. The style this author uses is most likely intended to

(1) suggest that she is an authority on hospital care
(2) make the reader think twice about going to a hospital
(3) make the reader laugh
(4) make the reader take her advice seriously
(5) be suitable for publication in a medical journal

7. Which is the best meaning for the word "convalescents" (line 8)?

(1) people who like to talk a lot
(2) nurses
(3) orderlies
(4) troubled times
(5) people who are recovering from an illness

8. When the writer says that "your stay in the hospital will be the jolly, satisfying interlude it ought to be" (lines 6–7), she really means that

(1) people can have a lot of fun in a hospital
(2) people do not enjoy being in the hospital
(3) hospitals are becoming entertainment centers
(4) she is satisfied with the care she received
(5) hospital rooms are more comfortable than they used to be

Items 9 and 10 refer to the following excerpt from a poem by Daniel Mark Epstein.

WHO WAS AFRAID OF FLYING?

Miami

. . .

It started with the Bay Bridge.
He couldn't take that steel vault into the blue
above the blue, so much horizon!
Then it was the road itself, the rise and fall,
(5) the continual blind curve.
He hired a chauffeur, he took the train.
Then it was hotels, so many rooms
the same, he had to sleep with the light on.
His courage has shrunk to the size of a windowbox.

(10) Father who scared the witches and vampires
from my childhood closets, father
who walked before me like a hero's shield
through neighborhoods where hoodlums honed their knives
on concrete, where nerve was law,
(15) who will drive you home from Miami?
You're broke and I'm a thousand miles away
with frightened children of my own.
Who will rescue you from the garden
where jets flash like swords above your head?

Source: *The Book of Fortune.*

9. Which of the following is the best meaning of "where nerve was law" (line 14)?

   (1) where the police were nervous
   (2) where people were very calm
   (3) where people had to be brave to survive
   (4) where hoodlums made the rules
   (5) where the law was respected

10. According to this poem, when the speaker was young, his father had been a symbol of

    (1) evil
    (2) cowardice
    (3) hatred
    (4) fearlessness
    (5) justice

Items 11 and 12 refer to the following passage by Neil Simon.

DO THESE ROOMMATES AGREE ABOUT MOST THINGS?

FELIX: . . . (*Gets down on his knees, picks up chips and puts them into box.*) Don't forget I cook and clean and take care of this house. I save us a lot of money, don't I?

OSCAR: Yeah, but then you keep me up all night counting it.

(5) FELIX: (*Goes to table and sweeps chips and cards into box.*) Now wait a minute. We're not always going at each other. We have some fun too, don't we?

OSCAR: (*Crosses to couch.*) *Fun?* Felix, getting a clear picture on Channel Two isn't my idea of whoopee.

(10) FELIX: What are you talking about?

OSCAR: All right, what do you and I do every night? (*Takes off sneakers, dropping them on floor.*)

FELIX: What do we do? You mean after dinner?

OSCAR: That's right. After we've had your halibut steak and the
(15) dishes are done and the sink has been Brillo'd and the pans have been S.O.S.'d and the leftovers have been Saran-wrapped—what do we do?

FELIX: (*Finishes clearing table and puts everything on top of bookcase.*) Well, we read . . . we talk . . .

(20) OSCAR: (*Takes off pants and throws them on floor.*) No, no. *I* read and *you* talk! . . . I try to work and you talk. . . . I take a bath and you talk. . . . I go to sleep and you talk. We've got your life arranged pretty good but I'm still looking for a little entertainment.

(25) FELIX: (*Pulling upstage kitchen chairs away from table.*) What are you saying? That I talk too much?

OSCAR: (*Sits on couch.*) No, no. I'm not complaining. You have a lot to say. What's worrying me is that I'm beginning to listen. . . .

Source: *The Odd Couple*.

---

11. Which of the following sayings comes closest to stating the theme of this passage?

(1) Opposites attract.
(2) Beauty is only skin deep.
(3) Do unto others as you would have others do unto you.
(4) A chicken in every pot.
(5) Every rose has its thorn.

12. Which of the following would Felix probably enjoy least?

(1) trying a new recipe
(2) lying around all day
(3) organizing his dresser drawers
(4) balancing his checkbook
(5) dusting

To check your answers, turn to pages 132–133.

Answers and Explanations

Popular Literature Review (pages 126–131)

1. (Inferential Comprehension) **(1) a river** Although options (2), (3), (4), and (5) are possible, only option (1) fits the context of the passage as a whole. The author says the snake lived sixteen miles up the Brazos, and later that he was seen along the Brazos. Only a river really fits these descriptions. Also, the river ties in to the central event of the passage, which is the flood that brought the snake.

2. (Literal Comprehension) **(2) with her heart beating at a rate . . .** The heart beats faster when a person is scared. Option (1) refers to her anger at her son, not her fear. Option (3) is a statement of fact, not an indication of fear. Option (4) refers to the snake's action. Option (5) refers to the feel of the gun against her shoulder.

3. (Application) **(4) He would be unable to act in a time of crisis.** Option (4) best describes the way Quimper behaves in the passage. Thus, options (1) and (3) are unlikely. From the passage, it is doubtful that option (2) is true. There is no support for option (5).

4. (Inferential Comprehension) **(3) The author is fond of his cat.** The tone of the passage and the fact that the author attempts to please the cat support this. There is no comparison made to dogs, so option (1) is wrong. The cat clearly likes to eat, so option (2) is wrong. The references to Boston and old-fashioned are about the author, not the cat, so option (4) is wrong. Option (5) is wrong because the cat is acting on its own sense of time; it has not been trained to watch a clock.

5. (Literal Comprehension) **(2) the man had to figure out an easy way to feed the cat in the middle of the night** Option (1) is the opposite of what happens in the passage. The problem was about a late-night snack, not a diet, so option (3) is wrong. Options (4) and (5) are general statements that are suggested in the passage but do not cover the main idea.

6. (Analysis) **(3) make the reader laugh** The style is informal, lighthearted, and intended to be funny. Options (1) and (5) suggest the style is formal and serious, so both are wrong. There is no support for options (2) and (4).

7. (Inferential Comprehension) **(5) people who are recovering from an illness** She is talking as someone who has been in the hospital. Option (1) does not fit in the context. Options (2) and (3) are wrong because she is referring to patients, not people who work in a hospital. Option (4) is wrong because it does not refer to people.

8. (Analysis) **(2) people do not enjoy being in the hospital** The author uses sarcasm in saying the opposite of what she means, knowing that people will not take her literally. The rest of the passage does not suggest that people can have fun, so option (1) is wrong. The author is talking about the patient's attitude, not what the hospital provides, so options (3), (4), and (5) are wrong.

9. (Analysis) **(3) where people had to be brave to survive** Having nerve can be the same as having courage, and "law" refers to what was respected by otherwise lawless people. Option (1) gets the idea backward. Option (2) has nothing to do with nerve. Option (4) is true but is the reason that courage was required. Option (5) is the opposite of what is meant.

10. (Analysis) **(4) fearlessness** The father had faced all the real and imagined dangers of the speaker's childhood to protect his son. So options (1), (2), and (3) are wrong. Option (5) may have been true, but it is not illustrated in the poem.

11. (Analysis) **(1) Opposites attract.** Despite their differences, the two men seem to like each other. The passage focuses on the relationship between the two; options (2), (4), and (5) have nothing to do with that idea. Option (3) is not supported in the passage.

12. (Application) **(2) lying around all day** From what is suggested about his character, Felix likes to stay busy. Option (1) is wrong because he apparently likes to cook. Options (3), (4), and (5) are wrong because he seems to enjoy having everything clean and orderly.

Use the chart below to find your strengths and weaknesses in reading comprehension.

Skill	Area	Question	Lessons for Review
Literal Comprehension	Fiction Nonfiction	2 5	3 1 and 2
Inferential Comprehension	Fiction Nonfiction Nonfiction	1 4 7	4 5 4
Application	Fiction Drama	3 12	10 10
Analysis	Nonfiction Nonfiction Poetry Poetry Drama	6 8 9 10 11	6 7 8 9 11

- ◆ **autobiography**
  a person's life story told by that person

- ◆ **biography**
  a person's life story told by another person

- ◆ **essay**
  a short piece of nonfiction usually written from a personal point of view

The difference between classical literature and good popular literature is often hard to tell. One major difference is that classical literature has proven itself good enough to be read over and over by many people. A novel or poem has to be more than just well written to become classical literature. It also must be about experiences that are important to all people, not just to those of one culture or one time period. Popular literature is too recently written for us to know if people a hundred years from now will still enjoy it.

The word *classic* means a standard of excellence. It does not mean that something is old or hard to understand. A Model T Ford might be called a classic because it was well made to begin with and can still be easily driven and taken care of today. But how many of us remember a car called the Roamer? Classical literature endures. (It can also be fun to read.)

In the next seven lessons, you will be reading passages from classical fiction, nonfiction, poetry, and drama. As you read, you will be learning more skills that will help you understand and enjoy literature.

supporting details
information that describes or explains an idea

The selections in the first three lessons are fiction. Lesson 12 introduces cause and effect: the way that one event leads to another. Lesson 13 will review finding an unstated main idea. Now that you have had more practice in recognizing details and examples, unstated main ideas will be easier to discover. Lesson 14 presents another look at style and structure. You will study how a writer uses words to suggest an attitude about the subject without coming right out and saying it.

inference
an insight based on facts and suggestions

Another side of style is discussed in Lesson 15. Here you will learn about point of view, the angle from which a writer gets you to look at the subject. The subject in this lesson is people. The passages are nonfiction and have been taken from **biographies** and **autobiographies**.

mood
the emotional background in a literary work

Lesson 16 reviews drawing conclusions—making decisions based on **inferences** and **supporting details**. You will be reading nonfiction essays.

stage directions
the instructions an author includes in a play to describe actor's movements or manner; they also may describe the setting or costumes

In Lesson 17, you will be studying poetry. You will learn how a poet uses words to create a **mood**, or emotional background. Understanding the mood of a poem will help you understand the poet's purpose.

The last lesson uses drama to introduce characterization. Playwrights tell us about the personalities of the people in the play in several ways. You will learn that **stage directions** do more than just tell the actors where to stand.

LESSON 12 Comprehension Skills: Identifying Cause-and-Effect Relationships

Understanding cause-and-effect relationships helps you see the link between two specific pieces of information.

A **cause** is an initial action—a thought, word, or deed that makes something else happen. An **effect** is the consequence, or result, of that action. Sometimes the relationship between cause and effect is stated directly, as, for example, when the author uses words and phrases like "because," "led to," "brought about," or "due to." More often, however, fiction writers let events speak for themselves. Sometimes a writer tells you the cause first and then tells you about the effect. Other times, you read first about the effect and then about the cause. Whatever way an author sets up the information, there is a basic pattern: Cause A produces Effect B.

Cause and effect usually happen in chronological order—that is, in order of time. The cause happens before the effect: lightning strikes a utility pole and then the electricity in your house fails. But suppose it starts to rain heavily and then your windshield wipers quit working. Does this mean the rain is related to the wipers failing? Just because one event happened before the other does not mean the events are related as cause and effect.

The **plot** is what happens to the characters in a story. It is an unfolding series of events. The way one event or development leads to another is called **cause and effect**. Recognizing the relationship between causes and effects in a paragraph or longer piece of literature is called **understanding consequences**.

☞ *See Also: GED Exercise Book Literature and the Arts, pages 26–29*

Practicing Comprehension, Application, and Analysis Skills

Read the following passage by Kenneth Grahame.

WHY IS RABBIT RUNNING?

If he could only get away from the holes in the banks, he thought, there would be no more faces. He swung off the path and plunged into the untrodden places of the wood.

Then the whistling began.

(5) Very faint and shrill it was, and far behind him, when first he heard it; but somehow it made him hurry forward. Then, still very faint and shrill, it sounded far ahead of him, and made him hesitate and want to go back. As he halted in indecision it broke out on either side, and seemed to be caught up and passed on throughout the
(10) whole length of the wood to its farthest limit. They were up and alert and ready, evidently, whoever they were! And he—he was alone, and unarmed, and far from any help; and the night was closing in.

Then the pattering began.

He thought it was only falling leaves at first, so slight and deli-
(15) cate was the sound of it. Then as it grew it took a regular rhythm, and he knew it for nothing else but the pat-pat-pat of little feet, still a very long way off. Was it in front or behind? It seemed to be first one, then the other, then both. It grew and it multiplied, till from every quarter as he listened anxiously, leaning this way and that, it
(20) seemed to be closing in on him. As he stood still to hearken, a rabbit came running hard towards him through the trees. He waited, expecting it to slacken pace, or to swerve from him into a different course. Instead, the animal almost brushed him as it dashed past, his face set and hard, his eyes staring. "Get out of this, you fool, get
(25) out!" the Mole heard him mutter as he swung round a stump and disappeared down a friendly burrow.

Source: *The Wind in the Willows.*

Questions 1 and 2 refer to the passage. Circle the best answer for each question.

1. The speaker felt nervous because

  (1) he liked holes in the bank
  (2) he heard whistling
  (3) he was late for an appointment
  (4) the sounds were too faint
  (5) he wanted to see the faces he had imagined

2. The pattering made Mole feel

  (1) more relaxed
  (2) sick
  (3) delighted
  (4) even more nervous
  (5) as if he were at home

To check your answers, turn to page 142.

Read the following passage by Doris Lessing.

WILL THE LOCUSTS LEAVE ANYTHING BEHIND?

She went out to join the old man, stepping carefully among the insects. They stood and watched. Overhead the sky was blue, blue and clear.

"Pretty," said old Stephen with satisfaction.

(5) Well, thought Margaret, we may be ruined, we may be bankrupt, but not everyone has seen an army of locusts fanning their wings at dawn.

Over the slopes, in the distance, a faint red smear showed in the sky, thickened and spread. "There they go," said old Stephen. (10) "There goes the main army, off South."

And from the trees, from the earth all round them, the locusts were taking wing. They were like small aircraft, maneuvering for the take-off, trying their wings to see if they were dry enough. Off they went. A reddish brown stream was rising off the miles of bush, (15) off the lands, the earth. Again the sunlight darkened.

And as the clotted branches lifted, the weight on them lightening, there was nothing but the black spines of branches, trees. No green left, nothing. All morning they watched, the three of them, as the brown crust thinned and broke and dissolved, flying up to mass (20) with the main army, now a brownish-red smear in the Southern sky. The lands which had been filmed with green, the new tender mealie plants, were stark and bare. All the trees stripped. A devastated landscape. No green, no green anywhere.

Source: "A Mild Attack of Locust," from *The Habit of Loving*.

Questions 3 to 5 refer to the passage. Circle the best answer for each question.

3. What effect did the locusts have on the land?

(1) They left it bare of plants.
(2) They turned it brownish-red.
(3) They fertilized the new plants.
(4) They left it greener than before.
(5) They turned it into a runway.

4. Most farmers would regard the appearance of a swarm of locusts as

(1) a thrilling event
(2) an upsetting event
(3) a once-in-a-lifetime occurrence
(4) a yearly occurrence
(5) a colorful display

5. Which of the following best explains what might cause Margaret and her family to go bankrupt?

(1) The locusts were very hungry this year.
(2) They were not very good farmers.
(3) The farm was too big for them.
(4) Stephen would rather watch the locusts invade the field than work.
(5) The family would lose their income because the crops were destroyed.

To check your answers, turn to page 142.

Read the following passage by Joseph Conrad.

IS ELOPING WITH DIAMELEN WORTH ANY SACRIFICE?

We ran down to the water. I saw a low hut above the black
mud, and a small canoe hauled up. I heard another shot behind me.
I thought, "That is his last charge." We rushed down to the canoe; a
man came running from the hut, but I leaped on him, and we rolled
(5) together in the mud. Then I got up, and he lay still at my feet. I
don't know whether I had killed him or not. I and Diamelen pushed
the canoe afloat. I heard yells behind me, and I saw my brother run
across the glade. Many men were bounding after him. I took her in
my arms and threw her into the boat, then leaped in myself. When
(10) I looked back I saw that my brother had fallen. He fell and was up
again, but the men were closing round him. He shouted, "I am
coming!" The men were close to him. I looked. Many men. Then I
looked at her. Tuan, I pushed the canoe! I pushed it into deep water.
She was kneeling forward, looking at me, and I said, "Take your
(15) paddle," while I struck the water with mine. Tuan, I heard him cry.
I heard him cry my name twice; and I heard voices shouting, "Kill!
Strike!" I never turned back. I heard him calling my name again
with a great shriek, as when life is going out together with the
voice—and I never turned my head. My own name! . . . My brother!
(20) Three times he called—but I was not afraid of life. Was she not
there in that canoe? And could I not with her find a country where
death is forgotten—where death is unknown?

Source: *The Lagoon.*

Questions 6 to 8 refer to the passage. Circle the best answer for each question.

6. The narrator let his brother be killed
because the narrator

(1) relied on others to save him
(2) was busy saving the woman he
loved
(3) did not realize he was in trouble
(4) wanted to get him out of the way
(5) did not really care about him

7. Letting his brother die has made the
narrator feel

(1) secretly glad
(2) self-justified
(3) guilt-ridden
(4) nonchalant
(5) resentful

8. The brother dies while helping the
narrator

(1) escape from enemy prison
(2) rescue a maiden in distress
(3) kill his enemy
(4) complete a spying mission
(5) run away with his beloved

To check your answers, turn to page 142.

LESSON 12 Comprehension Skills: Identifying Cause-and-Effect Relationships **139**

GED Mini-Test

Directions: Choose the best answer to each item.

Items 1 to 6 refer to the following passage by Jane Austen.

ARE THESE TWO SISTERS HAVING THE SAME LUCK AT LOVE?

As soon as they were gone, Elizabeth walked out to recover her spirits; or in other words, to dwell without interruption on those subjects that must deaden them more. Mr. Darcy's behavior astonished and vexed her.

(5)   "Why, if he came only to be silent, grave, and indifferent," said she, "did he come at all?"

She could settle it in no way that gave her pleasure.

"He could be still amiable, still pleasing, to my uncle and aunt, when he was in town; and why not to me? If he fears me, why come (10) hither? If he no longer cares for me, why silent? Teasing, teasing, man! I will think no more about him."

Her resolution was for a short time involuntarily kept by the approach of her sister, who joined her with a cheerful look, which showed her better satisfied with their visitors, than Elizabeth.

(15)   "Now," said she, "That this first meeting is over, I feel perfectly easy. I know my own strength, and I shall never be embarrassed again by his coming. I am glad he dines here on Tuesday. It will then be publicly seen, that on both sides, we meet only as common and indifferent acquaintance."

(20)   "Yes, very indifferent indeed," said Elizabeth, laughingly. "Oh, Jane, take care."

"My dear Lizzy, you cannot think me so weak, as to be in danger now."

"I think you are in very great danger of making him as much (25) in love with you as ever."

Source: *Pride and Prejudice*.

1. Why is Elizabeth upset?

   (1) She is jealous of her sister.
   (2) Mr. Darcy had not paid much attention to her.
   (3) Mr. Darcy had paid too much attention to her.
   (4) She is embarrassed by her own shyness.
   (5) Mr. Darcy had been rude to her relatives.

2. In the future, Elizabeth probably will

   (1) never think about Mr. Darcy again
   (2) continue to think about Mr. Darcy
   (3) try to convince Jane to drop her boyfriend
   (4) stop speaking to her aunt and uncle
   (5) give up all hope of romance

3. In this passage, two sisters, Elizabeth and Jane, are

   (1) congratulating themselves on being good hostesses
   (2) discovering that they are in love with the same man
   (3) acting more friendly than either girl really feels
   (4) reacting to the visit of two men they are interested in
   (5) sharing their disappointment over their relationships

4. Which of the following is the best meaning of "amiable" (line 8)?

   (1) indifferent
   (2) silent
   (3) astonishing
   (4) teasing
   (5) pleasing

5. Jane's visitor has left her feeling

   (1) more sure of herself
   (2) indifferent to him
   (3) superior to him
   (4) overwhelmed by emotion
   (5) shy and awkward

6. Which of the following conclusions can be drawn from this passage?

   (1) Mr. Darcy used to act as if he cared for Elizabeth.
   (2) Mr. Darcy is in danger of falling in love with Jane.
   (3) The two girls will both be disappointed in love.
   (4) Mr. Darcy is dangerously insane.
   (5) Jane is better at flirting than Elizabeth is.

To check your answers, turn to page 143.

Answers and Explanations

Practicing Comprehension, Application, and Analysis Skills (pages 137–139)

1. (Inferential Comprehension) **(2) he heard whistling** The whistle was something he did not understand. Options (1) and (3) are not suggested. Options (4) and (5) do not explain why the character is nervous.

2. (Inferential Comprehension) **(4) even more nervous** Mole is already tense. The pattering is unexplained, so it adds to Mole's tension. Options (1), (3), and (5) are the opposite of what is suggested. There is no evidence that Mole felt ill, so option (2) is wrong.

3. (Inferential Comprehension) **(1) They left it bare of plants.** The result is described in the last paragraph. The color in option (2) refers to the swarm of locusts, not to the land. Options (3) and (4) are the opposite of what happened in the passage. Option (5) takes the figurative reference to aircraft literally.

4. (Application) **(2) an upsetting event** This is correct because it is upsetting that locusts leave the land barren. Options (1) and (5) might describe one aspect of a locust attack, but not the overall effect. There is no indication in the passage (or in nature) about the timing of a swarm of locusts, so options (3) and (4) are incorrect.

5. (Inferential Comprehension) **(5) The family would lose their income because the crops were destroyed.** The locusts had eaten the crops, and farmers make money only by selling what they grow. Option (1) might have been true, but it does not cause bankruptcy. There is no evidence for options (2) and (3). Option (4) is wrong because Stephen had little choice; the locusts had destroyed the reason for working.

6. (Inferential Comprehension) **(2) was busy saving the woman he loved** This inference is correct because the man looks at the woman right after hearing his brother. There is no evidence for options (1) and (4). Option (3) is wrong because he saw his brother fall and heard him call. The passion with which he speaks of his brother indicates that option (5) is wrong.

7. (Inferential Comprehension) **(3) guilt-ridden** Although the narrator does not come right out and say so, the narrator's feeling of guilt is made clear in the line "My own name! . . . My brother!" There is no support, direct or implied, in the passage for options (1), (2), (4), and (5).

8. (Inferential Comprehension) **(5) run away with his beloved** Although there is no mention of exactly whom they were running away from, they were definitely running away. There is no support for options (1), (3), and (4). There is no evidence of why Diamelen was there in the first place, so option (2) is wrong.

1. (Inferential Comprehension) **(2) Mr. Darcy had not paid much attention to her.** Elizabeth's thoughts supply this information. There is no evidence for option (1). Options (3) and (5) are the opposite of what is stated in the passage. It was Jane who had once felt embarrassed, so option (4) is wrong.

2. (Application) **(2) continue to think about Mr. Darcy** She is interested in him, and having to tell herself not to think about him suggests she will anyway, so option (1) is wrong. Option (3) is wrong because she is pleased for Jane. She has no reason for not speaking to her aunt and uncle, option (4). There is no support for option (5).

3. (Literal Comprehension) **(4) reacting to the visit of two men they are interested in** That the visitors were men is indicated by a man's name and a later reference to "he." There is no evidence in the passage for options (1), (2), and (3). Only Elizabeth, not Jane, is disappointed, and she does not share that feeling with Jane; thus option (5) is incorrect.

4. (Literal Comprehension) **(5) pleasing** This word is followed by the phrase "still pleasing" enclosed in commas, so the two are probably similar. Options (1) and (2) are wrong because they describe his behavior toward her, not toward her relatives. Options (3) and (4) make no sense in the context of the sentence.

5. (Inferential Comprehension) **(1) more sure of herself** This is supported by Jane's speech in lines 15–17. There is no evidence in the passage for options (2), (3), (4), or (5).

6. (Inferential Comprehension) **(1) Mr. Darcy used to act as if he cared for Elizabeth.** She thinks he no longer cares, implying that he did before. Option (2) is wrong because someone else is interested in Jane. There is no support for option (3). Option (4) overdramatizes Mr. Darcy's behavior. There is no evidence of flirtation, so option (5) is wrong.

LESSON 13 Comprehension Skills: Identifying an Unstated Main Idea

This skill will help you understand the most important point the author is making even when it is not directly stated.

As you learned in Lesson 2, the main idea of a paragraph or passage is not always directly stated. If you read a paragraph and do not find a sentence that generalizes about the details and examples, you will have to find the main idea yourself. Use your skills of restatement and understanding meaning from context to help you figure out what the author is saying. The best thing to do is to summarize—to say in your own words what the whole passage is about. Remember that you want to find what all the details and examples add up to, so do not include them in your summary. Also be sure that your summary, or general statement, includes all the ideas the details support.

In fiction, authors often do not state their main ideas. They rely on the reader's ability to understand the supporting details. The writer is telling a story and wants to entertain the reader as well as give information or make a point. The main ideas become clear as the plot develops through action and dialogue. As you read, also try to think about why the characters speak or act as they do. Sometimes this will help you to discover an unstated main idea.

As you study this lesson, remember that the main idea of a paragraph or a passage may be one of the general truths the author wants to express. Or it may be something more specific—a comment or piece of information the author wants you to have at this point. Whether it is general or specific, a paragraph's main idea is the most important, overall idea in that paragraph—its organizing principle.

Practicing Comprehension, Application, and Analysis Skills

Read the following passage from a short story by Willa Cather.

WHAT DOES ROSICKY THINK ABOUT THE GRAVEYARD?

It was a nice graveyard, Rosicky reflected, sort of snug and homelike, not cramped or mournful,—a big sweep all round it. A man could lie down in the long grass and see the complete arch of the sky over him, hear the wagons go by; in summer the mowing-
(5) machine rattled right up to the wire fence. And it was so near home. Over there across the cornstalks his own roof and windmill looked so good to him that he promised himself to mind the Doctor and take care of himself. He was awful fond of his place, he admitted. He wasn't anxious to leave it. And it was a comfort to think that he
(10) would never have to go farther than the edge of his own hayfield. The snow, falling over his barnyard and the graveyard, seemed to draw things together like. And they were all old neighbours in the graveyard, most of them friends; there was nothing to feel awkward or embarrassed about. Embarrassment was the most disagreeable
(15) feeling Rosicky knew. He didn't often have it,—only with certain people whom he didn't understand at all.

Source: "Neighbour Rosicky," from *The Signet Classic Book of Short Stories*.

Questions 1 and 2 refer to the passage. Circle the best answer for each question.

1. Which of the following best states the main idea of this passage?

(1) Rosicky thinks this graveyard would be a comfortable place to end up in.
(2) Rosicky's friends and neighbors are dead and buried.
(3) Rosicky is afraid of dying.
(4) The graveyard is a very depressing place.
(5) Rosicky is worried that the graveyard is too close to his barnyard.

2. The image of the snow on the graveyard and the barnyard supports the main idea by suggesting that

(1) winter is the season of death
(2) seasons affect how people act
(3) everything gets buried at one time or another
(4) the two places are not all that different
(5) people will start burying their dead in the barnyard

To check your answers, turn to page 150.

Read the following passage by Ambrose Bierce.

WHAT IS THE SIGNIFICANCE OF CARTER DRUSE'S DECISION?

The sleeping sentinel in the clump of laurel was a young Virginian named Carter Druse. He was the son of wealthy parents, an only child, and had known such ease and cultivation and high living as wealth and taste were able to command in the mountain
(5) country of western Virginia. His home was but a few miles from where he now lay. One morning he had risen from the breakfast-table and said, quietly but gravely: "Father, a Union regiment has arrived at Grafton. I am going to join it."

The father lifted his leonine head, looked at the son a moment
(10) in silence, and replied: "Well, go, sir, and whatever may occur do what you conceive to be your duty. Virginia, to which you are a traitor, must get on without you. Should we both live to the end of the war, we will speak further of the matter. Your mother, as the physician has informed you, is in a most critical condition; at the
(15) best she cannot be with us longer than a few weeks, but that time is precious. It would be better not to disturb her."

So Carter Druse, bowing reverently to his father, who returned the salute with a stately courtesy that masked a breaking heart, left the home of his childhood to go soldiering. By conscience and
(20) courage, by deeds of devotion and daring, he soon commended himself to his fellows and his officers; and it was to these qualities and to some knowledge of the country that he owed his selection for his present perilous duty at the extreme outpost.

Source: *A Horseman in the Sky*.

Questions 3 and 4 refer to the passage. Circle the best answer for each question.

3. The best statement of the main idea of this passage is

   (1) Carter Druse is a coward and a traitor to his country
   (2) Carter Druse acts on his beliefs no matter what the consequences
   (3) Carter's mother died of a broken heart
   (4) War is an evil thing
   (5) Carter Druse is a soldier in the Union army

4. Which of the following do you think Carter would be most likely to do?

   (1) run away from a battle
   (2) lie to one of his officers
   (3) keep a difficult promise
   (4) desert to the Southern army
   (5) steal from his father

To check your answers, turn to page 150.

Read the following passage by W. Somerset Maugham.

WILL BLANCHE LEAVE STRICKLAND?

"Oh, I'm so frightened. I know something is going to happen, something terrible, and I can do nothing to stop it."

"What sort of thing?" I asked.

"Oh, I don't know," he moaned, seizing his head with his
(5) hands. "I foresee some terrible catastrophe."

Stroeve had always been excitable, but now he was beside himself; there was no reasoning with him. I thought it probable enough that Blanche Stroeve would not continue to find life with Strickland tolerable, but one of the falsest of proverbs is that you
(10) must lie on the bed that you have made. The experience of life shows that people are constantly doing things which must lead to disaster; and yet by some chance manage to evade the result of their folly. When Blanche quarrelled with Strickland she had only to leave him, and her husband was waiting humbly to forgive and
(15) forget. I was not prepared to feel any great sympathy for her.

Source: *The Moon and Sixpence.*

Questions 5 to 8 refer to the passage. Circle the best answer for each question.

5. Why does the author have the speaker quote the proverb "You must lie on the bed that you have made" (lines 9–10)?

(1) because the speaker believes it
(2) to illustrate the opposite of the main idea
(3) to show how traditional the speaker is
(4) as a comfort to Stroeve
(5) as a criticism of Stroeve

6. Which of the following best explains and restates Stroeve's action of grabbing his head with his hands?

(1) The speaker says that Stroeve was beside himself.
(2) Stroeve has a terrible headache.
(3) Blanche is leaving Strickland.
(4) Stroeve attacks the speaker.
(5) Stroeve is willing to forgive Blanche.

7. Which of the following can be concluded from this passage?

(1) The speaker and Stroeve have just met.
(2) The speaker knows Stroeve well.
(3) The speaker has never met Strickland.
(4) The speaker has a lot of respect for Blanche.
(5) The speaker and Strickland are good friends.

8. The main idea of this passage is that the speaker believes

(1) Blanche is in danger
(2) Stroeve is right to worry about Blanche
(3) Blanche has no real problems
(4) many things lead to disaster
(5) Strickland is the best match for Blanche

To check your answers, turn to pages 150–151.

GED Mini-Test

Directions: Choose the best answer to each item.

Items 1 to 6 refer to the following passage from a short story by Zona Gale.

HAS ANYONE LIKE CALLIOPE EVER COME TO YOUR DOOR?

I watched Mis' Uppers in some curiosity while Calliope
explained that she was planning a dinner for the poor and
sick,—"the lame and the sick that's comfortable enough off to
eat,"—and could she suggest some poor and sick to ask? Mis'
(5) Uppers was like a vinegar cruet of mine, slim and tall, with a little
grotesquely puckered face for a stopper, as if the whole known
world were sour.

"I'm sure," she said humbly, "it's a nice i-dee. But I declare, I'm
put to it to suggest. We ain't got nobody sick nor nobody poor in
(10) Friendship, you know."

"Don't you know of anybody kind o' hard up? Or somebody
that, if they ain't down sick, feels sort o' spindlin'?" Calliope asked
anxiously.

"No," she said at length, "I don't know a soul. I think the
(15) church'd give a good deal if a real poor family'd come here to do for.
Since the Cadozas went, we ain't known which way to look for poor.
Mis' Ricker gettin' her fortune so puts her beyond the wolf. An'
Peleg Bemus, you can't *get* him to take anything. No, I don't know
of anybody real decently poor."

(20) "An' nobody sick?" Calliope pressed her wistfully.

"Well, there's Mis' Crawford," admitted Mis' Uppers; "she had a
spell o' lumbago two weeks ago, but I see her pass the house to-day.
Mis' Brady was laid up with toothache, too, but the *Daily* last night
said she'd had it out. An' Mis' Doctor Helman did have one o' her
(25) stomach attacks this week, an' Elzabella got out her dyin' dishes an'
her dyin' linen from the still-room—you know how Mis' Doctor
always brings out her nice things when she's sick, so't if she should
die an' the neighbours come in, it'd all be shipshape. But she got
better this time an' helped put 'em back. I declare it's hard to get up
(30) anything in the charity line here."

Source: "Nobody Sick, Nobody Poor," from *The Signet Classic Book
of Short Stories*.

1. Which of the following is the best statement of the main idea of this passage?

   (1) Mis' Uppers is very supportive of Calliope's idea.
   (2) Mis' Uppers does not want to admit she knows any poor people.
   (3) Friendship is a town badly in need of charity.
   (4) Calliope is having trouble finding people to be charitable to.
   (5) Women are more likely to be sick than men are.

2. Which of the following details best supports the main idea?

   (1) The speaker carefully watched Mis' Uppers.
   (2) The Cadozas got rich and left town.
   (3) The church cannot handle all of the poor people who come for help.
   (4) Mis' Uppers has a sour view of the world.
   (5) Calliope started to ask about people who were only slightly poor or sick.

3. Which of the following is probably true of Mis' Uppers?

   (1) She is a very stingy woman.
   (2) She knows most of the town's gossip.
   (3) She dislikes Calliope.
   (4) She thinks Mis' Crawford and Mis' Brady are exaggerating their illnesses.
   (5) She is in need of charity herself.

4. Which of the following would Mis' Doctor be most likely to have done if she were dying?

   (1) have the dishes and linens put away
   (2) have someone come in to clean the house
   (3) refuse visitors
   (4) go to a priest
   (5) go on a cruise

5. Which of the following best describes the organization of Mis' Uppers's reply to Calliope's questions?

   (1) She just rambles on and on.
   (2) She talks about the poor and the sick at the same time.
   (3) She answers only part of the question.
   (4) She talks about the poor first and then the sick.
   (5) She talks about the sick first and then the poor.

6. Which of the following best suggests the meaning of "puts her beyond the wolf" (line 17)?

   (1) Mis' Ricker keeps wolves as pets.
   (2) Mis' Ricker is dying.
   (3) Mis' Ricker has enough money for food.
   (4) Mis' Ricker is running from a wolf.
   (5) Mis' Ricker thinks she is a werewolf.

To check your answers, turn to page 151.

Answers and Explanations

Practicing Comprehension, Application, and Analysis Skills (pages 145–147)

1. (Literal Comprehension) **(1) Rosicky thinks this graveyard would be a comfortable place to end up in.** All of his thoughts about the grave-yard are pleasant. Option (2) assumes that the friends and neighbors there are the only ones he had. There is no support for options (3) and (4). Option (5) is wrong because he observes only how close they are; he does not seem worried.

2. (Literal Comprehension) **(4) the two places are not all that different** The drawing together applies not just to the land but to life and death. Option (1) is a figurative generalization that is not supported in this passage. Options (2) and (3) may be generally true but do not support the main idea. Option (5) has no support.

3. (Inferential Comprehension) **(2) Carter Druse acts on his beliefs no matter what the consequences** Carter fought for a cause he believed in even though it hurt his parents, and the strength of his convictions apparently made his officers trust him in a dangerous situa-tion. Druse is clearly brave and he turned against his state, not his coun-try, so option (1) is wrong. There is no support for option (3). Option (4) may be true, but it is a generalization that is not the main idea of the passage. Option (5) is a restatement of a sup-porting detail.

4. (Application) **(3) keep a difficult promise** Carter is clearly an honest and honorable man, so if he made a promise, he would keep it. It is not in his character as described in the pas-sage to do what is suggested by options (1), (2), and (5). As he has just made the decision in the face of opposition, option (4) is unlikely.

5. (Analysis) **(2) to illustrate the oppo-site of the main idea** The speaker states that the proverb is false and goes on to suggest the main idea, so option (1) is wrong. There is no support for option (3). The speaker does not say this either to Stroeve or about Stroeve, so options (4) and (5) are wrong.

6. (Literal Comprehension) **(1) The speaker says that Stroeve was beside himself.** The author restates Stroeve's action most clearly in lines 6–7. Options (2), (3), (4), and (5) do not explain the action.

7. (Inferential Comprehension) **(2) The speaker knows Stroeve well.** The speaker refers to previous experience with Stroeve and seems to know a lot about the circumstances with his wife. Option (1), then, is wrong. Options (3) and (5) are wrong because the speaker is able to make judgments about Strickland's character and they are not favorable ones. Option (4) is the opposite of what the speaker says.

8. (Literal Comprehension) **(3) Blanche has no real problems** He believes she has an easy way to get out of her present situation. Options (1) and (2) are wrong because he disagrees with Stroeve. He disagrees with what is suggested by options (4) and (5).

GED Mini-Test (pages 148–149)

1. (Literal Comprehension) **(4) Calliope is having trouble finding people to be charitable to.** Calliope has to ask about where she can find sick or poor people. Option (1) is the opposite of what is stated in the text. Option (2) is wrong because she does her best to think of someone. Option (3) suggests the opposite of the information given. There is no mention of men, so option (5) is wrong.

2. (Literal Comprehension) **(5) Calliope started to ask about people who were only slightly poor or sick.** Calliope had to change her ideas of whom she could help. Option (1) has nothing to do with the main idea. Option (2) is wrong because the Cadozas were a poor family when they left. Option (3) is wrong because the church would help if there were any need—which there is not. Mis' Uppers's expression does not support the main idea, so option (4) is wrong.

3. (Inferential Comprehension) **(2) She knows most of the town's gossip.** Her ability to report on the needs and illnesses of the town supports this conclusion. She is willing to help, so option (1) is wrong. There is no evidence for options (3) and (5). Option (4) is wrong because she says they recovered quickly.

4. (Application) **(2) have someone come in to clean the house** She would want to show her best if she were dying. Option (1) is the opposite of what is stated. Option (3) is wrong because she obviously expects people to visit. There is no evidence for options (4) and (5).

5. (Analysis) **(4) She talks about the poor first and then the sick.** She replied to the two-part question part by part. Options (1), (2), and (3) are not supported by the evidence. Option (5) is the opposite of her reply.

6. (Analysis) **(3) Mis' Ricker has enough money for food.** The phrase is based on "to keep the wolves from the door," which means that the people inside are not in danger of starving. This meaning, however, can be figured out from the context; she has just inherited money and so does not need a free meal. Options (1) and (4) are based on a literal reading of the phrase. Options (2) and (5) do not make sense in the context of the sentence.

LESSON 14 Analysis Skills: Identifying Elements of Style and Structure (Tone)

This skill will help you understand how authors use language and sentence structure to suggest how they feel and how they want you to feel.

When you talk to someone, the tone of your voice reveals your attitude—how you feel about your subject and your audience. Writers also use **tone** to suggest their feelings about a subject. The words used to talk about tone are emotional: serious or joking, angry or sympathetic, confused or positive. So when reading a passage, ask yourself how the writer feels about the ideas. Is the writer formal and distant? Is the writer informal and emotional?

Word choice is a clue to tone. If the writer uses formal or scientific words, the effect is unemotional and factual. Using direct language and slang creates a more informal tone. As you read, pay attention to the kinds of words the writer uses and think about what emotions you usually connect with those words.

The length and complexity of a sentence can also say something about tone. Short, simple sentences may suggest anxiety or urgency. Long sentences might suggest thoughtfulness.

Writers often let their characters create tone. So how a character says something gives you an idea of both how the character feels and how the author feels; however, the feelings of the author and of the characters are not always the same.

Tone is closely related to **mood,** the feeling the author wants the reader to experience. The same kind of words are used to describe mood as are used for tone, words that tell about emotion. Mood is the emotional atmosphere of the piece of literature. A writer often uses description to help create these feelings. As you read, look for these clues: how an author uses descriptive words and how a passage builds to its conclusion.

When reading a passage for style and structure, remember to ask yourself what feeling it conveys. Then look to see how the author structures the passages and uses (or does not use) descriptive words and images to create the mood.

Practicing Comprehension, Application, and Analysis Skills

Read the following passage by Ernest Hemingway.

WHAT IS THE BOY'S SECRET FEAR?

"Don't think," I said. "Just take it easy."

"I'm taking it easy," he said and looked straight ahead. He was evidently holding tight onto himself about something.

"Take this with water."

(5) "Do you think it will do any good?"

"Of course it will."

I sat down and opened the *Pirate* book and commenced to read, but I could see he was not following, so I stopped.

"About what time do you think I'm going to die?" he asked.

(10) "What?"

"About how long will it be before I die?"

"You aren't going to die. What's the matter with you?"

"Oh, yes, I am. I heard him say a hundred and two."

"People don't die with a fever of one hundred and two. That's a

(15) silly way to talk."

"I know they do. At school in France the boys told me you can't live with forty-four degrees. I've got a hundred and two."

He had been waiting to die all day, ever since nine o'clock in the morning.

(20) "You poor Schatz," I said. "Poor old Schatz. It's like miles and kilometers. You aren't going to die. That's a different thermometer. On that thermometer thirty-seven is normal. On this kind it's ninety-eight."

"Are you sure?"

(25) "Absolutely," I said. "It's like miles and kilometers. You know, like how many kilometers we make when we do seventy miles in the car?"

Source: "A Day's Wait," from *Winner Take Nothing*.

Questions 1 and 2 refer to the passage. Circle the best answer for each question.

1. The absence of descriptive images in this passage gives it

(1) a cold, scientific effect
(2) a dull, ho-hum feeling
(3) a direct, factual impact
(4) a dry, scholarly quality
(5) a dreamy, poetic mood

2. Like the boy's fear, the passage

(1) remains mysterious throughout
(2) fails to reach a climax
(3) awakens little sympathy
(4) is about something trivial
(5) builds up and relaxes

To check your answers, turn to page 158.

Read the following passage by Katherine Anne Porter.

WHAT KIND OF PERSON IS GRANNY WETHERALL?

Doctor Harry spread a warm paw like a cushion on her forehead where the forked green vein danced and made her eyelids twitch. "Now, now, be a good girl, and we'll have you up in no time."

"That's no way to speak to a woman nearly eighty years old
(5) just because she's down. I'd have you respect your elders, young man."

"Well, Missy, excuse me." Doctor Harry patted her cheek. "But I've got to warn you, haven't I? You're a marvel, but you must be careful or you're going to be good and sorry."

"Don't tell me what I'm going to be. I'm on my feet now,
(10) morally speaking. It's Cornelia. I had to go to bed to get rid of her."

Her bones felt loose, and floated around in her skin, and Doctor Harry floated like a balloon around the foot of the bed. He floated and pulled down his waistcoat and swung his glasses on a cord. "Well, stay where you are, it certainly can't hurt you."

(15) "Get along and doctor your sick," said Granny Wetherall. Leave a well woman alone. I'll call for you when I want you. . . . Where were you forty years ago when I pulled through milk-leg and pneumonia? You weren't even born. Don't let Cornelia lead you on," she shouted, because Doctor Harry appeared to float up to the
(20) ceiling and out. "I pay my own bills, and I don't throw money away on nonsense!"

Source: "The Jilting of Granny Wetherall," from *Flowering Judas and Other Stories*.

Questions 3 to 5 refer to the passage. Circle the best answer for each question.

3. The best way to describe the doctor's tone is

(1) understanding but firm
(2) distant and scientific
(3) gentle and unsure
(4) serious and gloomy
(5) bright and cheery

4. Which of the following best states Granny Wetherall's attitude?

(1) respectful
(2) afraid
(3) sulky
(4) timid
(5) scolding

5. Which of the following is probably true about Granny?

(1) She really is as well as she says.
(2) She is much sicker than she says she is.
(3) She believes that doctors are well worth the money.
(4) She is able to get around easily on her own.
(5) She thinks Cornelia is a fine woman.

To check your answers, turn to page 158.

Read the following passage from a short story by McKnight Malmar.

WHY IS THIS WOMAN ALONE AT NIGHT?

She felt the familiar constriction about the heart as she held it in her hands. What these envelopes contained she never had known. What she did know was their effect on Ben. After receiving one— one came every month or two—he was irritable, at times almost ugly.
(5) Their peaceful life together fell apart. At first she had questioned him, had striven to soothe and comfort him; but she soon had learned that this only made him angry, and of late she had avoided any mention of them. For a week after one came they shared the same room and the same table like two strangers, in a silence that was morose
(10) on his part and a little frightened on hers.

This one was postmarked three days before. If Ben got home tonight he would probably be cross, and the storm would not help his mood. Just the same she wished he would come.

She tore the envelope into tiny pieces and tossed them into the
(15) fireplace. The wind shook the house in its giant grip, and a branch crashed on the roof. As she straightened, a movement at the window caught her eye.

She froze there, not breathing, still half-bent toward the cold fireplace, her hand still extended. The glimmer of white at the win-
(20) dow behind the sheeting blur of rain had been—she was sure of it—a human face. There had been eyes. She was certain there had been eyes staring in at her.

The wind's shout took on a personal, threatening note. She was rigid for a long time, never taking her eyes from the window. But
(25) nothing moved there now except the water on the windowpane; beyond it there was blackness, and that was all. The only sounds were the thrashing of the trees, the roar of water, and the ominous howl of the wind.

Source: "The Storm," from *Story and Structure*, 6th edition.

Questions 6 and 7 refer to the passage. Circle the best answer for each question.

6. Which of the following best describes the effect of this passage?

(1) joyful
(2) regretful
(3) calm
(4) suspenseful
(5) humorous

7. Which of the following introductions would this writer be most likely to use?

(1) once upon a time
(2) the purpose of the following discussion
(3) 'twas a dark and stormy night
(4) the reader cannot fail to appreciate
(5) a funny thing happened on the way . . .

To check your answers, turn to page 158.

GED Mini-Test

Directions: Choose the best answer to each item.

Items 1 to 6 refer to the following passage from a short story by Mary Wilkins Freeman.

WHO IS THE NEW CHOIR SOLOIST?

In the centre of the row of women singers stood Alma Way. All the people stared at her, and turned their ears critically. She was the new leading soprano. Candace Whitcomb, the old one, who had sung in the choir for forty years, had lately been given her

(5) dismissal. The audience considered that her voice had grown too cracked and uncertain on the upper notes. There had been much complaint, and after long deliberation the church-officers had made known their decision as mildly as possible to the old singer. She had sung for the last time the Sunday before, and Alma Way had been

(10) engaged to take her place. With the exception of the organist, the leading soprano was the only paid musician in the large choir. The salary was very modest, still the village people considered it large for a young woman. Alma was from the adjoining village of East Derby; she had quite a local reputation as a singer.

(15) Now she fixed her large solemn blue eyes; her long, delicate face, which had been pretty, turned paler; the blue flowers on her bonnet trembled; her little thin gloved hands, clutching the singing-book, shook perceptibly; but she sang out bravely. That most formidable mountain-height of the world, self-distrust and timidity,

(20) arose before her, but her nerves were braced for its ascent. In the midst of the hymn she had a solo; her voice rang out piercingly sweet; the people nodded admiringly at each other; but suddenly there was a stir; all the faces turned toward the windows on the south side of the church. Above the din of the wind and the birds,

(25) above Alma Way's sweetly straining tones, arose another female voice, singing another hymn to another tune.

"It's her," the women whispered to each other; they were half aghast, half smiling.

Candace Whitcomb's cottage stood close to the south side of the

(30) church. She was playing on her parlor organ, and singing, to drown out the voice of her rival.

Source: "A Village Singer," from *Great American Short Stories*.

1. In this passage, the author's style is

   (1) dry and scholarly
   (2) flat and unemotional
   (3) informal and joking
   (4) informal and serious
   (5) complex and confused

2. The mood of the first paragraph is best described as

   (1) gloomy
   (2) expectant
   (3) triumphant
   (4) peaceful
   (5) festive

3. Which of the following details from the passage does help the reader to understand the emotional atmosphere in the church?

   (1) turned their ears critically
   (2) her voice had grown too cracked
   (3) considered it large for a young woman
   (4) flowers on her bonnet trembled
   (5) shook perceptibly

4. What is the best explanation of why Candace Whitcomb stayed home and played the organ?

   (1) She did not feel well that day.
   (2) The pastor had wanted the new soloist to sing alone.
   (3) She felt she needed the practice for next Sunday.
   (4) She was jealous of the new soloist.
   (5) She was happy to have someone else take her place.

5. Which of the following can be learned about Alma's personality from this passage?

   (1) She is willing to face a challenge.
   (2) She is sure that her looks will influence people.
   (3) She enjoys mountain climbing.
   (4) Her singing is admired.
   (5) She is paid too much.

6. What does the comparison of self-distrust and timidity with the mountain (lines 18–20) suggest?

   (1) Self-distrust and timidity are difficult to overcome.
   (2) Singing requires the same skills as mountain climbing.
   (3) Alma cannot hit the high notes.
   (4) Self-doubt is a good thing.
   (5) Self-distrust is necessary for climbing mountains.

To check your answers, turn to page 159.

Answers and Explanations

Practicing Comprehension, Application, and Analysis Skills (pages 153–155)

1. (Analysis) **(3) a direct, factual impact** Because we have little more than dialogue to go on, the revelation of the boy's secret fear comes as a shock. The tense and down-to-earth nature of the scene rules out options (1), (2), (4), and (5).

2. (Analysis) **(5) builds up and relaxes** The underlying structure of the passage matches the buildup and resolution of the boy's fear, step for step. Options (1), (2), (3), and (4) are wrong because the fear is explained (line 18), reaches a climax (lines 16–17), awakens our sympathy, and is clearly not trivial.

3. (Analysis) **(1) understanding but firm** The effect of the doctor's words is soothing but carries a hint of warning. The words he uses are informal and simple, so option (2) is wrong. Although "gentle" might be right, the doctor is sure of himself, so option (3) is wrong. Option (4) is too extreme, even though the doctor warns Granny. Because of the warning, option (5) is incorrect.

4. (Analysis) **(5) scolding** Granny's speech is fairly abrupt and direct. By calling the doctor "young man," she is putting him in his place. Option (1) is the opposite of what is suggested in the passage. Her words and sentence structure are too confident and forceful for options (2), (3), and (4).

5. (Inferential Comprehension) **(2) She is much sicker than she says she is.** The description of how her bones felt and how her vision was acting suggest that she is very ill, so options (1) and (4) are wrong. There is no evidence to support option (3). Option (5) is wrong because she has nothing good to say about Cornelia.

6. (Analysis) **(4) suspenseful** The images suggest fear, uncertainty, and threat. These are the opposites of options (1), (3), and (5). Option (2) may be part of how the woman feels but is not the attitude the author wants to suggest for the whole scene.

7. (Application) **(3) 'twas a dark and stormy night** The writer would probably choose something that immediately suggested mystery or the setting for a scary story. Option (1) is wrong because it sounds like a fairy tale. Options (2) and (4) are wrong because they set up a dry and formal tone. Option (5) suggests humor, which does not match the gloom of the passage.

1. (Analysis) **(4) informal and serious** The language is not stiff or technical, so option (1) is wrong. Option (2) is wrong because description is used. There is no suggestion of humor, so option (3) is wrong. The language is direct and informative, so option (5) is wrong.

2. (Analysis) **(2) expectant** The whole passage suggests that the churchgoers are waiting to see how Alma performs and what will happen when she does. Options (1) and (3) are both too extreme for the content. The slight suggestion of tension makes option (4) wrong. There is no support for option (5).

3. (Analysis) **(2) her voice had grown too cracked** This detail refers to the reason the other soloist had been replaced. Options (1) and (3) suggest that the congregation is waiting to judge the new soloist. Options (4) and (5) show that Alma realizes the church folk are expecting her to justify their choice.

4. (Inferential Comprehension) **(4) She was jealous of the new soloist.** This is suggested by the last paragraph, so option (5) is wrong. There is no evidence for option (1). Option (2) is probably true but does not answer the question. Option (3) is wrong because Candace no longer sings at church.

5. (Inferential Comprehension) **(1) She is willing to face a challenge.** Alma is nervous, but she sings well anyway. Option (2) is wrong because she is not thinking about her looks. Option (3) refers to a literal reading of figurative language. Options (4) and (5) have nothing to do with Alma's personality.

6. (Analysis) **(1) Self-distrust and timidity are difficult to overcome.** The mountain represents an obstacle that needs to be faced with courage. There is no support for options (2) and (3). Option (4) is the opposite of what is suggested by the comparison. Option (5) is wrong because "self-distrust" is the figurative mountain.

LESSON 15 Analysis Skills: Identifying Techniques (Point of View)

This skill will help you understand who is telling the story or explaining an idea.

Understanding the **point of view** means that you know who is talking and can figure out how this person's own background and opinions will affect what is said about the subject. The speaker is not always the author. The speaker may be either the person who is being described or someone who knew that person well enough so that the reader can believe what is said.

Autobiography, told in the first person, is likely to have a special quality of immediacy and emotional truth. No one else knows as much about that person's thoughts, feelings, and experiences as the "I" who is telling the story. Biographies, which are told in the third person ("he" or "she"), naturally lack some of the intimacy and immediacy of autobiographies. However, they can be just as exciting and dramatic.

In some cases, the biographer has actually known or interviewed the person whose life story is being told. In other cases, where the subject of the biography is a historical figure, the biographer may bring the story to life with imagined details based on careful research of the people and the period. The author of the passage on page 161 lived 150 years after the subject; but notice how she brings the scene to life with descriptive details about the weather, the physical setting, and the actions of both Hancock and Washington.

Remember, in an autobiography a person uses the first person to tell his or her own story. In a biography one person tells another person's story. Both biographies and autobiographies are concerned with real people and events. They differ in the point of view from which they are told.

☞ *See Also: GED Exercise Book Literature and the Arts, pages 30–32*

Practicing Comprehension, Application, and Analysis Skills

Read the following passage by Catherine Drinker Bowen.

IS WASHINGTON'S NOMINATION SURPRISING?

John worked hard. By the middle of June, he decided the moment was ripe. On a dull, muggy morning, he walked alone to Congress, determined to nominate Washington before the noon bell sounded from the tower. As soon as the members were seated, John
(5) rose and spoke briefly for the establishment of a Continental army, outlining the present dangers, chief of which was that the forces at Cambridge might dissolve entirely. What was to prevent the British from profiting by this delay, marching out of Boston and "spreading desolation as far as they could go"? For commander-in-chief of a
(10) Grand American Army he would like, John finished, to suggest "*a gentleman whose skill as an officer, whose independent fortune, great talents and universal character would command the respect of America and unite the full exertions of the Colonies better than any other person alive.*"
(15) All the time he was speaking, Hancock wore a look of pleased, even radiant, expectancy. Facing the room in his chair behind the President's table, he was plainly visible to everyone, including John, who stood near the front. No one loved glory more than Hancock; he had the vanity of a child, open and vulnerable. John saw his face and
(20) hastened on, raising his voice a little: "A gentleman *from Virginia*, who is among us here, and well known to all."

Hancock shrank as at a blow. ("I never," John wrote later, "remarked a more sudden and striking change of countenance. Mortification and resentment were expressed as forcibly as his face could
(25) exhibit them.") Washington, who was on the south side of the room, left his seat at the word *Virginia* and slipped quietly out the door before his name was pronounced.

Source: *The Young John Adams.*

Questions 1 and 2 refer to the passage. Circle the best answer for each question.

1. The incident in this passage is described

(1) from Hancock's viewpoint
(2) in the third person
(3) from Washington's viewpoint
(4) in the first person
(5) in the interviewer's words

To check your answers, turn to page 166.

2. What tells us how Hancock's face looked in response to the nomination?

(1) Adams's own words
(2) Washington's memoirs
(3) a newspaper account
(4) a painting of the event
(5) the biographer's imagination

Read the following passage by Booker T. Washington.

WHAT WAS IT LIKE TO BE A SLAVE DURING THE WAR?

I had no schooling whatever while I was a slave, though I
remember on several occasions I went as far as the schoolhouse
door with one of my young mistresses to carry her books. The
picture of several dozen boys and girls in a schoolroom engaged in
(5) study made a deep impression upon me, and I had the feeling that
to get into a schoolhouse and study in this way would be about the
same as getting into paradise.

So far as I can now recall, the first knowledge that I got of the
fact that we were slaves, and that freedom of the slaves was being
(10) discussed, was early one morning before day, when I was awakened
by my mother kneeling over her children and fervently praying that
Lincoln and his armies might be successful, and that one day she
and her children might be free. In this connection I have never been
able to understand how the slaves throughout the South, com-
(15) pletely ignorant as were the masses so far as books or newspapers
were concerned, were able to keep themselves so accurately and
completely informed about the great National questions that were
agitating the country. From the time that Garrison, Lovejoy, and
others began to agitate for freedom, the slaves throughout the South
(20) kept in close touch with the progress of the movement. Though I
was a mere child during the preparation for the Civil War and during
the war itself, I now recall the many late-at-night whispered discussions that I heard my mother and the other slaves on the planta-
tion indulge in. These discussions showed that they understood the
(25) situation, and that they kept themselves informed of events by what
was termed the "grape-vine" telegraph.

Source: *Up From Slavery.*

Questions 3 to 6 refer to the passage. Circle the best answer for each question.

3. During the Civil War, the author was

    (1) starting school
    (2) an old man
    (3) a soldier
    (4) a young man
    (5) still a child

4. This passage is told

    (1) by a biographer
    (2) in the present tense
    (3) in the first person
    (4) by a newspaper reporter
    (5) in the third person

5. The author thought of school as

    (1) a form of slavery
    (2) a terrifying challenge
    (3) the gateway to society
    (4) a kind of heaven
    (5) an arena for protest

6. The author remains impressed by

    (1) how religious his mother was
    (2) how kind his masters were
    (3) his schooling as a slave
    (4) how hard slaves had to work
    (5) how informed the slaves were

To check your answers, turn to page 166.

Read the following excerpt from the autobiography of Black Elk as told through John G. Neihardt (Flaming Rainbow).

WHAT DOES BLACK ELK DO ON THE HUNT?

I was well enough to go along on my pony, but I was not old enough to hunt. So we little boys scouted around and watched the hunters; and when we would see a bunch of bison coming, we would yell "Yuhoo" like the others, but nobody noticed us.

(5) When the butchering was all over, they hung the meat across the horses' backs and fastened it with strips of fresh bison hide. On the way back to the village all the hunting horses were loaded, and we little boys who could not wait for the feast helped ourselves to all the raw liver we wanted. Nobody got cross when we did this.

(10) During this time, women back at camp were cutting long poles and forked sticks to make drying racks for the meat. When the hunters got home they threw their meat in piles on the leaves of trees.

Then the advisers all went back into the council tepee, and from all directions the people came bringing gifts of meat to them, (15) and the advisers all cried "Hya-a-a-a!," after which they sang for those who had brought them the good gifts. And when they had eaten all they could, the crier shouted to the people: "All come home! It is more than I can eat!" And people from all over the camp came to get a little of the meat that was left over.

(20) The women were all busy cutting the meat into strips and hanging it on the racks to dry. You could see red meat hanging everywhere. The people feasted all night long and danced and sang. Those were happy times.

Source: *Black Elk Speaks*.

Questions 7 to 9 refer to the passage. Circle the best answer for each question.

7. At the time this person is telling his story, he probably is

(1) a boy
(2) a hunter
(3) a grown man
(4) very happy
(5) quite healthy

8. The style of this passage is

(1) very formal
(2) simple and direct
(3) complex and confusing
(4) wordy but lively
(5) informal and humorous

9. Which of the following is not true according to this passage?

(1) Everyone in camp gets some of the bison meat.
(2) The meat is prepared on drying racks.
(3) The advisers receive the first meat from the hunt.
(4) Everyone in the village goes on the hunt.
(5) The boys are allowed to watch the hunt.

To check your answers, turn to pages 166–167.

GED Mini-Test

Directions: Choose the best answer to each item.

Items 1 to 6 refer to the following passage by Theodora Kroeber.

WHERE WILL ISHI GO?

The black face of the white man's Demon rushed toward the platform, pouring out clouds of sparks and smoke, and filling the ears with its hollow, moaning voice. Mill Creek and Deer Creek were within range of the sound of that voice; twice a day Ishi had
(5) heard it ever since he could remember, and he had watched the train hundreds of times as it snaked along below him, bellowing and belching. His mother had reassured him as a small boy when he was afraid of it, telling him that it was a Demon who followed white men wherever they went, but that Indians need have no fear
(10) of it; it never bothered them.

Today, Ishi wondered. He had not been so near it before; it was larger and noisier and speedier than he had realized. Would the Demon know that he was Indian? He was wearing white men's clothes, and his hair was short like theirs. It might be as well to
(15) watch from a little distance, from the shelter of a tree or bush, as he was accustomed to, at least until he made sure that his friend was correct in his assurance that the Demon always stayed in its own old tracks, and that it carried people safely from place to place. He stepped behind a cottonwood tree alongside the platform. The
(20) Demon drew up beside the station and came to a halt. Ishi saw that it was as his friend had said—it did not leave its tracks. The white men who should have the most reason to be afraid, showed no signs of uneasiness, rather they climbed in and out of it, and one of them sat in its head waving to those below. Ishi came back onto the plat-
(25) form, and made no objection to going aboard with Waterman. He had committed himself too far to turn back, nor did he wish to do so; where his new friend led he would follow.

Source: *Ishi in Two Worlds: A Biography of the Last Wild Indian in North America.*

1. According to the passage, Ishi is

    (1) a demon
    (2) used to riding on trains
    (3) about to get on the train
    (4) not going to board the train
    (5) sure the train will leave its
        tracks

2. The passage is written

    (1) as if the author knows what the
        character is thinking
    (2) in Ishi's own words
    (3) in the form of a diary
    (4) by a person who did not
        understand Ishi
    (5) by another Indian

3. Which of the following best describes
    how the author feels about the
    subject?

    (1) fearful
    (2) confused
    (3) sympathetic
    (4) bored
    (5) angry

4. The author uses her description of the
    train to

    (1) explain why white men like
        trains
    (2) emphasize how Ishi saw the train
        as being alive
    (3) prove that trains are evil
    (4) make the reader uneasy
    (5) suggest the reason for the failure
        of the railroad

5. From the passage you can infer that

    (1) Ishi misses his mother
    (2) Waterman is not familiar with
        trains
    (3) Waterman is Ishi's brother
    (4) Ishi had never expected to ride a
        train
    (5) the train had arrived on schedule

6. The phrase "hollow, moaning voice"
    (line 3) probably refers to

    (1) the noise of the passengers
    (2) the clank of the train's wheels
    (3) a noise Ishi made as a child
    (4) the hooting of the train's whistle
    (5) the clouds of smoke and sparks

To check your answers, turn to page 167.

Answers and Explanations

Practicing Comprehension, Application, and Analysis Skills (pages 161–163)

1. (Analysis) **(2) in the third person** The biographer describes the incident from Adams's viewpoint. Since it is someone other than Adams telling the story, we know that it is told from the third-person point of view. Therefore, options (1), (3), and (4) are wrong. Option (5) is wrong because the people were not interviewed.

2. (Literal Comprehension) **(1) Adams's own words** Adams's own words are quoted about the look on Hancock's face (lines 22–25). There is no evidence for options (2), (3), (4), and (5).

3. (Literal Comprehension) **(5) still a child** In lines 21–22, the author describes himself as "a mere child" during the war; therefore, options (2), (3), and (4) are wrong. Option (1) is wrong because the author did not go to school when he was a slave.

4. (Analysis) **(3) in the first person** As is clear from the author's use of "I," the passage is told in the first person, rather than in the third, by a biographer. Therefore, options (1) and (5) are wrong. The author uses the past tense, so option (2) is wrong. Option (4) is wrong because we do not know if he is a reporter.

5. (Literal Comprehension) **(4) a kind of heaven** In lines 6–7, the author says that going to school would be like "getting into paradise." There is no evidence for options (1), (2), (3), and (5).

6. (Inferential Comprehension) **(5) how informed the slaves were** Although he probably was impressed by his mother's prayer, option (1), the main point he makes here is how amazing it was that the slaves managed to keep themselves informed. There is no evidence for options (2), (3), and (4).

7. (Inferential Comprehension) **(3) a grown man** He is remembering an event from his boyhood, so option (1) is wrong. Option (2) is wrong because there is no evidence of what he does. Options (4) and (5) are wrong because there is no suggestion of how he feels emotionally or physically at the time he tells the story.

8. (Analysis) **(2) simple and direct** The sentences are short and to the point, so option (3) is wrong. The language is plain and easy to understand, so options (1) and (4) are wrong. Although the style is informal, there is no attempt at humor, so option (5) is wrong.

9. (Literal Comprehension) **(4) Everyone in the village goes on the hunt.** The small boys are not allowed to hunt, and the women stay behind to prepare the drying racks. Options (1), (2), (3), and (5) are stated in the passage.

GED Mini-Test (pages 164–165)

1. (Literal Comprehension) **(3) about to get on the train** This information is given in lines 24–25. Option (1) refers to what Ishi calls the train. Options (2) and (4) are the opposite of what is stated. Option (5) refers to something Ishi finds is not true.

2. (Analysis) **(1) as if the author knows what the character is thinking** The passage is written in the third person. The biographer is writing as if she sees through Ishi's eyes. Option (2) is wrong because Ishi is not telling his own story. Option (3) has no support. The author seems to know Ishi well, so option (4) is wrong. There is no evidence for option (5).

3. (Analysis) **(3) sympathetic** The description of the man's nervousness shows understanding. Option (1) might refer to Ishi at one point, but not to the author. There is no support for options (2), (4), and (5).

4. (Analysis) **(2) emphasize how Ishi saw the train as being alive** The words in the description refer to the train as if it had human characteristics. There is no support for option (1). Option (3) is suggested by calling the train a demon, but the author is not saying that trains are evil. There is no support for option (4). Option (5) has nothing to do with the passage.

5. (Inferential Comprehension) **(4) Ishi had never expected to ride a train** The passage as a whole suggests this idea. It is supported by Ishi's mother telling him that trains had nothing to do with Indians. Option (1) might have been true, but it is not suggested in the passage. Option (2) is the opposite of what is suggested. Option (3) is not true; Waterman is a new friend. There is no mention of time, so option (5) is wrong.

6. (Analysis) **(4) the hooting of the train's whistle** This phrase refers to the noise the train makes as it comes into the station. Option (1) is wrong because it is the train's noise, not that of people. Option (2) is wrong because a clank is different from a moan. The noise is not Ishi's, so option (3) is wrong. A cloud does not make a sound, so option (5) is wrong.

LESSON 16 Comprehension Skills: Identifying an Implication and Drawing a Conclusion

This skill helps you develop a two-part process of reading. First you find out what an author is suggesting, and then you make a decision based on your own understanding of what the writer said indirectly.

In Lesson 5, you learned about drawing conclusions. You learned to consider the facts and information you had been given in order to make a logical decision about what it all added up to. But sometimes the facts are not spelled out. The reader must then make a decision based on stated and suggested information. This is called **making an inference**.

Just as a writer often draws conclusions from things he or she has inferred, a reader will sometimes first have to make inferences before coming to a conclusion about what the writer is saying. A writer may **imply** something—that is, state something indirectly. In such a case, the author is assuming the reader will be able to understand the meaning of what is suggested and also be able to connect several ideas into a whole.

An essay is usually about a single topic. The style of the essay depends on the topic's seriousness and on the personality of the writer. Formal essays are often used to discuss abstract principles and issues. Informal essays often tell personal stories and include many colorful details drawn from life. The passage on page 169, by Robert Frost, is an example of an informal essay. Reading it is almost like having a conversation with the author himself.

When reading an essay, look first for the ideas that are stated directly. Then look for other, equally important ideas that are implied. In the passage that follows, Frost tells us directly how he grades his students, for instance. However, indirectly he also tells us something about the abstract nature of poetry. This is implied in his use of the phrase "coming close to" (line 1) and in his description of the inexact way he arrives at a mark for his students.

Practicing Comprehension, Application, and Analysis Skills

Read the following passage from an essay by Robert Frost.

HOW DOES A TEACHER AND POET DECIDE HOW TO GRADE HIS STUDENTS?

There are two ways of coming close to poetry. One is by writing poetry. And some people think I want people to write poetry, but I don't; that is, I don't necessarily. I only want people to write poetry if they want to write poetry. I have never encouraged anybody to
(5) write poetry that did not want to write it, and I have not always encouraged those who did want to write it. That ought to be one's own funeral. It is a hard, hard life, as they say. . . .

. . . There is another way to come close to poetry, fortunately, and that is in the reading of it, not as linguistics, not as history, not
(10) as anything but poetry. It is one of the hard things for a teacher to know how close a man has come in reading poetry. How do I know whether a man has come close to Keats in reading Keats? It is hard for me to know. I have lived with some boys a whole year over some of the poets and I have not felt sure whether they have come near
(15) what it was all about. One remark sometimes told me. One remark was their mark for the year; had to be—it was all I got that told me what I wanted to know. And that is enough, if it is the right remark, if it came close enough. I think a man might make twenty fool remarks if he made one good one some time in the year. His
(20) mark would depend on that good remark.

Source: "Education by Poetry," from *The Selected Prose of Robert Frost.*

Questions 1 and 2 refer to the passage. Circle the best answer for each question.

1. When Frost talks about "coming close to poetry," he means

   (1) being near great poets
   (2) leading a poetic life
   (3) being able to recite it
   (4) understanding its meaning
   (5) doing a translation of it

2. We can conclude that, for Frost, both teaching and understanding poetry

   (1) are inexact and unscientific
   (2) require historical knowledge
   (3) benefit from religious faith
   (4) are a waste of time
   (5) are subjects for linguists

To check your answers, turn to page 174.

Read the following passage from an essay by Virginia Woolf.

WHO IS THIS FINE YOUNG COUPLE?

So now at the turn of the road I saw one of these pictures. It might have been called "The Sailor's Homecoming" or some such title. A fine young sailor carrying a bundle; a girl with her hand on his arm; neighbours gathering round; a cottage garden ablaze with
(5) flowers; as one passed one read at the bottom of that picture that the sailor was back from China, and there was a fine spread waiting for him in the parlour; and he had a present for his young wife in his bundle; and she was soon going to bear him their first child. Everything was right and good and as it should be, one felt about
(10) that picture. There was something wholesome and satisfactory in the sight of such happiness; life seemed sweeter and more enviable than before.

So thinking I passed them, filling in the picture as fully, as completely as I could, noticing the colour of her dress, of his eyes,
(15) seeing the sandy cat slinking round the cottage door.

For some time the picture floated in my eyes, making most things appear much brighter, warmer, and simpler than usual; and making some things appear foolish; and some things wrong and some things right, and more full of meaning than before. At odd moments
(20) during that day and the next the picture returned to one's mind, and one thought with envy, but with kindness, of the happy sailor and his wife; one wondered what they were doing, what they were saying now.

Source: "Three Pictures," from *The Death of the Moth and Other Essays*.

Questions 3 and 4 refer to the passage. Circle the best answer for each question.

3. If the author continued to "fill in the picture," which of the following would she be most likely to come up with?

(1) a fight between the sailor and his wife
(2) a quarrel between the couple and their neighbors
(3) a happy scene around the fireplace
(4) the girl cleaning the oven while the sailor watches television
(5) the sailor discovering that he cannot find a job

4. This author draws a conclusion from the four details in lines 3–5 when she says that

(1) the sight was satisfactory
(2) the scene could be called "The Sailor's Homecoming"
(3) life seemed sweeter than it had before
(4) she noticed the sandy cat at the cottage door
(5) she thought about the couple with envy and kindness

To check your answers, turn to page 174.

Read the following passage from an essay by Joseph Mitchell.

WHAT DID LOUIE ACHIEVE IN LIFE?

Louie left Recco in 1905, when he was close to eighteen. "I loved my family," he says, "and it tore me in two to leave, but I had five brothers and two sisters, and all my brothers were younger than me, and there were already too many fishermen in Recco, and
(5) the bathhouse brought in just so much, and I had a fear kept persisting there might not be enough at home to go around in time to come, so I got passage from Genoa to New York scrubbing pots in the galley of a steamship and went straight from the dock to a chophouse on East 138th Street in the Bronx that was operated by a man
(10) named Capurro who came from Recco. Capurro knew my father when they both were boys." . . . For the next twenty-three years, [Louie] worked as a waiter in restaurants all over Manhattan and Brooklyn. . . . In the winter of 1930, he decided to risk his savings and become his own boss. "At that time," he says, "the stockmarket
(15) crash had shook everything up and the depression was setting in, and I knew of several restaurants in midtown that could be bought at a bargain—lease, furnishings, and good will. All were up-to-date places. Then I ran into a waiter I used to work with and he told me about this old run-down restaurant in an old run-down building in
(20) the fish market that was for sale, and I went and saw it, and I took it. The reason I did, Fulton Fish Market reminds me of Recco. There's a world of difference between them. At the same time, they're very much alike—the fish smell, the general gone-to-pot look, the trading that goes on in the streets, the roofs over the sidewalks, the cats in
(25) corners gnawing on fish heads, the gulls in the gutters, the way everybody's on to everybody else, the quarreling and the arguing."

Source: "Up in the Old Hotel," from *Read to Write*.

Questions 5 and 6 refer to the passage. Circle the best answer for each question.

5. Which is the best conclusion about why Louie left Recco (an Italian town)?

(1) He was eighteen, of legal age.
(2) There was no room in the house.
(3) He did not want to support his younger brothers and sisters.
(4) There was not enough work in Recco to support his family.
(5) He did not want to live much longer with the problems of five brothers and two sisters.

6. Which is the best reason for the use of Louie's own words in this essay?

(1) It helps make the character of Louie come alive.
(2) It contrasts with the informal style of the essay.
(3) It hides the fact that the author did not understand Louie.
(4) It emphasizes the formal tone.
(5) It shows how Louie disagrees with the author.

To check your answers, turn to page 174.

Directions: Choose the best answer to each item.

Items 1 to 6 refer to the following passage by E. B. White.

IS IT POSSIBLE TO RECAPTURE THE PLEASURES OF THE PAST?

One summer, along about 1904, my father rented a camp on a lake in Maine and took us all there for the month of August. We all got ringworm from some kittens and had to rub Pond's Extract on our arms and legs night and morning, and my father rolled over in
(5) a canoe with all his clothes on; but outside of that the vacation was a success and from then on none of us ever thought there was any place in the world like that lake in Maine. We returned summer after summer—always on August 1st for one month. I have since become a salt-water man, but sometimes in summer there are days
(10) when the restlessness of the tides and the fearful cold of the sea water and the incessant wind which blows across the afternoon and into the evening make me wish for the placidity of a lake in the woods. A few weeks ago this feeling got so strong I bought myself a couple of bass hooks and a spinner and returned to the lake where
(15) we used to go, for a week's fishing and to revisit old haunts.

I took along my son, who had never had any fresh water up his nose and who had seen lily pads only from train windows. On the journey over to the lake I began to wonder what it would be like. I wondered how time would have marred this unique, this holy spot—
(20) the coves and streams, the hills that the sun set behind, the camps and paths behind the camps. I was sure the tarred road would have found it out and I wondered in what other ways it would be desolated. It is strange how much you can remember about places like that once you allow your mind to return into the grooves which lead back.
(25) You remember one thing, and that suddenly reminds you of another thing. I guess I remembered clearest of all the early mornings, when the lake was cool and motionless, remembered how the bedroom smelled of the lumber it was made of and of the wet woods whose scent entered through the screen. The partitions in the camp were
(30) thin and did not extend clear to the top of the rooms, and as I was always the first up I would dress softly so as not to wake the others, and sneak out into the sweet outdoors and start out in the canoe, keeping close along the shore in the long shadows of the pines. I remembered being very careful never to rub my paddle against the
(35) gunwale for fear of disturbing the stillness of the cathedral.

Source: "Once More to the Lake," from *Essays of E. B. White.*

---

1. We know that this passage is from an informal essay because it

   (1) is very serious and dignified
   (2) reads like a scientific report
   (3) deals with abstract principles
   (4) has an easygoing, chatty style
   (5) takes a cool, impersonal tone

2. The author decided to return to the lake in order to

   (1) visit his elderly father
   (2) enjoy some saltwater fishing
   (3) visit the cathedral there
   (4) teach his son canoeing
   (5) re-experience its peacefulness

3. Before going to the lake, the author was afraid "the tarred road would have found it out" (lines 21–22). By this he means he feared that

   (1) the road would no longer be there
   (2) civilization had come to this secluded spot of nature
   (3) a tar factory would have been started there
   (4) there would have been little change there
   (5) no one had paved the road yet

4. Which of the following details was not part of the author's memories of the lakeside camp?

   (1) fishing for bass
   (2) riding horses
   (3) the scent of the pine woods
   (4) the stillness of the lake
   (5) getting up very early

5. By "incessant wind" (line 11), the author means that the wind

   (1) never stopped blowing
   (2) was polluted
   (3) brought thunderstorms
   (4) blew in gale-force gusts
   (5) could not be counted on

6. The main implication in this passage, which the author does not state directly, is his

   (1) religious feeling about nature
   (2) disapproval of all signs of progress
   (3) longing to recapture the joys of youth
   (4) disillusionment with vacations by the sea
   (5) passion for freshwater fishing

To check your answers, turn to page 175.

Answers and Explanations

Practicing Comprehension, Application, and Analysis Skills (pages 169–171)

1. (Analysis) **(4) understanding its meaning** For Frost "coming close to poetry" means understanding what it is all about (lines 8–10). There is no evidence for options (1), (2), (3), and (5).

2. (Inferential Comprehension) **(1) are inexact and unscientific** The fact that, for Frost, the best indication of a student's grasp of poetry is a "right remark" (line 17) shows how inexact and unscientific both teaching it and understanding it are. There is no evidence for options (2), (3), (4), and (5).

3. (Application) **(3) a happy scene around the fireplace** The author has said they were the picture of happiness, so her image would be a happy and cozy one. Options (1), (2), and (4) are not pictures of a happy and loving home. Option (5) would turn the peaceful scene into a tragedy.

4. (Inferential Comprehension) **(2) the scene could be called "The Sailor's Homecoming"** She first infers that the girl was his wife and the cottage their home; then she connects all four details into a logical conclusion. Options (1) and (3) are the author's opinions about her conclusion, not the conclusion itself. Option (4) is an observation of fact. Option (5) is the author's feeling about her conclusion.

5. (Inferential Comprehension) **(4) There was not enough work in Recco to support his family.** Louie implies that work was scarce by talking about the fishermen and the bathhouse; that, combined with the mention of his large family, leads to the conclusion in option (4). Option (1) is a fact that does not answer the question. Option (2) may have been true but is not implied in the passage. There is no support for options (3) and (5).

6. (Analysis) **(1) It helps make the character of Louie come alive.** Using Louie's own speech makes him seem more real than just a character being described. Option (2) is wrong because Louie's language is even more informal than the author's. The author seems to understand Louie fairly well, so option (3) is wrong. Option (4) is wrong because the tone is casual. Option (5) is wrong because there is no evidence of disagreement.

1. (Analysis) **(4) has an easygoing, chatty style** The author's chatty, conversational style is typical of an informal essay. There is no evidence for options (1), (2), (3), and (5).

2. (Literal Comprehension) **5) re-experience its peacefulness** In lines 9–13 the author states his reason for going back to the lake. Though he might also wish to teach his son canoeing, option (4), that is not his main reason. There is no evidence for options (1), (2), and (3).

3. (Inferential Comprehension) **(2) civilization had come to this secluded spot of nature** First, "the tarred road" has to be understood as being a paved highway and "found it out" as meaning "found its way there." A paved road would provide easy access; so what the author feared can be concluded. There is no support for options (1) and (3). Options (4) and (5) are the opposite of what worried the author.

4. (Literal Comprehension) **(2) riding horses** There is no mention of riding of any kind. All the other details are mentioned.

5. (Inferential Comprehension) **(1) never stopped blowing** "Incessant" means constant. The context clue is that the wind blew all afternoon and continued in the evening. Option (2) is wrong because this place seems to be untouched. Options (3), (4), and (5) do not make sense in the context of the sentence or passage.

6. (Inferential Comprehension) **(3) longing to recapture the joys of youth** In line 15 the author refers to revisiting old haunts. In lines 17–36 he reviews memories obviously dear to him and wonders wistfully if things will still be the same. His fear that things may have changed suggests how much he wants to recapture his youth. There is some evidence for options (1), (2), (4), and (5), but only option (3) expresses implication, with the most support in the passage.

LESSON 17 Analysis Skills: Identifying Techniques (Mood)

This skill helps you to recognize the mood of a poem and to understand how the poet created that mood.

Remember that poetry is a compact way of talking about experience. People experience things in several ways: through physical senses like sight and touch, through getting and understanding information, through imagining and creating things, and through emotion. The **mood** of a poem or story is basically the emotion that the author wants the reader to experience. The poet uses figurative language and images to describe the world and the events that happen in it in order to create an atmosphere. For example, the color gray may be used to suggest gloom, or yellow may be used to suggest happiness. Look back at the passage by McKnight Malmar on page 155 to see how the descriptions in the last paragraph help to create an atmosphere of fear and tension.

The poet's most effective tool in creating mood is **imagery**—word-pictures that bring a scene vividly to life. "Velvet Shoes," on page 177, is about a walk in the snow. Each of the poem's images helps to share that experience with us by appealing to our senses of sight, touch, and sound.

Other techniques a poet uses to remind you of feelings you have had are the **sound** of words and the **rhythm** of the verse. Some sounds are more pleasing than others. The sound of "great gray wings" is more soothing to the ear than "huddled, hungry hordes." The rhythm of speech, the natural rise and fall of the voice, also has an effect on our emotions. Think of the way music uses rhythm to make us feel sad or romantic or joyful.

To become more aware of a poem's rhythm and word sounds, read it aloud quietly. Do the lines hurry along breathlessly, or do they make you pause as you read them? Are there many words containing short vowel sounds—words like "giggle," "tickle," "funny," "whistle"? Or are there many words that make you slow down as you pronounce them—words like "moan," "cold," "sad," "sighing"? Trust your own emotions. Sometimes a poem's mood comes across more clearly than its meaning—especially on first reading.

☞ *See Also: GED Exercise Book Literature and the Arts, pages 33–36*

Practicing Comprehension, Application, and Analysis Skills

Read the following poem by Elinor Wylie.

DOES THIS REMIND YOU OF A WINTER DAY?

Velvet Shoes

Let us walk in the white snow
    In a soundless space;
With footsteps quiet and slow,
    At a tranquil pace,
(5)   Under veils of white lace.

I shall go shod in silk,
    And you in wool,
White as a white cow's milk,
    More beautiful
(10)   Than the breast of a gull.

We shall walk through the still town
    In a windless peace;
We shall step upon white down,
    Upon silver fleece,
(15)   Upon softer than these.

We shall walk in velvet shoes:
    Wherever we go
Silence will fall like dews
    On white silence below.
(20)   We shall walk in the snow.

Source: *The Collected Poems of Elinor Wylie*.

Questions 1 and 2 refer to the poem. Circle the best answer for each question.

1. The mood expressed in the poem is one of

  (1) creeping terror
  (2) deep depression
  (3) hidden anxiety
  (4) wild joy
  (5) quiet delight

2. All the images used in the poem have something in common. It is

  (1) deafness and blindness
  (2) the innocence of animals
  (3) softness, whiteness, silence
  (4) the first signs of winter
  (5) the feel of various textures

To check your answers, turn to page 182.

Read the following poem by Alfred, Lord Tennyson.

WHAT HAS MADE THE POET FEEL THIS WAY?

Break, Break, Break

Break, break, break,
   On thy cold gray stones, O Sea!
And I would that my tongue could utter
   The thoughts that arise in me.

(5) O well for the fisherman's boy,
   That he shouts with his sister at play!
O well for the sailor lad,
   That he sings in his boat on the bay!

And the stately ships go on
(10)   To their haven under the hill;
But O for the touch of a vanished hand,
   And the sound of a voice that is still!

Break, break, break,
   At the foot of thy crags, O Sea!
(15) But the tender grace of a day that is dead
   Will never come back to me.

Source: "Break, Break, Break."

Questions 3 to 6 refer to the passage. Circle the best answer for each question.

3. Music for this poem would most likely be

(1) romantic
(2) joyful
(3) triumphant
(4) sad
(5) harsh

4. The speaker is longing for

(1) the days of his childhood
(2) his youth as a fisherman
(3) his home by the sea
(4) his lost skills as a writer
(5) a loved one who has died

5. The words "cold gray stones" suggest

(1) a wild rage
(2) hopeless sadness
(3) a kinship with nature
(4) a peaceful mind
(5) gentle rest

6. The importance of the boy and girl and the sailor is that they

(1) remind the speaker of life's joys
(2) remind the speaker of his boyhood
(3) are a contrast to the speaker's sorrow
(4) are like the speaker's sad story
(5) are a frustrating distraction

To check your answers, turn to page 182.

Read the following poem by Theodore Roethke.

WAS THE SPEAKER'S CHILDHOOD A HAPPY ONE?

My Papa's Waltz

The whiskey on your breath
Could make a small boy dizzy;
But I hung on like death:
Such waltzing was not easy.

(5) We romped until the pans
Slid from the kitchen shelf;
My mother's countenance
Could not unfrown itself.

The hand that held my wrist
(10) Was battered on one knuckle;
At every step you missed
My right ear scraped a buckle.

You beat time on my head
With a palm caked hard by dirt,
(15) Then waltzed me off to bed
Still clinging to your shirt.

Source: *The Collected Poems of Theodore Roethke.*

Questions 7 to 9 refer to the passage. Circle the best answer for each question.

7. When read aloud, the rhythm of this poem is

(1) smooth and gliding
(2) sad and slow
(3) gentle and dreamy
(4) sweeping and exalted
(5) abrupt and jerky

8. The father danced with the boy

(1) when he was drunk
(2) to celebrate a new job
(3) after a fight with his wife
(4) to annoy the neighbors
(5) after an accident at work

9. The scene depicted in the poem

(1) illustrates how not to bring up a child
(2) describes a bittersweet childhood memory
(3) generates a happy mood of nostalgia
(4) contains nothing "poetic" enough to call it a poem
(5) is the speaker's way of getting back at his parents

To check your answers, turn to page 182.

GED Mini-Test

Directions: Choose the best answer to each item.

Items 1 to 6 refer to the following poem by Ezra Pound.

HOW DOES THIS YOUNG WIFE IN CHINA FEEL?

The River Merchant's Wife: A Letter

While my hair was still cut straight across my forehead
I played about the front gate, pulling flowers.
You came by on bamboo stilts, playing horse,
You walked about my seat, playing with blue plums.
(5) And we went on living in the village of Chokan:
Two small people, without dislike or suspicion.

At fourteen I married My Lord you.
I never laughed, being bashful.
Lowering my head, I looked at the wall.
(10) Called to, a thousand times, I never looked back.

At fifteen I stopped scowling.
I desired my dust to be mingled with yours
Forever and forever and forever.
Why should I climb the look out?

(15) At sixteen you departed,
You went into far Ku-to-yen, by the river of swirling eddies,
And you have been gone five months.
The monkeys make sorrowful noise overhead.

You dragged your feet when you went out.
(20) By the gate now, the moss is grown, the different mosses,
Too deep to clear them away!
The leaves fall early this autumn, in wind.

The paired butterflies are already yellow with August
Over the grass in the West garden;
(25) They hurt me. I grow older.
If you are coming down through the narrows of the river Kiang,
Please let me know beforehand,
And I will come out to met you
As far as Cho-fu-Sa.

(by Rihaku)

Source: *Personae*.

1. The couple in the poem knew each other as children. They were

   (1) schoolmates
   (2) enemies
   (3) sweethearts
   (4) rivals
   (5) playmates

2. The overall mood created by the poem is one of

   (1) wistful longing
   (2) passionate love
   (3) quiet despair
   (4) businesslike restraint
   (5) hidden anxiety

3. By saying "Why should I climb the look out?" (line 14), the girl means

   (1) It is hopeless for me to try to escape.
   (2) Being happy, why should I look elsewhere?
   (3) My husband is not coming home, so why look for him?
   (4) My life is over. Why torture myself by looking outside?
   (5) Why should I have to man the watchtower?

4. The gathering moss at the front gate suggests that

   (1) the girl is actually dead and speaking from the grave
   (2) the husband has abandoned his young wife
   (3) the girl is a prisoner in her own home
   (4) the servants refuse to work in the husband's absence
   (5) the woman is leading a lonely and isolated life

5. The falling leaves and pairs of yellowing butterflies "hurt" the girl because they remind her that

   (1) winter is on its way
   (2) her husband may be in danger
   (3) her happy childhood is over
   (4) life is short and she is alone
   (5) she has no children

6. How did the couple's youthful marriage come about?

   (1) They fell in love with each other at age fourteen.
   (2) The girl was already her husband's servant.
   (3) The marriage was arranged by their families.
   (4) A local ruler commanded that they get married.
   (5) They had to marry because the girl was pregnant.

To check your answers, turn to page 183.

Answers and Explanations

Practicing Comprehension, Application, and Analysis Skills (pages 177–179)

1. (Analysis) **(5) quiet delight** The underlying emotion in the poem is pleasure; the poet is expressing her sense of hushed delight in the new-fallen snow. There is no support for options (1), (2), and (3). Option (4) is too extreme for the images presented.

2. (Analysis) **(3) softness, whiteness, silence** The poem's images are all designed to underscore the snow's essential softness and whiteness, as well as the silence it creates. Option (1) suggests a lack of sensation. There is no support for option (2). Winter is already advanced, so option (4) is wrong. Not all the images appeal to the sense of touch, so option (5) is wrong.

3. (Application) **(4) sad** Since the mood of the poem is one of mournful sadness, music that is romantic, option (1); joyful, option (2); triumphant, option (3); or harsh, option (5), would be incorrect.

4. (Inferential Comprehension) **(5) a loved one who has died** Though the speaker mentions a boy and girl, a sailor, and the sea, it is clear from lines 11–12 that he has lost someone he loved. There is no evidence for options (1), (2), (3), and (4) in the poem.

5. (Analysis) **(2) hopeless sadness** The long-drawn-out "o" sounds of these words plus the bleak image they bring up suggest hopeless sadness. There is no evidence for options (1), (3), (4), and (5) in the poem.

6. (Analysis) **(3) are a contrast to the speaker's sorrow** Though these sights and sounds may remind the speaker of days gone by and remind us that life holds pleasures, options (1) and (2), they mainly serve as a contrast to the speaker's own sorrow. There is no evidence for options (4) and (5) in the poem.

7. (Analysis) **(5) abrupt and jerky** The rhythm of the poem has a driving, jerky beat, much like the motion of the drunken father as he "waltzed" his son around the kitchen. For this reason, options (1), (2), (3), and (4) are incorrect.

8. (Literal Comprehension) **(1) when he was drunk** We know from the first two lines that the father was drunk when he danced with his son. Whatever other reasons he may have had for dancing are not stated or implied, so options (2), (3), (4), and (5) are not supported by the poem.

9. (Inferential Comprehension) **(2) describes a bittersweet childhood memory** The scene described—and the father in it—are both rough and loving, scary and tender. The combination makes for a memory that is both sweet and bitter. The mood is neither nostalgic nor critical, ruling out options (1), (3), and (5). The poem shows that any subject is worthy of a poem, so option (4) is wrong.

GED Mini-Test (pages 180–181)

1. (Inferential Comprehension) **(5) play-mates** School is not mentioned, so option (1) is incorrect. Lines 2–6 describe their happy, friendly relationship as childhood playmates; therefore, options (2) and (4) are wrong. There is no evidence for option (3).

2. (Analysis) **(1) wistful longing** The letter's references to their past happiness and to the passing season give it a sense of wistful longing. The letter, while expressing her love, is neither passionate, option (2); despairing, option (3); nor anxious, option (5). It is obviously not businesslike, option (4).

3. (Inferential Comprehension) **(2) Being happy, why should I look elsewhere?** Lines 11–13 tell us that at fifteen the girl fell in love with her husband. Her evident happiness with him rules out options (1), (4), and (5). There is no evidence for option (3).

4. (Inferential Comprehension) **(5) the woman is leading a lonely and isolated life** The gathering moss at the gate suggests that, in her husband's absence, the girl neither goes out nor receives visitors; she is, therefore, very isolated and lonely. There is no evidence for options (1), (2), (3), and (4) in the poem.

5. (Analysis) **(4) life is short and she is alone** The fact that the butterflies are in pairs and the season is passing remind her that life is short and her husband is away. She does not appear concerned about the arrival of winter, option (1). There is no evidence to suggest that she is worried about her husband's safety or about not having children, options (2) and (5). She does not seem to miss her childhood, option (3).

6. (Inferential Comprehension) **(3) The marriage was arranged by their families.** We know that they were not in love when they married, so option (1) is wrong. There is no evidence that she was his servant or that she was pregnant, options (2) and (5). A ruler's command, option (4), is not mentioned. We conclude, therefore, that the marriage was arranged by their families.

LESSON 18 Analysis Skills: Identifying Techniques (Characterization)

This skill will help you to understand the personalities of characters in literature and to make decisions about them.

In Lesson 10, you learned that you can find out about characters in plays, just as you can about people in real life, by paying attention to what they say. You can also learn about characters through their actions, which may or may not match their words. So look for clues in both speech and action. Understanding motivation—why people are doing something—will help you better understand the purpose of the whole play. Use your imagination. Since plays are written to be acted out, the dialogue only carries part of the author's ideas.

In most plays, there are a few places in which you can learn about the characters by what the author says about them. The stage directions and character descriptions may give you some information. Once in a while, a play has a character who serves as the narrator, or the voice of the playwright, but this is rare.

The stage directions (the words in parentheses and italics) tell you where people are, how they are dressed, what they are doing, and how they are doing it. In the passage on page 185, you will notice the way Mama speaks—"*Still quietly.*" This stage direction tells you that, despite the situation, she does not raise her voice. What can this tell you about her character?

So, you can understand **characterization** in two ways. In this passage, you will learn about Walter **directly,** through his mother's description of his behavior, and **indirectly**, through his words and the stage directions.

After you read the passage, ask yourself how you would play Walter. Then go back and look for clues in *all* the characters' speeches that help you determine what kind of person Walter is.

☞ *See Also: GED Exercise Book Literature and the Arts, pages 37–39*

Practicing Comprehension, Application, and Analysis Skills

Read the following passage from a play by Lorraine Hansberry.

IS THIS MAN ACTING LIKE AN ADULT?

WALTER: I'm going out!

RUTH: Where?

WALTER: Just out of this house somewhere—

RUTH: (*Getting her coat*) I'll come too.

(5) WALTER: I don't want you to come!

RUTH: I got something to talk to you about, Walter.

WALTER: That's too bad.

MAMA: (*Still quietly*) Walter Lee—(*She waits and he finally turns and looks at her*) Sit down.

(10) WALTER: I'm a grown man, Mama.

MAMA: Ain't nobody said you wasn't grown. But you still in my house and my presence. And as long as you are—you'll talk to your wife civil. Now sit down.

RUTH: (*Suddenly*) Oh, let him go out and drink himself to death! He

(15) makes me sick to my stomach! (*She flings her coat against him*)

WALTER: (*Violently*) And you turn mine too, baby! (RUTH *goes into their bedroom and slams the door behind her*) That was my greatest mistake—

MAMA: (*Still quietly*) Walter, what is the matter with you?

(20) WALTER: Matter with me? Ain't nothing the matter with *me*!

MAMA: Yes there is. Something eating you up like a crazy man. Something more than me not giving you this money. The past few years I been watching it happen to you. You get all nervous acting and kind of wild in the eyes—(WALTER *jumps up*

(25) *impatiently at her words*) I said sit there now, I'm talking to you!

WALTER: Mama—I don't need no nagging at me today.

Source: *A Raisin in the Sun*.

Questions 1 and 2 refer to the passage. Circle the best answer for each question.

1. As portrayed in this scene, Walter is

(1) loud and drunk
(2) acting like a criminal
(3) lazy and cowardly
(4) angry and defensive
(5) depressed and withdrawn

2. Walter's mother comes across as

(1) patient and long-suffering
(2) hard and domineering
(3) passive and easygoing
(4) whiny and complaining
(5) strong and caring

To check your answers, turn to page 190.

Read the following passage from a play by Tennessee Williams.

IS AMANDA REALLY CONCERNED ABOUT HER DAUGHTER'S FEELINGS?

AMANDA: I thought that you were an adult; it seems that I was mistaken. (*She crosses slowly to the sofa and sinks down and stares at* LAURA.)

LAURA: Please don't stare at me, Mother.

(5) (AMANDA *closes her eyes and lowers her head. Count ten.*)

AMANDA: What are we going to do, what is going to become of us, what is the future?

LAURA: Has something happened, Mother? (AMANDA *draws a long breath and takes out the handkerchief again. Dabbing process.*)

(10) Mother, has—something happened?

AMANDA: I'll be all right in a minute, I'm just bewildered—(*Count five*)—by life. . . .

LAURA: Mother, I wish that you would tell me what's happened!

AMANDA: As you know, I was supposed to be inducted into my office

(15) at the D.A.R. [Daughters of the American Revolution, a patriotic society] this afternoon. But I stopped off at Rubicam's business college to speak to your teachers about your having a cold and ask them what progress they thought you were making down there.

(20) LAURA: Oh. . . .

AMANDA: I went to the typing instructor and introduced myself as your mother. She didn't know who you were. "Wingfield," she said. "We don't have any such student enrolled at the school!"

I assured her she did, that you had been going to classes

(25) since early in January.

"I wonder," she said, "if you could be talking about that terribly shy little girl who dropped out of school after only a few days' attendance?"

Source: *The Glass Menagerie.*

Questions 3 and 4 refer to the passage. Circle the best answer for each question.

3. Why did Laura drop out of school?

(1) to embarrass her mother
(2) because she really is shy
(3) because she loves school
(4) to go dancing instead
(5) to make Amanda angry

4. Amanda says the lines beginning "What are we going to do . . ." (lines 6–7)

(1) because she is really worried
(2) to make a dramatic effect
(3) to comfort Laura
(4) because a tragedy has happened
(5) to show she is proud of Laura

To check your answers, turn to page 190.

Read the following passage from a play by Henrik Ibsen.

WHAT HAS NORA DONE FOR HER HUSBAND?

MRS. LINDE: . . . A wife can't borrow without her husband's consent.

NORA: (*tossing her head*) Ah, but when it happens to be a wife with a bit of a sense of business . . . a wife who knows her way about things, then . . .

(5) MRS. LINDE: But, Nora, I just don't understand. . . .

NORA: You don't have to. I haven't said I did borrow the money. I might have got it some other way. (*Throws herself back on the sofa.*) I might even have got it from some admirer. Anyone as reasonably attractive as I am . . .

(10) MRS. LINDE: Don't be so silly!

NORA: Now you must be dying of curiosity, Kristine.

MRS. LINDE: Listen to me now, Nora dear—you haven't done anything rash, have you?

NORA: (*sitting up again*) Is it rash to save your husband's life?

(15) MRS. LINDE: I think it was rash to do anything without telling him. . . .

NORA: But the whole point was that he mustn't know anything. Good heavens, can't you see! He wasn't even supposed to know how desperately ill he was. It was me the doctors came and told his life was in danger, that the only way to save him was to go South
(20) for a while. Do you think I didn't try talking him into it first? I began dropping hints about how nice it would be if I could be taken on a little trip abroad, like other young wives. I wept, I pleaded, I told him he ought to show some consideration for my condition, and let me have a bit of my own way. And then I sug-
(25) gested he might take out a loan. But at that he nearly lost his temper, Kristine. He said I was being frivolous, that it was his duty as a husband not to give in to all these whims and fancies of mine—as I do believe he called them. All right, I thought, somehow you've got to be saved. And it was then I found a way.

Source: *A Doll's House.*

Questions 5 and 6 refer to the passage. Circle the best answer for each question.

5. From the speeches in this scene, Nora could be described as

(1) humble and obedient
(2) hysterical and panicky
(3) arrogant and evil
(4) resourceful and determined
(5) childish and impulsive

6. When Nora's husband called her "frivolous" (line 26), he meant she was

(1) the life of the party
(2) impractical
(3) scatterbrained
(4) hard to say no to
(5) flirtatious

To check your answers, turn to page 190.

GED Mini-Test

Directions: Choose the <u>best answer</u> to each item.

<u>Items 1 to 6</u> refer to the following passage from a play by Lillian Hellman.

CAN THIS CHILD BE TRUSTED?

MARY: I *did* pick the flowers near Conway's. You never believe me. You believe everybody but me. It's always like that. Everything I say you fuss at me about. Everything I do is wrong.

KAREN: You know that isn't true. (*Goes to* MARY, *puts her arm around*
(5)   *her, waits until the sobbing has stopped*) Look, Mary, look at me. (*Raises* MARY'S *face with her hand*) Let's try to understand each other. If you feel that you *have* to take a walk, or that you just *can't* come to class, or that you'd like to go into the village by yourself, come and tell me—I'll try to understand. I don't say
(10)   that I'll always agree that you should do exactly what you want to do, but I've had feelings like that, too—everybody has—and I won't be unreasonable about yours. But this way, this kind of lying you do, makes everything wrong.

MARY: (*looking steadily at* KAREN) I got the flowers near Conway's
(15)   cornfield.

KAREN: (*looks at* MARY, *sighs, moves back toward desk and stands there for a moment*) Well, there doesn't seem to be any other way with you; you'll have to be punished. Take your recreation periods alone for the next two weeks. No horseback riding and
(20)   no hockey. Don't leave the school grounds for any reason whatsoever. Is that clear?

MARY: (*carefully*) Saturday, too?

KAREN: Yes.

MARY: But you said I could go to the boat races.

(25) KAREN: I'm sorry, but you can't go.

MARY: I'll tell my grandmother. I'll tell her how everybody treats me here and the way I get punished for every little thing I do. I'll tell her. I'll—

MRS. MORTAR: Why, I'd slap her hands! . . .

(30) KAREN: (*wearily*) Go upstairs now.

MARY: I've got a pain. I've had it all morning. It hurts right here. (*Pointing vaguely in the direction of her heart*) Really it does.

KAREN: Ask Miss Dobie to give you some hot water and bicarbonate of soda.

(35) MARY: It's a bad pain. I've never had it before. My heart! It's my heart! It's stopped or something. I can't breathe.

Source: *The Children's Hour.*

1. Which of the following phrases best describes Karen?

   (1) prim and proper
   (2) harsh and demanding
   (3) kindly and forgiving
   (4) reasonable and firm
   (5) easily intimidated

2. Which of the following phrases best describes Mary?

   (1) lonely and misunderstood
   (2) pathetic and victimized
   (3) friendly and open
   (4) slow-witted and dull
   (5) sneaky and uncooperative

3. Which of the following is Mary most capable of?

   (1) admitting mistakes
   (2) helping others
   (3) getting her own way
   (4) accepting punishment
   (5) obeying orders

4. The passage creates a sense of

   (1) harmony
   (2) suspense
   (3) conflict
   (4) sorrow
   (5) amusement

5. Karen, as the teacher, is responsible for Mary. This fact

   (1) makes it easy for Karen to control Mary's behavior
   (2) explains why Mary is being so difficult
   (3) makes the whole conflict of wills unnecessary
   (4) makes it easy for Mary to manipulate Karen's responses
   (5) makes Karen's job seem carefree and appealing

6. Given what we know about Mary, we can anticipate that later in the play she will

   (1) experience a change of heart
   (2) take revenge on Karen
   (3) become class president
   (4) become an honors student
   (5) become best friends with Karen

To check your answers, turn to page 191.

Answers and Explanations

Practicing Comprehension, Application, and Analysis Skills (pages 185–187)

1. (Analysis) **(4) angry and defensive** Walter's anger shows in the way he treats his wife and in his defensive response to his mother. There is no support for options (1), (2), (3), and (5).

2. (Analysis) **(5) strong and caring** Mama's concern for her son and his wife comes through in the strong stand she takes about his behavior. Options (1) and (3) are wrong because calm is not the same as patience or passiveness, and Mama is not simply tolerating Walter's behavior. Options (2) and (4) suggest the opposite of her character.

3. (Inferential Comprehension) **(2) because she really is shy** A painful scene like this one is clearly not what Laura had in mind, so options (1) and (5) are wrong. Her timidity in this scene makes it unlikely that she would have quit to do something as social as dancing, option (4). If she loved school, option (3), she would not have quit; therefore, she probably left because of her shyness.

4. (Inferential Comprehension) **(2) to make a dramatic effect** Amanda is acting as if something awful has happened just to get Laura's attention. Options (1) and (4) are wrong because the incident is not really tragic. Options (3) and (5) are wrong because she is trying to make Laura feel uncomfortable.

5. (Inferential Comprehension) **(4) resourceful and determined** Nora is clearly not humble and obedient, option (1); hysterical, option (2); or evil, option (3). While she may have an impulsive streak, option (5), her determination and resourcefulness are her most obvious qualities.

6. (Inferential Comprehension) **(2) impractical** When Nora's husband called her frivolous, he meant that she was being silly and impractical. There is no evidence for options (1), (3), (4), and (5).

1. (Inferential Comprehension) **(4) reasonable and firm** Karen does her best to reason with Mary, but she is also firm with her. She is not prim, option (1); harsh, option (2); or easily intimidated, option (5). Nor is she overly forgiving toward the girl, ruling out option (3).

2. (Inferential Comprehension) **(5) sneaky and uncooperative** Mary's tears and tantrums, threats, and steady refusal to tell the truth tell us that she is hard to control. She may be lonely and misunderstood as well, option (1), but those are not her chief traits. There is no evidence for options (2), (3), and (4).

3. (Inferential Comprehension) **(3) getting her own way** Mary has proved that she can get her own way; she has also proved that she cannot admit mistakes, option (1); accept punishment, option (4); or obey orders, option (5). There is no evidence that she would be good at helping others, option (2).

4. (Analysis) **(3) conflict** The clash of wills between Mary and Karen makes this a scene full of conflict. There is no evidence for options (1), (2), (4), or (5).

5. (Inferential Comprehension) **(4) makes it easy for Mary to manipulate Karen's responses** Karen's responsibility for Mary makes her vulnerable to Mary's accusations and phony heart attack; Karen must ask herself if she is being unfair or unfeeling at the same time that she is trying to discipline Mary. Therefore, option (1) is wrong. The conflict between them is both real and unavoidable, so option (3) is wrong. There is no support for options (2) and (5).

6. (Application) **(2) take revenge on Karen** What we already know about Mary does not suggest the possibility of her changing much, option (1). It is more likely that Mary will find a way to get revenge on Karen. There is no support for options (3), (4), and (5).

Review: Classical Literature

In this section you have studied fiction, drama, biography, autobiography, poetry, and essays. You have learned to recognize main ideas, implications, consequences, and supporting details. You have learned to identify elements of style and structure, mood, characterization, and point of view. And you have practiced these skills by reading the passages and answering the questions that accompanied them.

The following exercises give you an additional opportunity to review some of the literary forms you have been learning about and a chance to continue practicing the reading strategies you have studied.

Directions: Choose the best answer to each item.

Items 1 and 2 refer to the following passage by Jack London.

WHAT HAS THIS NEWCOMER OVERLOOKED?

The man flung a look back along the way he had come. The Yukon lay a mile wide and hidden under three feet of ice. On top of this ice were as many feet of snow. It was all pure white, rolling in gentle undulations where the ice jams of the freeze-up had formed.
(5) North and south, as far as the eye could see, it was unbroken white, save for a dark hairline that curved and twisted from around the spruce-covered island to the south, and that curved and twisted away into the north, where it disappeared behind another spruce-covered island. The dark hairline was the trail—the main trail—
(10) that led south five hundred miles to the Chilkoot Pass, Dyea, and salt water; and that led north seventy miles to Dawson, and still on to the north a thousand miles to Nulato, and finally to St. Michael on Bering Sea, a thousand miles and half a thousand more.

But all this—the mysterious, far-reaching hairline trail, the
(15) absence of sun from the sky, the tremendous cold, and the strangeness and weirdness of it all—made no impression on the man. It was not because he was long used to it. He was a newcomer in the land, a *chechaquo*, and this was his first winter. The trouble with him was that he was without imagination. He was quick and
(20) alert in the things of life, but only in the things, and not in the significances. Fifty degrees below zero meant eighty-odd degrees of frost. Such fact impressed him as being cold and uncomfortable, and that was all.

Source: "To Build a Fire."

1. The writing style of this author could be described as

   (1) graceful and poetic
   (2) witty and amusing
   (3) ornate and elaborate
   (4) exciting and descriptive
   (5) hysterical and overwrought

2. From the evidence in the text, we can conclude that this story is taking place

   (1) on a spruce-covered island
   (2) in the far north
   (3) in the man's imagination
   (4) in prehistoric times
   (5) on some other planet

Items 3 and 4 refer to the following passage by John Steinbeck.

WOULD YOU BUY A USED CAR FROM THIS MAN?

A stout, slow man sat in an office waiting. His face was fatherly and benign, and his eyes twinkled with friendship. He was a caller of good mornings, a ceremonious shaker of hands, a jolly man who knew all jokes and yet who hovered close to sadness, for in the
(5) midst of a laugh he could remember the death of your aunt, and his eyes could become wet with sorrow for your loss. This morning he had placed a flower in a vase on his desk, a single scarlet hibiscus, and the vase sat beside the black, velvet-lined pearl tray in front of him. He was shaved close to the blue roots of his beard, and his hands
(10) were clean and his nails polished. His door stood open to the morning, and he hummed under his breath while his right hand practiced legerdemain. He rolled a coin back and forth over his knuckles and made it appear and disappear, made it spin and sparkle. The coin winked into sight and as quickly slipped out of sight, and the man
(15) did not even watch his own performance. The fingers did it all mechanically, precisely, while the man hummed to himself and peered out the door. Then he heard the tramp of feet of the approaching crowd, and the fingers of his right hand worked faster and faster until, as the figure of Kino filled the doorway, the coin flashed and
(20) disappeared.

"Good morning, my friend," the stout man said. "What can I do for you?"

Source: *The Pearl*.

---

3. At the beginning of the passage, what kind of man do we think the dealer is?

   (1) greedy and secretive
   (2) shy and timid
   (3) two-faced and tricky
   (4) serious and scholarly
   (5) softhearted and friendly

4. Which image best suggests the main idea of this passage?

   (1) a Venus's-flytrap, a flower that traps insects attracted by its scent
   (2) an animal trap set in the woods
   (3) a magician pulling rabbits out of a hat
   (4) a pleasantly decorated waiting room at a doctor's office
   (5) flypaper hanging on a wall

Items 5 and 6 refer to the following passage from an essay by Henry David Thoreau.

WOULD YOU HIRE THIS MAN?

As for my own business, even that kind of surveying which I could do with most satisfaction my employers do not want. They would prefer that I should do my work coarsely and not too well, ay, not well enough. When I observe that there are different ways of
(5) surveying, my employer commonly asks which will give him the most land, not which is most correct. I once invented a rule for measuring cordwood, and tried to introduce it in Boston; but the measurer there told me that the sellers did not wish to have their wood measured correctly—that he was already too accurate for them, and
(10) therefore they commonly got their wood measured in Charlestown before crossing the bridge.

The aim of the laborer should be, not to get his living, to get "a good job," but to perform well a certain work; and, even in a pecuniary sense, it would be economy for a town to pay its laborers
(15) so well that they would not feel that they were working for low ends, as for a livelihood merely, but for scientific, or even moral ends. Do not hire a man who does your work for money, but him who does it for love of it.

Source: "Life Without Principle," from *Major Writers of America*.

---

5. The author sometimes feels unsatisfied with his work because

(1) he is not paid well enough
(2) he does not need the money
(3) the customers do not always want his best effort
(4) the customers often go to other surveyors
(5) he has not been able to invent a better measuring rule

6. Which of the following is the best meaning of "pecuniary" (line 14)?

(1) peculiar
(2) inaccurate
(3) having to do with measuring
(4) having to do with money
(5) a means of surveying

WILL THIS AUTHOR EVER GO BACK TO SCHOOL?

The morning came, without any warning, when my sisters surrounded me, wrapped me in scarves, tied up my bootlaces, thrust a cap on my head, and stuffed a baked potato in my pocket.

"What's this?" I said. . . .

(5) They picked me up bodily, kicking and bawling, and carried me up to the road.

"Boys who don't go to school get put into boxes, and turn into rabbits, and get chopped up Sundays."

I felt this was overdoing it rather, but I said no more after that.

(10) I arrived at the school just three feet tall and fatly wrapped in my scarves. The playground roared like a rodeo, and the potato burned through my thigh. Old boots, ragged stockings, torn trousers and skirts, went skating and skidding around me. The rabble closed in; I was encircled; grit flew in my face like shrapnel. Tall girls with

(15) frizzled hair, and huge boys with sharp elbows, began to prod me with hideous interest. They plucked at my scarves, spun me round like a top, screwed my nose, and stole my potato. . . .

"What's the matter, Loll? Didn't he like it at school, then?"

"They never gave me the present!"

(20) "Present? What present?"

"They said they'd give me a present."

"Well, now, I'm sure they didn't."

"They did! They said: 'You're Laurie Lee, ain't you? Well, just you sit here for the present.' I sat there all day but I never got it. I

(25) ain't going back there again!"

But after a week I felt like a veteran and grew as ruthless as anyone else. Somebody had stolen my baked potato, so I swiped somebody else's apple. . . . This tiny, white-washed Infants' room was a brief but cosy anarchy. In that short time allowed us we played

(30) and wept, broke things, fell asleep, cheeked the teacher, discovered the things we could do to each other, and exhaled our last guiltless days.

Source: *Cider With Rosie.*

---

7. The theme of this passage is

(1) school is dreadful
(2) school is wonderful
(3) schooling should not be forced
(4) people adapt to new situations
(5) young teachers are understanding

8. The author now regards his early schooling with

(1) fear and distaste
(2) anger and disbelief
(3) fond amusement
(4) reluctant admiration
(5) bitter resentment

Items 9 and 10 refer to the following poem by Walt Whitman.

WHAT IS ORDINARY ABOUT A MIRACLE?

Miracles

Why, who makes much of a miracle?
As to me I know of nothing else but miracles,
Whether I walk the streets of Manhattan,
Or dart my sight over the roofs of houses toward the sky,
(5) Or wade with naked feet along the beach just in the edge of the
    water,
Or stand under the trees in the woods,
Or talk by day with any one I love,
Or sit at table at dinner with the rest,
(10) Or look at strangers opposite me riding in the car,
Or watch honeybees busy around the hive of a summer forenoon,
Or animals feeding in the fields,
Or birds, or the wonderfulness of insects in the air,
Or the wonderfulness of the sundown, or of stars shining so quiet
(15)   and bright,
Or the exquisite delicate thin curve of the new moon in spring;
These with the rest, one and all, are to me miracles,
The whole referring, yet each distinct and in its place.
To me every hour of the light and dark is a miracle,
(20) Every cubic inch of space is a miracle,
Every square yard of the surface of the earth is spread with the
    same,
Every foot of the interior swarms with the same.

To me the sea is a continual miracle,
(25) The fishes that swim—the rocks—the motion of the waves—
    the ships with men in them,
What stranger miracles are there?

Source: "Miracles."

9. Which of the following does the poet not list as a miracle

  (1) walking barefoot on the beach
  (2) sharing a dinner table
  (3) the hours of day and night
  (4) walking along city streets
  (5) the sound of train whistles

10. By saying "What stranger miracles are there?" (line 27), the poet means

  (1) there are no miracles
  (2) everything we take for granted is really very special
  (3) the things we see every day are not very miraculous
  (4) even stranger miracles occur
  (5) hoping for miracles is strange

HOW DO THESE TWO WOMEN REVEAL THEIR CHARACTERS?

MRS. DUDGEON: . . . Oh, it's you, is it, Mrs. Anderson?

JUDITH: (*very politely—almost patronizingly*) Yes. Can I do anything for you, Mrs. Dudgeon? Can I help to get the place ready before they come to read the will?

(5) MRS. DUDGEON: (*stiffly*) Thank you, Mrs. Anderson, my house is always ready for anyone to come into.

JUDITH: (*with complacent amiability*) Yes, indeed it is. Perhaps you had rather I did not intrude on you just now.

MRS. DUDGEON: Oh, one more or less will make no difference this (10) morning, Mrs. Anderson. Now that you're here, you'd better stay. If you wouldn't mind shutting that door! (JUDITH *smiles, implying "How stupid of me!" and shuts it with an exasperating air of doing something pretty and becoming.*) That's better. I must go and tidy myself a bit. I suppose you don't mind (15) stopping here to receive anyone that comes in until I'm ready.

JUDITH: (*graciously giving her leave*) Oh yes, certainly. Leave that to me, Mrs. Dudgeon; and take your time. (*She hangs up her cloak and bonnet.*)

MRS. DUDGEON: (*half sneering*) I thought that would be more in (20) your way than getting the house ready.

Source: *The Devil's Disciple*.

---

11. Mrs. Dudgeon's words and actions in this scene show her to be

(1) patient and long-suffering
(2) gentle and easygoing
(3) pure and high-minded
(4) stingy and tightfisted
(5) rude and huffy

12. According to the stage directions, Judith is best described as

(1) sweet and self-sacrificing
(2) smug and self-satisfied
(3) high-strung and sensitive
(4) depressed and withdrawn
(5) angry and defensive

13. Which of the following best states the main idea of this passage?

(1) Judith arrived early for a party.
(2) Judith is an unexpected guest for the reading of a will.
(3) Judith and Mrs. Dudgeon are trying to become friends.
(4) Politeness can make an awkward meeting easier.
(5) Mrs. Dudgeon is pleased that Judith has come to help.

14. Which of the following best describes the mood of this passage?

(1) mournful
(2) tense
(3) lighthearted
(4) depressing
(5) cheerful

Answers and Explanations

Classical Literature Review (pages 192–197)

1. (Analysis) **(1) graceful and poetic**
Option (1) best sums up the author's style. Although he describes the weather and terrain, option (4), he supplies the reader with these facts in an almost poetic way. There is no support for options (2), (3), and (5).

2. (Inferential Comprehension) **(2) in the far north** The details—Yukon, unbroken views of ice and snow, among others—lead to the conclusion that the story takes place in the far north. Although option (1) is mentioned, it is only a detail that is seen. There is no evidence for options (3), (4), and (5).

3. (Analysis) **(5) softhearted and friendly** The dealer appears to be softhearted and friendly in the first paragraph because he is fatherly and kindly and jokes or sympathizes with those he meets. Although options (1) and (3) are closer to his true nature, the reader does not know this at the beginning of the passage. Options (2) and (4) do not reflect his personality.

4. (Application) **(1) a Venus's-flytrap, a flower that traps insects attracted by its scent** The flower lures its victims by appearing innocent. Options (2) and (5) are wrong because their purpose is not disguised. Option (3) is wrong because even though a magician deceives, he does it to entertain. Option (4) is wrong because the room is intended to reassure people, not to deceive them.

5. (Inferential Comprehension) **(3) the customers do not always want his best effort** The example suggests that customers are more interested in saving or making money than in quality; the author is more interested in quality. Options (1) and (2) are wrong because money is not his main concern and because we do not know how much he makes or needs. There is no evidence for option (4). Option (5) is not true.

6. (Inferential Comprehension) **(4) having to do with money** The context is about work and money. The sentence that follows suggests how a town should best spend its money. Options (1), (2), (3), and (5) do not make sense in that context.

7. (Analysis) **(4) people adapt to new situations** Although the author touches on options (1), (2), (3), and (5) as he tells about his early school days, the idea of adapting to new situations is the theme. Lines 26–28 support this.

8. (Analysis) **(3) fond amusement** The tone of this passage is humorous. The word choice and examples are designed to be funny. Although his initial reaction, when he was faced with his first day of school, was anger and disbelief, option (2), his remembrance of the experience as a whole is warm and positive. There is no support for options (1), (4), and (5).

9. (Literal Comprehension) **(5) the sound of train whistles** Options (1), (2), (3), and (4) are all mentioned in the poem.

10. (Literal Comprehension) **(2) everything we take for granted is really very special** All the miracles he lists are ordinary things. Option (1) is the opposite of the main idea. Option (3) is the opposite of what is meant. There is no support for options (4) and (5).

11. (Analysis) **(5) rude and huffy** Mrs. Dudgeon's actions and statements toward Judith reveal this. Options (1), (2), and (3) are incorrect. Though she may also be stingy, option (4), there is no evidence of that trait in this passage.

12. (Analysis) **(2) smug and self-satisfied** Although her words are sweet, the stage directions suggest that Judith has a very high opinion of herself. If the reader had only the character's speeches to rely on, option (1) would be correct. There is no support for options (3), (4), and (5).

13. (Literal Comprehension) **(2) Judith is an unexpected guest for the reading of a will.** Mrs. Dudgeon is surprised to see Judith but says, not very nicely, that she can stay. The occasion is stated in line 4. Option (1) has no support. Options (3) and (5) are the opposite of what is suggested. Option (4) might be true, but it is too general and does not describe the situation.

14. (Analysis) **(2) tense** These two women are barely managing to be polite to each other. Options (1) and (4) are wrong because there is no evidence of sadness. Options (3) and (5) both suggest a pleasantness not found in this passage.

Use the chart below to find your strengths and weaknesses in reading comprehension.

Skill	Area	Question	Lessons for Review
Literal Comprehension	Poetry	9	3
	Poetry	10	1 and 13
	Drama	13	1 and 13
Inferential Comprehension	Fiction	2	16
	Nonfiction	5	16
	Nonfiction	6	4
Application	Fiction	4	9
Analysis	Fiction	1	14
	Fiction	3	10
	Nonfiction	7	11
	Nonfiction	8	14
	Drama	11, 12	18
	Drama	14	17

COMMENTARY

♦ **opinion**
   a personal belief or viewpoint about a particular subject; it is not always based on facts or rational thought

♦ **fact**
   a statement that is based on reality and can be proven to most people's satisfaction

When writers talk about a work of literature or art, we call what they say commentary. Commentaries come in several forms. One that you will be familiar with is the review. A review is intended to tell you what the reviewer, or critic, thinks of the book, television show, movie, play, or artwork. Usually reviews are written in an informal, sometimes humorous style. Sometimes reviews are very serious. The subject matter and the intended audience affect the writer's approach.

The purpose of a commentary often is to help the reader by giving some information about a work that the reader has not seen yet. The review or commentary tells such things as what the work is, who created it, who appears in it, and what it is about, as well as how the writer feels about it.

Reviews are usually found in newspapers and magazines. Commentaries of a more general nature can also be found in books, especially if the author is writing about a well-known creative work, artist, writer, or filmmaker. Reviews and commentaries are not limited to works recently produced. At times, older works or artists are discussed because they are once again of public interest.

- **implication**
  an idea that is suggested, rather than stated directly, by other facts or ideas

- **point of view**
  the personal interests and background that influence a person's opinions

- **consequence**
  the result of actions or decisions

The most important thing to be aware of when you read a review is that you are reading the author's **opinion**. The purpose of a review is not just to give you some **facts** but to persuade you to accept the author's judgment about the facts. Often a review will have more opinions than facts. It will be up to you to sort out facts from opinions. Then you can make a decision whether or not to trust the reviewer's opinion. This skill is taught in Lesson 19.

In Lesson 20, cause-and-effect relationships are reviewed in order to show how critics talk about their ideas. These relationships are most often important when the writer is talking about the author or artist of the work under discussion.

In lesson 21, you will see how reviewers use **implications** to make their point. Many reviewers do not state their opinions directly; therefore, it is up to the reader to infer what the idea is and then draw a conclusion.

You will be reminded about **point of view** in Lesson 22. The reviewer's point of view is very important because it involves the writer's likes and dislikes and background in the field. You need to pay attention to the way the writer talks about what is being reviewed. Is the reviewer fair or too critical?

Lesson 23 focuses on understanding a **consequence**. Results are very important in a review. Reviewers often talk about the consequences of the way the film or program or artwork is made. Remember to pay attention to the effects of how something is made or presented.

LESSON 19 Analysis Skills: Distinguishing Fact From Opinion

This skill will help you understand the difference between fact and opinion.

Writers of reviews and commentaries begin by looking at facts, but the published material expresses the writers' opinions about those facts. People read reviews and commentaries to help them make judgments about the quality of a certain book, movie, or artwork, for example. Because writers often try to get you to agree with them, you need to be able to **evaluate** what the writers have said. That is, you need to be able to recognize the difference between a fact and an opinion.

A **fact** is something that actually has happened or actually exists. A fact is based on reality and can be proved. I can say, "There is an apple orchard on my land," and you can come to my house and see the apple orchard. That is a fact. The apple trees are there to see.

An **opinion** is a personal judgment, viewpoint, or belief. An opinion is usually based on facts, but it is an interpretation of the facts. My opinion of the apple orchard may not be the same as someone else's. I might say that my orchard is a pain in the neck, requires too much work, and should be cut down and replaced with grass. Someone else might think that the orchard is useful, gives fruit every year, and is pretty to look at. Both of these statements are opinions. An opinion states how a person feels about a fact.

Usually a writer has strong feelings concerning the subject you are reading about and will try to persuade you that those feelings are right. It is up to you to first figure out what is fact and what is opinion. Then you can evaluate the reviewer's opinion and form your own opinion. You may find that the author has not given you enough facts, so you may not want to agree with him or her.

It is important to remember that sometimes opinions are based not on facts but on other beliefs. If a writer says that doctors are over-paid, that person is making a generalization that is probably not based on fact. It may be true that some doctors are overpaid, but other doctors may be working for very little money. You as the reader must ask yourself if the writer is referring to all of the facts—in this case, does the writer know the salaries of all doctors and what their services are worth?

☞ *See Also: GED Exercise Book Literature and the Arts, pages 44–46*

Practicing Comprehension, Application, and Analysis Skills

Read the following review by Jack Kroll.

WHY DID THE NEANDERTHALS ADOPT AYLA?

The Clan of the Cave Bear is dog. Jean M. Auel write big best seller about Neanderthals who live 35,000 years ago. Holly-wood-heads buy movie rights, screw up movie. Holly-woodheads even more primitive than Neanderthals. Book make cave people talk in
(5) plain English. Holly-woodheads make cave people talk in fake ugga-mugga lingo like old Johnny Weissmuller movies, while audience read subtitles. Book like ice-age soap opera (no, soapless opera, cave people pretty grungy). Movie no zip, no zap, no zing. John Sayles good writer, why his screenplay so dull? Director Michael Chapman
(10) great camera man, why his movie so dull? Alan Silvestri write music sound like "Chariots of Fire," dumb Holly-woodhead move.

Daryl Hannah play Ayla, girl from new Cro-Magnon people. Neanderthals found her when little child after big earthquake. Short dark Neanderthals uneasy with tall blond Cro-Magnon girl. But
(15) foster mother Iza (Pamela Reed), foster father Creb (James Remar) very kind to orphan girl. Ayla break Neanderthal taboos, use male weapons, become first woman hunter, defy male chauvinist pig Broud (Thomas G. Waites). Ayla become prehistoric Gloria Steinem. Daryl Hannah look great in animal skins, try hard show deep feeling
(20) in ugga-mugga talk. Pamela Reed look very hairy. James Remar more primitive as mob boss Dutch Schultz in *The Cotton Club*. Jean Auel very mad at Holly-woodheads for screwing up her book. She bring suit. No, not animal-skin suit, legal suit. Good luck, Jean. Ugga-mugga.

Source: "When a Bear Is a Dog," *Newsweek*.

Questions 1 and 2 refer to the review. Circle the best answer for each question.

1. How does the reviewer feel about the film?

(1) Jean Auel is a superb writer.
(2) The film made the subject seem silly.
(3) The book deserved big sales.
(4) Books should not be made into films.
(5) He enjoyed reading the novel.

2. The review is written in the cavemanlike style to

(1) emphasize the reviewer's dislike of the film
(2) show how much the reviewer liked the film
(3) make fun of ordinary English
(4) imitate the way Jean Auel wrote
(5) help us remember our childhood

To check your answers, turn to page 208.

Read the following review by David Patrick Stearns.

IS *HENRY V* A SUCCESS?

Shakespeare's plays rarely translate into great cinema, because they're either made on low budgets or look like filmed stage plays. So it's quite a surprise that *Henry V*, not Shakespeare's best, is one of the few movies in which Shakespeare seems not only a great
(5) playwright, but a seasoned screenwriter.

A lot of it has to do with Kenneth Branagh, a little-known English actor whose identification with Henry V is like Laurence Olivier's with Hamlet. He plays the title role, directs and adapts this play dealing with his psychological transition from Prince Hal to
(10) King Henry during the ruler's heroic campaigns into France.

Branagh is young enough that his face has a boyish fleshiness, but old enough to project the charisma of a king. Even if you gasp to keep up with the Elizabethan language, his natural, eloquent in-flections and the details of his direction clearly convey what he—and
(15) the large cast—is talking about.

The film is full of beautifully photographed images, but they're never just decorative. In fact, it has a rough, primitive medieval look in keeping with its 15th-century setting. Though the battle sequences are sweeping, their details show the suffering, sorrow and pettiness
(20) of Henry's men. The film even inspires us with their battle heroism. After all, their wars were more a sport than a means of annihilation.

Henry V emerges a first-class epic film, so entertaining that it needs no apologies for being based on a 400-year-old play. The only disappointments: Paul Scofield, whose portrayal of the French king
(25) is surprisingly dour, and the last 10 minutes, which turn needlessly cute as Henry courts his future wife, Katherine. But that's as much Shakespeare's fault as Branagh's.

Source: "Majestic *Henry V* Does Justice to the Bard," *USA Today*.

Questions 3 and 4 refer to the review. Circle the best answer for each question.

3. According to the passage, which is a fact about Kenneth Branagh?

   (1) He is a talented director.
   (2) He plays the part of Henry V.
   (3) He is the reason for the success of the film.
   (4) His voice is perfect for Shakespearean dialogue.
   (5) He is very young.

4. Which statement best expresses the reviewer's opinion of the movie *Henry V*?

   (1) It is based on a 400-year-old play.
   (2) It is about King Henry's campaigns into France.
   (3) It is an entertaining film.
   (4) It is a poor translation of the original play.
   (5) It has a large cast.

To check your answers, turn to page 208.

Read the following excerpt from a review by Ari Korpivaara.

IS THE WORLD WAITING FOR MS. RAMBO?

Sly Stallone and Arnold Schwarzenegger had better get out of town. Sigourney Weaver is ready to take over as the number-one action hero. As Ripley in *Aliens*, she is just as brave and competent with weaponry as the male Rambos. She is also smarter and capa-
(5) ble of feeling. She is as close to believable as you can get in science fiction. That's because Weaver can act—more than can be said for the muscle-bound Katzenjammer Kids.

. . . Ripley . . . returns as a consultant with a fighting force of Marines to the planet taken over by the aliens. The human colonists
(10) have been wiped out, except for a little girl named Newt.

. . . The "top gun" pilot is a woman. The outfit's best fighting machine is a well-muscled woman named Vasquez, who in barracks-style banter puts the men in their place. A male Marine, eyeing her bulging biceps with envy: "Ever been mistaken for a man?"
(15) Vasquez: "No, have you?"

When the going gets rough, a number of the men come apart—panic-stricken, hysterical, cowardly. The women do not. Despite her own fear (something the thickheaded Rambo never feels), Ripley takes control from the mission's commander, paralyzed by the horror
(20) of it all, and, driving a space-age tank, rescues the Marines trapped inside the aliens' incubation room. It's a pleasure to root for her.

Source: "Roll Over, Rambo," *Ms.* magazine.

Questions 5 to 7 refer to the excerpt. Circle the best answer for each question.

5. Which of the following best states the reviewer's use of facts?

    (1) The review is full of facts.
    (2) Each opinion is supported by a fact.
    (3) There are no facts in this review.
    (4) Facts are used in the plot summary.
    (5) Several facts are used in the description of Weaver's acting.

6. What is implied in the opening paragraph?

    (1) Male heroes dominate action films.
    (2) War is heroic.
    (3) Flying is for men.
    (4) Female pilots are cowardly.
    (5) Women make poor soldiers.

7. According to the passage, the aliens killed all the human colonists except

    (1) a male Marine
    (2) a Japanese space scientist
    (3) the Katzenjammer Kids
    (4) a female child
    (5) all women over six feet

To check your answers, turn to page 208.

GED Mini-Test

Directions: Choose the best answer to each item.

Items 1 to 4 refer to the following movie review by Ralph Novak.

WHAT IS THE PLOT OF THIS MOVIE?

This movie [*A Shock to the System*] about mid-life-crisis murder
exists as much to be a vehicle for [Michael] Caine as all those '40s
Westerns with titles like *Song of Nevada*, *Heart of the Golden West*
and *Springtime in the Sierras* existed to be vehicles for Roy Rogers.
(5) While a lot of other actors could play the part, it's hard to imagine
many of them making this much out of this little.

Caine, as a New York City marketing executive passed over for
a promotion he deserves at the office and buried under nagging he
doesn't deserve at home, gleefully gets into the fury of his character.
(10) He's on screen almost the whole time.

The role of a young subordinate who becomes Caine's lover
seems far too passive and slight for an actress of [Elizabeth]
McGovern's talent and experience. But she has a vivid moment or
two, as do Peter (*Local Hero*) Riegert as the ruthless young competi-
(15) tor who one-ups Caine at the office, Swoosie Kurtz as Caine's unsat-
isfiable wife and Will (*No Way Out*) Patton as a persistent state
police detective.

There's too little plot as it is to reveal any of it. Let's just say
that this is the sort of mildly twisty story that Alfred Hitchcock
(20) could have boiled down to a half hour for his old TV series. In this
case, veteran TV director Jan Egleson and debuting writer Andrew
Klavan let things run on an hour longer and leave loopholes gaping.

Source: *People* magazine.

---

1. The reviewer uses the example of the
   Roy Rogers films to support the
   opinion that

   (1) this film would be worthless
   without Michael Caine
   (2) this film will be very popular
   (3) Roy Rogers would have been good
   in the lead role
   (4) Hollywood should remake some
   of the old cowboy movies
   (5) any actor could have done as well
   as Michael Caine

2. Which of the following can be inferred
   from this review?

   (1) The reviewer likes detective
   movies.
   (2) The movie was intended to be a
   thriller.
   (3) The movie is a comedy.
   (4) Alfred Hitchcock had already
   used the plot of this movie.
   (5) The reviewer does not like
   Caine's acting.

3. According to this review, Michael Caine plays

   (1) a police detective
   (2) a veteran TV director
   (3) an unhappy executive
   (4) a happy husband
   (5) a ruthless competitor

4. Which of the phrases from the review is <u>not</u> used to express an opinion?

   (1) this much out of this little
   (2) far too passive
   (3) onscreen almost the whole time
   (4) could have boiled down
   (5) leave loopholes gaping

Items 5 and 6 refer to the following review by Art Durbano.

IS THIS HOW TO PASS HISTORY?

Southern California—the fictitious mall-and-waterslide heaven of San Dimas, to be precise—is a main character in one of '89's biggest sleeper hits, *Bill and Ted's Excellent Adventure*. Bill and Ted (played with hilarious gusto by Alex Winter and Keanu Reeves) are a pair
(5) of high-school nincompoops on the verge of flunking history. (These guys are so slow they think "Ceasar was that salad-dressing dude.") Their final oral exam is tomorrow and, to make a long story short, that "report had better be something *very* special." With a little help from some new friends, it becomes just that. George Carlin (as
(10) an excellent dude from the future) imparts to Bill and Ted the ways and means of time travel (don't ask why) and off they go, collecting speakers for their exam: Napoleon (whom Bill and Ted learn was someone other than that "short, dead dude"), Billy the Kid, Socrates and—for extra credit—Sigmund Freud, Genghis Khan, Beethoven,
(15) Joan of Arc and Abraham Lincoln. The stunning effects these people have on San Dimas make up the last third of this irresistible romp.

Source: *TV Guide*.

5. Which of the following is a valid conclusion based on all the facts and opinions from this review?

   (1) California is the setting for the movie.
   (2) The education system needs to be improved.
   (3) The main characters of the movie are flunking history.
   (4) Time travel is really possible.
   (5) Movies about high school nincompoops can be funny.

6. Which of the following probably made the author laugh most?

   (1) naming the town San Dimas
   (2) the idea that boys can flunk history
   (3) the assignment of an oral exam
   (4) calling Napoleon a "short, dead dude"
   (5) the idea of time travel

To check your answers, turn to page 209.

Answers and Explanations

Practicing Comprehension, Application, and Analysis Skills (pages 203–205)

1. (Analysis) **(2) The film made the subject seem silly.** The reviewer does not describe the book, option (1), or even say if he read it, option (5). Option (3) is not mentioned in the review. The reviewer criticizes the movie, not the fact that it was based on a book, option (4).

2. (Analysis) **(1) emphasize the reviewer's dislike of the film** The reviewer is making fun of the film's poor use of language. This is supported in lines 4–7. The reviewer did not like the movie, so option (2) is wrong. Option (3) is the opposite of what is meant. Option (4) is wrong because Auel had her characters speak in plain English. Option (5) has no support.

3. (Literal Comprehension) **(2) He plays the part of Henry V.** This is stated in the second paragraph. Options (1), (3), and (4) are suggested but are all opinions of the reviewer. There is no evidence for option (5).

4. (Analysis) **(3) It is an entertaining film.** The reviewer's opinion can be found in lines 22–23. Options (1), (2), and (5) are facts. Option (4) is an opinion, but it is not held by the reviewer.

5. (Literal Comprehension) **(4) Facts are used in the plot summary.** Most of the review is opinion, so option (1) is wrong. The reviewer does not support the opinions with facts, so options (2) and (5) are wrong. The summary of the plot is supported with facts, so option (3) is wrong.

6. (Analysis) **(1) Male heroes dominate action films.** You know from comparisons made in the opening sentences that the reviewer is enthusiastic about seeing women in action films. The main idea is that such roles have been limited to men in the past. Options (2), (3), (4), and (5) are not supported by the passage.

7. (Literal Comprehension) **(4) a female child** This detail is mentioned in lines 9–10. The only colonist who has not been killed by the aliens is "a little girl named Newt." No other survivors are mentioned, so options (1), (2), (3), and (5) are wrong.

GED Mini-Test (pages 206–207)

1. (Analysis) **(1) this film would be worthless without Michael Caine** Because there is almost no plot, something has to hold the viewer's attention. In this case, it is Michael Caine; Roy Rogers used to do the same for some weak Westerns. There is no support for options (2) and (3). There is no suggestion of option (4). Option (5) is the opposite of what is stated.

2. (Inferential Comprehension) **(2) The movie was intended to be a thriller.** This is suggested by the characters involved, including a "persistent state police detective." The reviewer also mentions that Alfred Hitchcock, the director of many classic thrillers, could have used the plot. There is no evidence for option (1). Considering the characters and general description of the movie, option (3) is unlikely. Option (4) is not true. Option (5) is the opposite of the reviewer's opinion.

3. (Literal Comprehension) **(3) an unhappy executive** This is stated in lines 7–9. Options (1) and (5) refer to other characters. Option (2) refers to the filmmaker. Option (4) is the opposite of what is suggested.

4. (Analysis) **(3) onscreen almost the whole time** This refers to a fact about Caine that could be observed by anyone. Options (1), (2), (4), and (5) all refer to personal opinions of the author.

5. (Analysis) **(5) Movies about high school nincompoops can be funny.** The reviewer enjoyed the movie and the characters. Options (1) and (3) are mere facts given in the passage. Option (2) is not related to the movie. There is no suggestion of option (4).

6. (Inferential Comprehension) **(4) calling Napoleon a "short, dead dude"** The author liked the phrase so much he included it in a short review. Options (1), (2), (3), and (5) are not likely to appeal to one's sense of humor.

LESSON 20 Analysis Skills: Identifying Cause-and-Effect Relationships

When you understand a cause-and-effect relationship, you understand the connection between something that happened and what made it happen.

Asking questions is a natural way of looking at the world. Two common questions are "Why did such and such happen?" and "What was the result of such and such?" We even have traditional sayings that use the cause-and-effect relationship: Haste makes waste; April showers bring May flowers. People like to have explanations for the way things are ordered in the world.

Remember that the link between a cause and an effect is not always obvious or direct. Sometimes we have to stop to think about what we know of the world in order to figure out the real cause of something or the real effect of something. This is especially important when there is more than one cause for a result, or when several things make something happen. As you read, ask yourself questions like "Was Cause A really responsible for making Effect B happen?" and "If Cause A had not happened, would Effect B have happened anyway?"

It is possible to mistake other relationships for cause and effect. For example, in the passage about pop art on page 211, two related ideas are mentioned. First, the media helped make pop art what it is—popular and easy to understand—by giving it publicity. Second, critics attacked pop art for its *commercialism*—in a sense, for being what it is! Would the art itself have been popular without all the media attention? Did the media give the art publicity because it *was* popular? And would critics have hated it if it were *not* so popular? It is not always easy to see cause-and-effect relationships between events and ideas, so read and think carefully.

When reading for cause and effect, watch for clue words: *because, since, therefore, as a result,* and *consequently*. These are words that show cause and effect.

☞ *See Also: GED Exercise Book Literature and the Arts, pages 47–49*

Practicing Comprehension, Application, and Analysis Skills

Read the following passage by Norbert Lynton.

WHERE DID POP ART GET ITS NAME?

Pop suggests popular. The movement got a lot of publicity from the media who saw that it was news, easy to enjoy and easy to write about. It was the time when pop stars like Elvis Presley and the Beatles were emerging, and this art in many instances was
(5) responding to that world rather than the world of deep human feelings and problems. Its idiom was in many cases borrowed from the media: whereas art normally proceeded by taking ideas from art and making something new of them, this came from commercial art and so was speaking a language created by experts to reach the
(10) whole consumer society. For the same reason many commentators, especially in the United States, hated it. It denied, or seemed to deny, all seriousness and attached itself to commonplace fantasies and the hard sell.

Source: *A History of Art*.

Questions 1 and 2 refer to the excerpt. Circle the best answer for each question.

1. According to the passage, the term "pop art" means that it

   (1) appealed only to fans of rock and roll
   (2) was not expensive
   (3) was easy to understand
   (4) dealt with important issues
   (5) was favored by religious groups

2. One reason that some people objected to pop art was that

   (1) it was too romantic
   (2) it lacked serious content
   (3) pop artists copied Picasso
   (4) it had no humor
   (5) the subject matter was unpleasant

To check your answers, turn to page 216.

Read the following excerpt from a review by John Russell.

WHY HAS JOHN MARTIN MADE A COMEBACK?

Fifty years ago it was possible to buy a painting by John Martin for next to nothing. As for the books that he illustrated, they turned up on book barrows all over England and cost only pennies. Born in the year of the French Revolution, Martin lived until 1854, had
(5) moments of celebrity in his lifetime and then somehow fell through the floorboards of art history. The fact that he was a visionary artist who could match himself against the Old Testament and go the distance without apparent effort counted for nothing in the 1920's and 1930's.

(10) But in our own time, John Martin has come all the way back again. Curators, connoisseurs and book collectors stand in line for his work when it appears on the market. His visions were true visions—fiery and never-failing, with direct access to heaven, hell and all regions between.

Source: *New York Times*.

Questions 3 to 5 refer to the excerpt. Circle the best answer for each question.

3. Anyone could have bought a Martin painting fifty years ago

   (1) for millions of dollars
   (2) with great difficulty
   (3) for practically nothing
   (4) for a moderate price
   (5) by lining up at auctions

4. By referring to the Old Testament, the reviewer probably means that Martin

   (1) looked like Moses
   (2) was very religious
   (3) painted until he was very old
   (4) was a visionary like the prophets
   (5) painted only biblical scenes

5. Which of the following best explains why Martin "fell through the floorboards of art history" (lines 5–6)?

   (1) Martin's paintings were cheap.
   (2) Martin painted religious pictures.
   (3) Art collectors of the 1920s and 1930s were not interested in visionary art.
   (4) People in the 1920s and 1930s did not have enough money to spend on expensive artworks.
   (5) A painter does not become popular until he or she has been dead for at least fifty years.

To check your answers, turn to page 216.

Read the following excerpt from a review by Jack Kroll.

WHY DOES THIS 73-YEAR-OLD PAINT?

The American folk artist Howard Finster once announced that God had shown him how to paint a picture of a fabulous factory. This industrial plant, said Finster, will be "the world's 8th wonder. . . . It will run until it wears out without one single employee. . . . It will
(5) store one square mile of our largest aircraft. . . . The picture will be beautiful even if rejected."

Not many of Finster's pictures have been rejected. By his own count this 73-year-old former revivalist preacher from Georgia has created more than 10,000 works of "sacred art." He's been interviewed
(10) by an amazed Johnny Carson, has designed rock-music albums, is the subject of an eye-popping retrospective at New York's Paine Webber Art Gallery, and is one of the hottest properties in the field of folk art. As the quotation above indicates, Finster is a painter of visions. His pictures combine almost every kind of graphic medium
(15) with words ranging from Bible quotations to snatches of his own wisdom. In *Four Presidents* (1983), he depicts Washington, Lincoln, Jefferson and Kennedy beneath a message that reads: "Our great nation came up through great leaders. Shall we stand by and let it turn to monsters?"
(20) Finster's work is riding the current accelerated expansion of interest in 20th-century folk art. Say "folk art" and most Americans will think of Grandma Moses landscapes, duck decoys, quilts and weather vanes. But the innocuous term "folk" masks many problems that have spawned additional labels including, in one scholar's list:
(25) "primitive, native, amateur, . . . country, popular, . . . innocent, provincial, anonymous, visionary, homemade, . . . ethnic, nonacademic." As Robert Bishop, director of the Museum of American Folk Art in New York, puts it: "When you have something that difficult to classify, it makes you nervous."

Source: "The Outsiders Are In," *Newsweek*.

Questions 6 and 7 refer to the excerpt. Circle the best answer for each question.

6. It can be inferred from the long list of terms for folk art that

(1) art critics are not quite sure what folk art is
(2) folk art is complicated and slick
(3) folk artists are highly trained
(4) anyone can become a folk artist
(5) folk art does not really belong in museums and galleries

7. Which would you be most likely to find in a folk art museum?

(1) a painting by an art student
(2) a hand-painted Easter egg
(3) an architect's blueprint
(4) a factory-made teapot
(5) a child's first drawing

To check your answers, turn to pages 216.

GED Mini-Test

Directions: Choose the best answer to each item.

Items 1 to 6 refer to the following excerpt from a review by Maggie Malone.

WHAT ARE OUTDOOR ROOMS?

Elyn Zimmerman makes serene oases of stone and water where people can sit and "see the everyday." Most are small, circular hideaways, one is boulder-studded and as long as a football field. Zimmerman began her career as a painter but after a trip to India,
(5) where she saw intricate temples carved into giant rock formations, she realized that she wanted to "make rooms in the out-of-doors." Her latest piece, "Keystone Island," in Miami, is 45 feet in diameter. It's designed to act as a buffer between Arquitectonica's new high-tech Dade County Courthouse and a peaceful nearby estuary. She
(10) chose a blond fossilized limestone indigenous to Florida because it will darken in an interesting way over time.

Though her works are useful as well as beautiful, Zimmerman warns that "too often artists are being asked to become designers and to forget their art. You have to hold on to your specific vision."
(15) Indeed, according to tile muralist Malou Flato, one arts commission seemed so taken with eliminating artists' individual demands that they tried to locate several who might be willing to get together and concoct a public space that would ultimately come out looking like *none* of their work. Meanwhile, some architects grumble that they're
(20) creative enough to devise their own plaza seating, thank you. And a handful of landscape architects are shaking up that profession with experimental earthworks and phony foliage. It seems that public art has truly jumped down from its pedestal. "It's a bouillabaisse. Everybody wants to be an artist now," complains public artist Robert
(25) Irwin. But to many in the art world that isn't a problem—it's a fresh new direction.

Source: "The Great Outdoors," *Newsweek*.

1. What was the result of Elyn Zimmerman's trip to India?

   (1) She became a painter.
   (2) She decided to move to Florida.
   (3) She started building houses.
   (4) She decided to work in stone.
   (5) She began carving intricate temples.

2. Which of the following is <u>not</u> a fact about Zimmerman?

   (1) She used limestone in a Florida piece.
   (2) Her work is sometimes large.
   (3) Her work is sometimes small.
   (4) She has opinions about what artists should do.
   (5) Her work is beautiful.

3. Which of the following is true about the reaction to artists making "useful" art?

   (1) Artists are refusing to become designers.
   (2) Some artists are becoming landscape architects.
   (3) Some architects are unhappy about the situation.
   (4) Architects are encouraging the artists.
   (5) Public spaces are getting cluttered.

4. Why might Zimmerman be a good example of "a fresh new direction" (line 26) in art?

   (1) She believes artists must have specific visions.
   (2) She is willing to work with other artists and give up her individual style.
   (3) She is experimenting with artificial plants.
   (4) Everybody can become an artist now.
   (5) She successfully left painting to make useful pieces out of stone.

5. Which of the following is suggested by "public art has truly jumped down from its pedestal" (lines 22–23)?

   (1) We used to think of art as something just to look at, and now we can use it.
   (2) Public art is not as good as it used to be.
   (3) Statues are being taken off their pedestals.
   (4) The ground has shaken so much that public artworks are falling down.
   (5) There is no longer enough stone to make stands for public artworks.

6. If you came across one of Zimmerman's latest artworks, you could expect to

   (1) take it home with you
   (2) be uncomfortable
   (3) sit down and feel peaceful
   (4) see it hanging on a wall
   (5) be in India

To check your answers, turn to page 217.

Answers and Explanations

Practicing Comprehension, Application, and Analysis Skills (pages 211–213)

1. (Inferential Comprehension) **(3) was easy to understand** The meaning of the word "pop" is suggested throughout the paragraph. It was given a lot of publicity and was accepted by the public. There is no evidence to support options (1) and (5). The price of the art is not mentioned, so option (2) is wrong. Many criticized pop art for not being serious, so option (4) is wrong.

2. (Analysis) **(2) it lacked serious content** The passage describes how some people disliked it because it was too commercial and trivial. There is no evidence to support options (1), (3), (4), and (5).

3. (Literal Comprehension) **(3) for practically nothing** The passage says the artist's work sold for "next to nothing" (line 2). Options (1) and (2) state the opposite. Option (4) is not supported by the passage. Option (5) is true now but was not the case fifty years ago.

4. (Analysis) **(4) was a visionary like the prophets** The reviewer is restating what he means by "visionary artist." The Old Testament is full of visions and fantastic imagery. There is no support for options (1) and (3). Option (2) may be true, but it is a very general point. The specific content of Martin's paintings is not discussed, so option (5) is wrong.

5. (Analysis) **(3) Art collectors of the 1920s and 1930s were not interested in visionary art.** If art collectors are not interested in a type of painting, it will often be ignored and forgotten. Martin's paintings were cheap because they were not popular, not the other way around, so option (1) is wrong. It was lack of interest, not the subject of the paintings themselves, that was the cause, so option (2) is wrong. Options (4) and (5) may be partly true, but both are too general and neither is related to why Martin's work was forgotten for a while.

6. (Inferential Comprehension) **(1) art critics are not quite sure what folk art is** The words in the list suggest a number of different qualities. Options (2) and (3) are wrong because the one thing most of the words on the list have in common is simplicity. There is no support for options (4) and (5).

7. (Application) **(2) a hand-painted Easter egg** In addition to being a traditional European folk art, egg painting would meet the requirements of being handmade, ethnic, nonacademic, and from the country. Options (1) and (3) refer to art produced by training. Option (4) is a manufactured object. Option (5) is wrong because there is no reference to children's art being folk art.

1. (Analysis) **(4) She decided to work in stone.** She was inspired by the stonework she had seen. Option (1) refers to what she had been before. There is no support for options (2), (3), and (5).

2. (Analysis) **(5) Her work is beautiful.** This is the reviewer's opinion. Options (1), (2), and (3) are facts stated in the excerpt. Option (4) is supported by the quotation in lines 13–14.

3. (Literal Comprehension) **(3) Some architects are unhappy about the situation.** This is a restatement of lines 19–20. Option (1) is the opposite of what is stated in the review. There is no support for options (2) and (5). Option (4) is the opposite of the reaction.

4. (Inferential Comprehension) **(5) She successfully left painting to make useful pieces out of stone.** She is following a fresh new direction. Option (1) is true but does not answer the question. Options (2) and (3) are not true. There is no support for option (4), even though Irwin believes everybody wants to be an artist.

5. (Analysis) **(1) We used to think of art as something just to look at, and now we can use it.** Saying something is on a pedestal is a figurative way of saying it is untouchable. Now it is literally down to earth. There is no support for option (2). Options (3), (4), and (5) all result from misunderstanding the figurative language.

6. (Application) **(3) sit down and feel peaceful** Zimmerman's new work is designed for restful sitting. Option (1) would be impossible. Option (2) is the opposite of what is intended. Option (4) refers to painting, which she no longer does. Option (5) is highly unlikely.

LESSON 21 Comprehension Skills: Drawing a Conclusion

This skill helps you make a decision about the facts and opinions you have read.

When you studied understanding the main idea, locating context clues, finding cause and effect, and separating fact from opinion, you were restating and organizing what you had read. When you **draw a conclusion,** you use those skills to interpret the information and make a single, logical decision.

When you read a review and want to draw a conclusion, you need to understand the facts, understand any implied ideas, and make judgments about the opinions the reviewer presents. You also need to be aware of what facts, implications, and opinions are necessary to come to that conclusion. Often you will have to sort out the unnecessary information first.

For example: If Linda finishes washing the car before noon, I will take her to lunch.

     Opinion: Linda is a very careful worker.
     Fact: Linda finished washing the car before noon.
     Conclusion: I took Linda to lunch.

The fact that Linda is a careful worker is not needed to come to the conclusion.

Most reviewers also form conclusions based on facts and their opinions. You can agree or disagree with the reviewer based on your own interpretation of the information. So pay attention to what the reviewer relies on and judge whether the reviewer's opinions are valid or misleading. Ask yourself if the information leads you to the same conclusion.

☞ *See Also: GED Exercise Book Literature and the Arts, pages 44–46*

Practicing Comprehension, Application, and Analysis Skills

Read the following passage from a commentary by Dan Hurley.

SO WHY DON'T THEY JUST ASK US?

Who's more popular than Michael J. Fox, Clint Eastwood, Vanna White or Angela Lansbury? The California Raisins, of course! Their Q score—the quotient of people recognizing them who rate them as one of their favorites—is 54, beaten only by Bill Cosby's 57.

(5) That's just one of the stranger facts that come from the popularity ratings taken for the past 25 years by Marketing Evaluations/TV Q, a Long Island–based company that polls approximately 6000 Americans on their favorite actors, series, cartoon characters and consumer products. Surpassed in importance only by the Nielsen

(10) ratings, yet shrouded in mystery, the Q scores have drawn the ire of actors, producers and directors who hate the idea of popularity ratings so much that attempts have been made to outlaw them. But the Q ratings have also been credited with saving series that would otherwise have been cancelled and with transforming unknown

(15) actors into stars. . . .

"The whole idea of TV Q is to get into the consumers' heads, into their state of mind," says Steven Levitt, the 48-year-old president of the company. . . . A questionnaire is mailed to each household that agrees to participate, and next to the name of each per-

(20) former or show, respondents are asked whether they recognize the name. If they do, they write in whether the performer or show is one of their favorites, very good, good, fair, or poor.

Source: "Those Hush-Hush Q Ratings—Fair or Foul?" *TV Guide*.

Questions 1 and 2 refer to the passage. Circle the best answer for each question.

1. From this passage you can conclude

 (1) people recognize TV characters only if they watch the shows
 (2) there is no good way to find out what shows the viewers like
 (3) the popularity of certain TV characters does not depend on the popularity of their shows
 (4) few people are willing to give a new show a chance
 (5) the Q questionnaire is not fair

To check your answers, turn to page 224.

2. From this passage, you can conclude that the television industry

 (1) is going to outlaw the Q ratings
 (2) has learned how to get into the viewers' heads
 (3) makes important decisions based on viewer ratings
 (4) does not put much faith in the Q ratings
 (5) prefers the Q ratings to the Nielsen ratings

Read the following review by Karen Ridgeway.

SO WHAT IS THE NEWS?

Who says PBS' *Sesame Street* is all reading, 'riting, and 'rithmetic? This season's topics read like news headlines:

Working mothers battle day-care dilemma. Recycling on the rise. Teens struggle in job market. Fire threatens inner-city
(5) neighborhood.

TV's make-believe miniworld begins its third decade today, preparing school-bound viewers for life after the ABCs.

Three-month-old Gabriela—born to newlyweds Luis and Maria at the end of last season—enters day care. Toddling Muppets also
(10) spend weekdays with Mrs. Edwards (Lillias White), a new neighbor.

Miles—the adopted son of Susan and Gordon—enters kindergarten, while storekeeper Gina finishes high school. A new teen—Ward Sacton as Mike—gets a part-time job at the Fix-It
(15) shop.

Another new cast member: Mr. Hanford (Leonard Jackson), a retired firefighter who will run Mr. Hooper's store. His fire safety messages are crucial when fire breaks out in the basement of 123 Sesame St.
(20) Careful research ensures that the episode won't frighten young viewers—Burt and Ernie, who live in the basement apartment, are on vacation. Through voice-overs, a sleeping Miles wakes to the smell of smoke and recalls emergency measures. He will "stop, drop and roll" out of danger.
(25) *Street*'s growing curriculum includes geography and ecology this year.

"We hope to raise a generation of anti-litter advocates," says director of research Valeria Lovelace.

Source: "*Sesame Street* Paves New Ground," *USA Today*.

Questions 3 and 4 refer to the review. Circle the best answer for each question.

3. According to the review, which of the following probably would <u>not</u> be featured on *Sesame Street*?

(1) safety training
(2) reading and arithmetic
(3) basic living skills
(4) political arguments
(5) environmental awareness

4. When new characters appear on this program, they

(1) are always grown-ups
(2) have an educational purpose
(3) do not stay very long
(4) are always guest stars
(5) are always puppets

To check your answers, turn to page 224.

Read the following excerpt from a review by Brian Donlon.

WHO IS GOING TO WIN THE BATTLE?

Two of the hottest-selling shows this year are *American Gladiators* and *Rollergames*. Both are weekly programs using action and athletics—taking a note from the World Wrestling Federation.

Gladiators is a sort of a battle of network stars against real
(5) people; *Rollergames* is an updated, glitzed-up version of roller derby.

"We're doing this in such a way to make it a legitimate sporting event," says Ray Solley, vice president of development at Samuel Goldwyn Television, producer of *Gladiators*.

Rollergames executive producer David Sams says athletic com-
(10) petition is part of his program's appeal. But there are a bunch of gimmicks, too.

Aside from the inevitable brawls that break out, rock concerts will be held featuring the likes of Lita Ford and Debbie Harry.

A live alligator pit is also on the track for use in sudden-death
(15) overtime.

Why the gators? "We had to sell the show," Sams says.

"The fact is that if we would have gone out with just roller derby as it was and not sizzled it up a little bit we would have been on a small bunch of UHF stations."

(20) Instead, *Rollergames* has been picked up by 144 stations. In most markets, it will go against NBC's weekend hit *Saturday Night Live*.

Gladiators—on 112 stations—also is expected to air against *SNL* and may run in tandem with *Rollergames* in some areas.

(25) An *SNL* replacement on NBC, wrestling's *Saturday Night's Main Event* gets some of the credit for the advent of this new competition.

"It was clear that viewers had an appetite for event program-ming because of *Main Event*," says Sams.

Source: "Fun and Games for Night Owls," *USA Today*.

Questions 5 and 6 refer to the review. Circle the best answer for each question.

5. Which of the following best describes the tone of this passage?

  (1) straightforward and casual
  (2) humorously exaggerated
  (3) formal and indifferent
  (4) serious and persuasive
  (5) confused and amazed

6. Which of the following can be con-cluded about *Main Event*?

  (1) It is better than other shows.
  (2) It has a large audience.
  (3) It features roller skaters.
  (4) It is more popular than *Saturday Night Live*.
  (5) It has gone off the air.

To check your answers, turn to page 224.

GED Mini-Test

Directions: Choose the <u>best answer</u> to each item.

<u>Items 1 to 6</u> refer to the following excerpt from a review by Merrill Panitt.

DOESN'T THIS NEST SEEM FULL?

Susan Harris creates situation comedies that she and her partners (her husband, Paul Junger Witt, and Tony Thomas) produce. If we had our way there would be a 25-foot statue of her in front of that new television academy building they're planning in

(5) North Hollywood.

Harris's shows don't always earn sensational ratings, but she does come up with shows that not only are funny, but make sense. After seeing one, you don't have that slightly guilty feeling of having wasted a half hour watching silly people do and say silly

(10) things.

Harris's new show is NBC's *Empty Nest*, about a pediatrician widower who lives near *The Golden Girls* (another Harris creation) in Miami and whose three daughters have left home. It's a simple premise, but it's vintage Harris, and like everything else she does,

(15) *Empty Nest* has been meticulously thought out and superbly cast. Each of the regulars (there are five plus Dreyfuss, a wonderful dog who plays straight canine for star Richard Mulligan) is carefully drawn, consistently realized.

Mulligan, whom you'll remember as nutty Burt Campbell of

(20) Susan Harris's *Soap* and the wild producer in the movie *S.O.B.*, plays Dr. Harry Weston. His youngest daughter is off somewhere in college. The other daughters are Barbara (Kristy McNichol), a police officer, and Carol (Dinah Manoff), who is still recovering from her two-year-old divorce. At the office Harry is kept in line by nurse

(25) LaVerne (Park Overall), fresh out of Arkansas, who drawls things like: "In mah town we didden have datin'. Ya washed yer hair evvy Satiddy night and then when yuh were 14 yuh married yer cousin."

Also dropping in occasionally, and for no apparent reason except to deliver a few overbearing-neighbor gags, is Charley, played

(30) by David Leisure, the lying Joe Isuzu of the auto commercials.

Harry is most appealing and the show's best moments come when he is chatting with Dreyfuss at home or administering to his young patients at the office. He usually winds up conspiring with the kids against their pushy mothers, a task Mulligan carries off

(35) with great charm.

As in all Harris comedies, there are serious plot lines as background for the comedy. Daughter Carol's high expectations when her philandering ex-husband asks for a date—and her disappoint-

ment after the date—concern Harry in one episode; in another he
(40) angers daughter Barbara after she's shot on duty by asking her
police superior to confine her to desk work; in the pilot episode his
best woman friend demands that he decide immediately whether or
not their once-a-week dinner dates are leading to a commitment.

Source: *TV Guide*.

1. According to this review, the author's favorite character on the show is

   (1) Harry Weston, the doctor
   (2) Barbara, the police officer
   (3) Carol, the divorced daughter
   (4) LaVerne, the nurse
   (5) Susan Harris, the creator

2. Which of the following best suggests the reviewer's opinion of some other situation comedies?

   (1) They are much better than *Empty Nest*.
   (2) They are a waste of time.
   (3) They have serious plot lines.
   (4) They are tastefully done.
   (5) They deal with important issues.

3. The actor who plays Charley on the show is probably familiar to many viewers because he

   (1) played a wild producer in *S.O.B.*
   (2) played the part of Burt in *Soap*
   (3) appears in TV ads
   (4) is the husband of the show's creator
   (5) used to be a movie producer

4. If you watched any of Susan Harris's other shows, you would most likely see

   (1) silly people doing silly things
   (2) a serious drama
   (3) a funny show with serious undertones
   (4) a tragedy-of-the-week show
   (5) a disappointing medical show

5. From this review, it can be concluded that the reviewer mainly wants to

   (1) discourage viewers from watching this show
   (2) comment on situation comedies
   (3) say this show is well worth watching
   (4) criticize Harris's creations
   (5) discuss the serious parts of the show

6. Which of the following is the best explanation for why the author would like to put up a 25-foot statue of Harris?

   (1) because she is so beautiful
   (2) because she seems to stand for what is best about TV
   (3) because her shows have brought in a lot of money
   (4) because the reviewer thinks it would be funny
   (5) because *Empty Nest* is the best show ever made

To check your answers, turn to page 225.

Answers and Explanations

Practicing Comprehension, Application, and Analysis Skills (pages 219–221)

1. (Inferential Comprehension) **(3) the popularity of certain TV characters does not depend on the popularity of their shows** This conclusion is drawn from the difference in the results of the rating systems. Option (1) may be true but is not supported here. No mention is made of how good the ratings are, so option (2) is wrong. There is no evidence for options (4) or (5).

2. (Inferential Comprehension) **(3) makes important decisions based on viewer ratings** Shows are canceled or kept based on ratings. Option (1) refers to what some people would like to have happen. Option (2) refers to something the marketing company hopes to do. Option (4) is wrong because the television industry does act on them. There is no evidence for option (5).

3. (Application) **(4) political arguments** The show is focusing on skills that help young people get along and will lead to a better life; politics is considered a more adult issue. Options (1), (2), (3), and (5) are mentioned in the article.

4. (Inferential Comprehension) **(2) have an educational purpose** Such characters as the new neighbor and the retired firefighter help to teach basic skills. There is no support for options (1) or (3). Option (4) is wrong because several of the new characters have become regulars. Option (5) is wrong because some new characters are people.

5. (Analysis) **(1) straightforward and casual** The writing describes the situation without much commentary. There is no evidence of exaggeration, so option (2) is wrong. The vocabulary is informal, so option (3) is wrong. The writer is not trying to influence the reader, so option (4) is wrong. Option (5) is wrong because the writer understands what is going on.

6. (Inferential Comprehension) **(2) It has a large audience.** Only a successful show would be imitated. There is no support for options (1), (3), (4), and (5).

1. (Inferential Comprehension) **(1) Harry Weston, the doctor** This is supported in lines 31–33. Fewer references are made to the other characters, so options (2), (3), and (4) are wrong. Option (5) refers to someone who is not a character on the show.

2. (Analysis) **(2) They are a waste of time.** This is supported by an indirect comparison in which the author suggests some other shows are silly. Options (1), (3), (4), and (5) are wrong because there is no other reference to situation comedies besides the ones the reviewer dislikes.

3. (Literal Comprehension) **(3) appears in TV ads** This is stated about Charley in lines 29–30. Options (1) and (2) are wrong because they refer to the star of the show. Option (4) is wrong because the husband is someone else. There is no support for option (5).

4. (Application) **(3) a funny show with serious undertones** The entire review supports option (3), especially the last paragraph. Option (1) refers to shows other than Harris's. As Harris's work is in comedy, options (2), (4), and (5) are unlikely.

5. (Inferential Comprehension) **(3) say this show is well worth watching** The review mainly praises the show and Harris, so options (1) and (4) are wrong. Option (2) is too general for the content of this review. Option (5) refers to a supporting detail, not the main intent.

6. (Inferential Comprehension) **(2) because she seems to stand for what is best about TV** The reviewer thinks Harris's shows are examples of how TV can be well done. There is no support for options (1) and (3). Option (4) is wrong because the reviewer is not making fun of Harris. The reviewer likes the new show, but option (5) is an overstatement.

LESSON 22 Analysis Skills: Identifying Techniques (Point of View)

This skill helps you recognize something about the author that will help you understand the purpose of the article or review.

Unlike fiction or nonfiction, where the point of view can vary, the point of view in commentary or a review is always the author's—that is, it is always written in the first person. Therefore, in writing about commentary, point of view takes on a more personal meaning. The tone of a commentary is often casual or conversational. By speaking directly to the reader, reviewers usually reveal something about themselves that can suggest why the review was written. You can find out if the reviewer is an expert in the field. If so, you can probably trust the opinions in the article. You can also find out if the reviewer likes or dislikes the subject.

The author's attitude toward the subject in general might influence how the specific topic is judged. (An attitude is sometimes called a *bias.*) For example, a dance critic may not like jazz dancing but may love ballet. This critic probably will tend to say more positive things about ballet in general than about jazz dance. As a reader, you might want to be careful about believing everything that critic has to say about jazz dance.

To figure out the author's point of view, you need to look for clues about the writer's background or interests. Pay attention to the vocabulary that is used. Do the terms used suggest that the writer knows a lot about the subject? Also look for details that point to the reviewer's likes and dislikes. If your likes or dislikes are not the same as the reviewer's, you may disagree with the conclusions he or she draws.

☞ *See Also: GED Exercise Book Literature and the Arts, pages 50–52*

Practicing Comprehension, Application, and Analysis Skills

Read the following excerpt from a review by Bill Barol.

IS THIS THE MAN WHO WROTE THAT FAMOUS SONG?

The story goes that Irving Berlin, desperate to get a new song down during a rehearsal, burst into a backstage room and asked for a piece of paper. A musician working there handed him a blank sheet of musical manuscript. "This is *music* paper," the songwriter said.

(5) "What am I supposed to do with that?"

Berlin may not have known how to write music, but there wasn't a thing he didn't know about songs. He understood instinctively that the popular song is a kind of tuning fork for the best traits in the American character: vivacity, industry, openheartedness, grit, senti-

(10) ment. Berlin himself lived the American dream. He was a poor kid who achieved fame and fortune, an unschooled craftsman who rose to the top of his profession, a patriot who loved his adopted country as only an immigrant can. So always, he aimed for the heart of the average American: "Not the highbrow nor the lowbrow," he once said,

(15) "but that vast intermediate crew which is the real soul of the country." When he died . . . at 101, Berlin left behind an astonishing number of great American songs: "Blue Skies," "Always," "Cheek to Cheek," "Isn't This a Lovely Day," "God Bless America," "White Christmas," "Let's Face the Music and Dance," "A Pretty Girl is Like a Melody,"

(20) "Easter Parade," "There's No Business Like Show Business" and "What'll I Do?" And more than 1,000 others.

Born Israel Baline in the Russian village of Temun on May 11, 1888, he fled the pogroms and settled with his parents and seven siblings on New York's Lower East Side. . . .

Source: "Irving Berlin, 1888–1989," *Newsweek*.

Questions 1 and 2 refer to the excerpt. Circle the best answer for each question.

1. The passage as a whole is presented from the point of view of

(1) a Russian immigrant
(2) a fellow songwriter
(3) a formal biographer
(4) a jealous musician
(5) a respectful admirer

To check your answers, turn to page 232.

2. The reviewer probably began with the story about Berlin (lines 1–5) to

(1) get the reader's interest with an unusual detail
(2) explain why Berlin could not read music
(3) present Berlin in a bad light
(4) show how an immigrant can succeed in America
(5) show why Americans liked his songs

Read the following review by John Waters.

CAN TOM WAITS TURN A PRINCESS INTO A FROG?

Tom Waits sings as if he doesn't change his underwear daily. I've always liked him. But then my musical tastes have never been to everybody's liking. I've had friends look through my five-hundred-plus record collection and say they can't find one they want to hear.

(5) I purchased only four LPs last year (*Glenn Gould: Wagner, Billy Stewart: The Greatest Sides,* Nico's *Camera Obscura,* and *The Wonderful World of Sonny and Cher*), but Tom Waits's newest, *Rain Dogs,* would have been my fifth. It should carry an "attitude warning" on the cover. If you're debating whether to go to sleep early so you

(10) can be productive the next day or to go out to a bar and get drunk, don't play this record. Tom Waits brings out the derelict in us all, but his sense of humor elevates him above being merely a cult figure who specializes in wrist-slashing cocktail/sleaze music.

. . . There's big talent playing behind him, but I'd be a fan even

(15) if he were singing with a high school combo. Imagine him terrorizing "New York, New York" or even "You Light Up My Life." Sometimes I wish he'd lighten up a bit and make us laugh out loud instead of through crocodile tears. But he's an original, all right; a white-trash prince in damaged armor who kisses the princess and turns her

(20) into a frog right before our bloodshot eyes.

Source: *Esquire* magazine.

Questions 3 and 4 refer to the review. Circle the best answer for each question.

3. To demonstrate Waits's originality (lines 19–20), the author describes him as a

(1) pirate king
(2) classical musician
(3) person who looks like a frog
(4) person with unexpected musical powers
(5) person from the Ice Age

4. Why does the author describe his record collection (lines 3–4) as uninteresting to his friends?

(1) to brag about its size
(2) to show that his friends are hard to please
(3) to compare Tom Waits to Glenn Gould
(4) to warn readers that he has offbeat musical tastes
(5) to make fun of Sonny and Cher

To check your answers, turn to page 232.

Read the following excerpt from a review by James T. Jones.

WHAT GIVES THESE WOMEN SOUL?

In a year dominated by soundalike R&B [rhythm and blues] producers producing sound-alike R&B singers, two women with new albums bring welcome relief to this overproduced genre.

Angela Winbush, once half of the hit-making duo Rene & Angela,
(5) made an impressive solo debut in 1987 with *Sharp* and its No. 1 black hit, "Angel." After producing Stephanie Mills, Ronald Isley and Sheena Easton, she returns with her own stunning sophomore effort, *The Real Thing.*

Hot on her heels is soulful torch singer Miki Howard. The for-
(10) mer lead singer of Side Effect and popular session singer (Grover Washington, Jr., Freddie Jackson, Dolly Parton), Howard has scored three top 5 black hits, including "Baby Be Mine" and "That's What Love Is," a duet with Gerald Levert of the pop/R&B trio LeVert. He rejoins her on her new self-titled LP, her third and best. . . .

(15) **Miki Howard**: *Miki Howard* (Atlantic)—She may not have the multioctave chops of Winbush, but Howard has enough church-bred, hard-edged soul to hold her own. This album is more R&B-based than her previous two. . . .

Primarily a balladeer, Howard surprisingly is releasing "Ain't
(20) Nuthin' in the World" as her first single. It's a fine enough dance tune; unfortunately, it's the only good one. "Love Me All Over" and "Mister" are predictable uptempo fare based on the rap-inspired new jack swing that's dominating too much of urban radio today.

But when the rap cliches and drum machines are turned down,
(25) Howard turns up. Maybe it's more than a coincidence that her label is the same one that made [Aretha] Franklin a legend.

Source: "Soulful Winbush, Howard Bring Some Sizzle to R&B," *USA Today*.

Questions 5 and 6 refer to the excerpt. Circle the best answer for each question.

5. It can be concluded from this review that Miki Howard

(1) is more talented than Angela Winbush
(2) will probably go far in the music world
(3) is not very talented
(4) is an excellent rap singer
(5) is a successful producer

6. Which of the following would this reviewer be <u>least</u> likely to want to hear on the radio?

(1) dance tunes
(2) saxophone music
(3) rap music
(4) ballads
(5) Aretha Franklin's songs

To check your answers, turn to page 232.

GED Mini-Test

Directions: Choose the best answer to each item.

Items 1 to 6 refer to the following review.

CYNDI LAUPER—KOOK OR COOKIE?

There's this Japanese snack, maybe it's even tasty. You boil a pot of water. Plop in a fistful of teensy eels. They'll fidget. Then, fast, throw in three or four very cold bean cakes. That's it for the eels, who'll burrow into the cool center, seeking refuge, though
(5) eventually that, too, gets hot. Cyndi Lauper's *True Colors* (Portrait) has one mischosen cover version, another tune puzzlingly revived from her time with Blue Angel. The sound lacks viscera. . . . The vocals don't front the arrangements like they should. The songs are laden with bland language. Somewhere inside the bean cake,
(10) though, there's this wriggling—this voice even more reckless than it was on *She's So Unusual*, a better album than *Houses of the Holy* or *The Best of Junior Parker*.

It's a willed blindness how so many—from zines that hate her to *Rolling Stone* scribes for whom she does no wrong—peg Lauper
(15) as simp kook or smart cookie. Either way the party line—*that Cyndi!*—makes her sound like the nurdish half of a double date where Madonna's on the other guy's arm. Lauper's more evasive than is realized and too few have seen how those crazy threads and beads keep things at a useful distance. Making a checkerboard on
(20) the side of her head . . . for the "Time After Time" video may label her as out to lunch, but this is a gambit: *you are not gonna figure her out*. No matter how many octaves she navigates, how she wails, the cartoonishness also makes fun of virtuosity. It doesn't sound like a *real* voice is supposed to. You can't trust the lyrics—Lauper
(25) wipes them out when she wants, but you have to trust the voice, which is anything but detached. The riotous operatics, the reverent nods to Ethel Merman and Big Maybelle, et al., are so furious and mutant in each song, the lines changing mood and character, she walks away from poses she hasn't defined yet.

Source: *Village Voice*.

1. The purpose of contrasting Cyndi Lauper's album with Japanese food is to

   (1) explain Lauper's popularity in Japan
   (2) indicate how many of Lauper's songs are about ethnic food
   (3) suggest the special qualities of Lauper's music
   (4) show the influence of Madonna
   (5) increase the album's sales abroad

2. In the author's view, the album *True Colors* is sometimes flawed by

   (1) poor choice of tunes
   (2) bland lyrics
   (3) problems with arrangements
   (4) unconvincing sound
   (5) all of the above

3. What is it about Lauper's appearance that might be misleading to audiences?

   (1) her green wig
   (2) her sunglasses
   (3) her clothing and jewelry
   (4) her Cubist make-up
   (5) her bare feet

4. The reviewer would most likely agree that

   (1) Cyndi Lauper is a first-rate actress
   (2) some pop stars cannot handle success
   (3) behind every star is a smart manager
   (4) Lauper's songs are thoroughly dated
   (5) some singers succeed better on videos

5. Which phrase best expresses the reviewer's conclusion about Lauper?

   (1) a Blue Angel
   (2) just like Ethel Merman
   (3) an untrustworthy voice
   (4) an operatic pop singer
   (5) a hard singer to explain

6. When the writer calls Lauper "simp kook or smart cookie" (line 15), he is stating

   (1) facts
   (2) his personal opinion
   (3) the public's opinion
   (4) Lauper's view of herself
   (5) quotes from a book

To check your answers, turn to page 233.

Answers and Explanations

Practicing Comprehension, Application, and Analysis Skills (pages 227–229)

1. (Analysis) **(5) a respectful admirer** The reviewer clearly thinks highly of Irving Berlin's songwriting and understanding of his audience. There is no evidence to suggest options (1) or (2). Option (3) refers to a singer who asked for a song. Option (4) is wrong because there is no evidence of jealousy or of the reviewer being a musician.

2. (Analysis) **(1) get the reader's interest with an unusual detail** That a songwriter cannot read music is definitely unusual. Option (2) is wrong because the story presents the fact but does not explain it. This detail also emphasizes the reviewer's respect for Berlin, so option (3) is wrong. Options (4) and (5) have nothing to do with the story.

3. (Analysis) **(4) person with unexpected musical powers** In the final sentence of the review, you learn that Waits strikes the author as a prince whose kiss might turn a princess into a frog, a twist on the old fairy tale. This is a way of saying that his music is unusual. There is no support for options (1), (2), (3), and (5).

4. (Analysis) **(4) to warn readers that he has offbeat musical tastes** Although the reviewer seems to be bragging, option (1), and complaining about his friends, option (2), the main point he is making is that listening to Tom Waits may not be for everybody. There is no support for options (3) and (5).

5. (Inferential Comprehension) **(2) will probably go far in the music world** The reviewer suggests this by his overall positive tone. Option (1) has no support. Option (3) is the opposite of what the reviewer states. Option (4) is wrong because the reviewer is least impressed with the rap songs. Option (5) refers to Winbush.

6. (Application) **(3) rap music** In lines 22–23, the reviewer says there is too much rap music on the radio. Options (1), (2), (4), and (5) refer to music he clearly enjoys.

1. (Analysis) **(3) suggest the special qualities of Lauper's music** The snack described is unusual, and the reviewer goes on to describe Lauper as being equally unusual. There is no support for options (1), (2), (4), and (5) in the review.

2. (Literal Comprehension) **(5) all of the above** Options (1), (2), (3), and (4) are supported in the review (lines 6–9); therefore, option (5) is correct.

3. (Inferential Comprehension) **(3) her clothing and jewelry** In lines 17–19 the reviewer says that not many viewers can see past her costume to the real Cyndi. There is no support for options (1), (2), (4), and (5).

4. (Application) **(1) Cyndi Lauper is a first-rate actress** Nowhere does the reviewer actually use the words "actress" or "role." However, he refers to "poses" (line 29) and the idea of acting is implied throughout. There is no evidence for options (2), (3), (4), and (5).

5. (Inferential Comprehension) **(5) a hard singer to explain** Option (5) is correct for two reasons: the writer states that people do not understand Lauper, and he calls attention to the idea by italicizing *"you are not gonna figure her out"* (lines 21–22). Option (3) is a supporting detail, not the conclusion. Options (1), (2), and (4) are wrong.

6. (Analysis) **(3) the public's opinion** Here you need to distinguish between provable and unprovable information. "Kook" and "smart cookie" reflect neither facts, option (1), nor the writer's own opinion, option (2). The best answer is option (3), public opinion. There is no evidence to support options (4) and (5).

LESSON 23 Comprehension Skills: Understanding a Consequence

This skill helps you use cause-and-effect relationships in order to understand consequences—the results of actions or decisions.

Just as you may read television and film reviews to help you decide what to watch, you can read a book review to help you decide if you would be interested in reading the book. A book review can give you information and opinions about both the author and the content of the book.

Book reviewers often refer to the consequences of either the actions or decisions of the author or of the characters in the book. As you saw in lessons 12 and 20, a cause is what makes something happen and an effect is the result. If you understand a basic cause-and-effect relationship, you will have no trouble discovering the consequence —that is, the result.

We usually use the word "consequence" when talking about people rather than about things. You have heard people say something like, "You need to consider the consequences of charging more on your credit card than you can afford to repay." The consequences here would be serious debt. But have you ever heard someone wonder, "What are the consequences of all this rain?" It would be more common to ask, "What is the effect of all this rain?" *Consequences* usually have to do with the results of people's behavior; *effects* are generally the results of events happening. Often, consequences are seen as negative results; effects, on the other hand, are generally neutral, neither positive nor negative.

Be sure to ask yourself two questions. If the author points to a result, ask what happened to lead up to that result. If the author points to certain acts or decisions, ask what will happen because of them.

☞ *See Also: GED Exercise Book Literature and the Arts, pages 41-43*

Practicing Comprehension, Application, and Analysis Skills

Read the following excerpt from a review by David Kirby.

HOW HAPPY WAS MICHELANGELO'S BRUSH CLEANER?

Even before she was given the 1983 Pulitzer Prize for *American Primitive*, much had been written about Mary Oliver's considerable powers as a nature poet and probably too little about the pain underlying her work. This is something she shares with others. . . .

(5) Thoreau went to Walden Pond to get away from a society that supported the Mexican War. The speakers in Ms. Oliver's *Dream Work* are troubled by more private concerns; for example, there is a father, brutal and unlovable, who shows up in two poems with telling titles, "Rage" and "A Visitor." Faced with such ugliness, one is given "the

(10) chance to love everything," to cite the title of a beautiful poem in which a camper is menaced by something huge and unseen (a bear, probably) and goes toward rather than away from it. . . .

One of Ms. Oliver's hallmarks is plain speech. The earnest questers in her poems know it is easy to state a goal—forgive the

(15) bad parent, seek out the bear—and hard to carry it out. They are ordinary people who are close to the elements. . . .

To work, to be a fisherman or a gardener or a writer, is exhausting, and in several of these poems there is an old and frightening idea—in the end art kills the artist. . . . It makes one

(20) uneasy to hear a fine poet say perhaps we should be like the man who did nothing more than clean Michelangelo's brushes every day, and lived to be 100 years old.

Source: *New York Times Book Review*.

Questions 1 and 2 refer to the excerpt. Circle the best answer for each question.

1. Which of the following is the best reason for Ms. Oliver's use of plain speech?

  (1) Her characters are ordinary people.
  (2) She was given the Pulitzer Prize.
  (3) Her speakers have a lot of worries.
  (4) She is imitating Thoreau.
  (5) Her poems are painful.

2. The reviewer is made uneasy by Ms. Oliver's idea that people get worn out when they

  (1) get physically or emotionally involved in their work
  (2) spend most of their lives working for other people
  (3) run away from society
  (4) refuse to face the ugliness of life
  (5) are constantly chased by bears

To check your answers, turn to page 240.

Read the following review by Jill Gerston.

WHAT DOES AUDREY SEE IN A MAN LIKE CHARLIE?

Danielle Steel's new romance novel is a delicious, lightweight treat. Audrey Driscoll, age 26, with her coppery hair, creamy skin, passion for exotic places and sizable fortune, hardly seems a candidate for spinsterhood, but that seems to be her fate in San
(5) Francisco in the 1930's. She rebels and sets off for Europe with her stylish clothes and treasured Leica. Aboard the *Mauretania*, she meets Lady Vi and Lord James, a young, rich, beautiful couple who persuade her to spend a few champagne-drenched weeks at their villa in Cap d'Antibes. Here, Audrey is introduced to all sorts of
(10) amusing folk, including Picasso (who proclaims her a talented photographer) and Charles Parker-Scott. He's a tall, dark, handsome travel writer who, like Audrey, has adventuring in his blood. Obviously, the two are destined for each other, if their respective wanderlusts don't keep them apart. Not one to sit home knitting
(15) while Charles traipses off to interview Chiang Kai-shek, Audrey embarks on her own adventures, which include running an orphanage in China, adopting a child, traveling to Nazi Germany. . . . The plot is implausible, of course, and the dialogue what one expects: "Don't leave me here. My whole life is with you Charlie, it
(20) always has been." The characters' credibility leaves a lot to the reader's blind faith. But to question why the bright, nifty Audrey would fall for the self-centered Charles is, perhaps, to take *Wanderlust* more seriously than we should.

Source: *New York Times Book Review*.

Questions 3 and 4 refer to the review. Circle the best answer for each question.

3. According to the reviewer, the plot of *Wanderlust* is "implausible" (line 18) because

(1) it is too sophisticated
(2) it is very silly
(3) its realism is overpowering
(4) the characters are true to life
(5) it deals with complex emotions

4. According to the review, reading *Wanderlust* would have the same effect on a reader as eating

(1) bacon and eggs
(2) meat and potatoes
(3) candy
(4) rice and beans
(5) bread and butter

To check your answers, turn to page 240.

Read the following review by Warren Kiefer.

IS THIS STORY AS TRUE AS HISTORY?

Lee Oliver Garland, this novel's hero and narrator, has been both a willing participant and a more-than-casual spectator to the calamitous events chronicled in [*Outlaw*], which spans nearly a century. As a child, he stares in stunned silence at what Apache warriors
(5) have done to his parents; barely a teenager, he rustles cattle and has half an arm chewed off by a wolf. He is a Teddy Roosevelt Rough Rider and survives battles against Pancho Villa, up San Juan Hill and across the Mexican plains. He kills a man, is double-crossed by a trusted partner, escapes the scandals of Teapot Dome, makes a for-
(10) tune from oil fields and loses it all at the gambling tables. In between he loved and lied as best and as often as he could.

Outlaw is the most colorful Western saga since *Lonesome Dove*. Written at a Pony Express pace by TV-film writer [Warren] Kiefer, it is the well-told story of Garland's life. The characters encoun-
(15) tered read as true as history, their lives driven along by the raw strength of the narrative, such as when Lee and a friend, Charlie Bruce, discuss the financial merits of a war with Spain:

"'The army will need meat, lots of it. What is a Texas steer worth today?'
(20) "'Around twenty dollars,' I tell him.
"'If there's a war, that price will shoot to a hundred. You should buy all the livestock you can get your hands on right now.'
"'I know something better,' I say. 'A Mexican steer sells for ten dollars. And if you can steal one, it's free.'"
(25) *Outlaw* has love, adventure, history and one of the most colorful heroes ever to fill the pages of any novel. So crunch down in your favorite chair and let Garland take you for a raucous ride.

Source: *People* magazine.

Questions 5 and 6 refer to the review. Circle the best answer for each question.

5. Which of the following probably did not contribute to turning Garland into an outlaw?

(1) rustling cattle as a teenager
(2) being a Rough Rider
(3) killing a man
(4) being double-crossed
(5) losing his fortune by gambling

6. The author uses the phrase "raucous ride" (line 27) to

(1) suggest that the book is boring
(2) make the reader think of cattle
(3) suggest the writing is bad
(4) refer to his image of the Pony Express
(5) refer to the Apaches

To check your answers, turn to page 240.

GED Mini-Test

Directions: Choose the <u>best answer</u> to each item.

<u>Items 1 to 6</u> refer to the following excerpt from a review by Katherine Ames.

WHAT IS HILLERMAN TRYING TO DO?

One of Tony Hillerman's New Mexican poker buddies read the proofs of his latest novel, *Talking God*, and was surprised to find a graphic four-letter word in it. "Did you think about that?" he asked. Hillerman, whose characters' cussing is usually mild, rewrote the
(5) sentence. "It's a small thing," he says. "In the right crowds, I've been known to sound like a yeoman second myself, but I think it's a bad habit. And I don't want to cause librarians and people who teach seventh grade not to use this book because they don't want to be endorsing that kind of language. All of a sudden I'm conscious
(10) that I have a heavier responsibility than I ever intended."

Published this month, *Talking God* is already a best seller. . . . The ninth in Hillerman's innovative mystery series centered on Joe Leaphorn and Jim Chee of the Navajo Tribal Police, it's more artistically daring than its predecessors. Woven as tightly as a Navajo
(15) blanket, set mostly in Washington, D.C., *Talking God* involves Third World terrorism and a mad hit man, Leroy Fleck. On their own turf, Leaphorn and Chee are loners: in this alien bureaucracy, they're uncomfortably alert, almost unearthly outsiders.

Hillerman is so accurate and unpatronizing in his portrayal of
(20) the Navajo way that many Navajo readers, including the school-children who bring him beat-up books to sign, are astonished to discover that he's white. Many also thank him: "Your books are us, and we win in them." Hillerman consistently evokes nature and place—particularly the beautiful desolation of the Southwest—with
(25) a brilliance that equals Arthur Upfield (whose antipodean mysteries influenced him). Examining the pain of cultural clashes, he creates morality plays that are as subtly colored as their landscape. "I want to write an entertaining book," says Hillerman, "and I'd like people to see the strength and dignity of a culture I admire. I want
(30) it to be seen by the kids in it. I don't want to put anything in it that's going to encourage something that I think is antisocial." Even his bad guys, he points out, aren't very bad.

Though critically acclaimed, the series had a merely respectable following until 1987, when Hillerman finally put Leaphorn
(35) (older, more cynical) and Chee (who is also a shaman) together in *Skinwalkers*.

Source: *Newsweek*.

1. What was the consequence of the criticism by Hillerman's poker buddy?

   (1) Hillerman stopped playing poker.
   (2) The four-letter word was taken out.
   (3) Hillerman gave up his bad habits.
   (4) The entire novel was rewritten.
   (5) Librarians started to complain.

2. According to this review, what was the consequence of putting Leaphorn and Chee together?

   (1) They did not get along.
   (2) The mystery was solved more quickly.
   (3) Book sales increased.
   (4) The books finally received critical acclaim.
   (5) Hillerman decided to give up writing.

3. Native American readers were surprised to find that Hillerman was white because

   (1) they thought he was an African American
   (2) he seemed to understand the Navajo way so well
   (3) he did not encourage antisocial actions
   (4) his writing was so descriptive
   (5) they had read his books

4. Which of the following is the best meaning for the word "predecessors" (line 14)?

   (1) dead people
   (2) police
   (3) bad language
   (4) the ones before it
   (5) terrorism

5. What is meant by the phrase "woven as tightly as a Navajo blanket" (lines 14–15)?

   (1) The novel is confusing.
   (2) The novel is well put together.
   (3) Blankets are not necessary.
   (4) Terrorism makes people nervous.
   (5) Good writing is hard to come by.

6. From the excerpt, you can conclude that the characters Leaphorn and Chee

   (1) do not feel comfortable in Washington, D.C.
   (2) cannot handle their assignment
   (3) are terrorists
   (4) feel right at home in Washington, D.C.
   (5) are as bad as they are portrayed

To check your answers, turn to page 241.

Answers and Explanations

Practicing Comprehension, Application, and Analysis Skills (pages 235–237)

1. (Analysis) **(1) Her characters are ordinary people.** The concerns of ordinary people are best talked about in plain language. Option (2) is the result of her use of language, not the cause. Options (3) and (5) have nothing to do with plain speech. Option (4) is wrong because she is like Thoreau in the way she feels, not in the way she writes.

2. (Inferential Comprehension) **(1) get physically or emotionally involved in their work** The reviewer seems to think that involvement in work is a good thing; however, the reviewer may be misunderstanding the point of Oliver's poetry. There is no support for option (2). Option (3) refers to Thoreau, not Oliver. Options (4) and (5) are not supported by the excerpt.

3. (Literal Comprehension) **(2) it is very silly** The reviewer suggests that the plot is very simple and not true to life. The characters act as if they do not know much about the world. Therefore, options (1), (3), (4), and (5) are wrong.

4. (Application) **(3) candy** In the opening lines, the reviewer likens *Wanderlust* to a delicious, delicate treat. Options (1), (2), (4), and (5) all suggest basic foods, which do not fit the description.

5. (Inferential Comprehension) **(2) being a Rough Rider** Being a soldier in the army does not necessarily lead to being an outlaw. Options (1), (3), (4), and (5) refer to crimes or to misfortunes that might lead to a life of desperation and crime.

6. (Analysis) **(4) refer to his image of the Pony Express** Even if you do not know the meaning of "raucous," the sound of it suggests "wild." The Pony Express image is meant to suggest a quick and frenzied ride. Options (1), (2), (3), and (5) do not make sense in terms of the word "ride."

1. (Inferential Comprehension) **(2) The four-letter word was taken out.** The author quotes the writer about this detail. There is no suggestion of options (1), (3), or (4). Option (5) refers to something Hillerman wanted to avoid.

2. (Inferential Comprehension) **(3) Book sales increased.** In lines 33–35 the reviewer says that more people started reading the books when the author paired the two men; therefore, you can infer that more books were sold. There is no support for options (1), (2), and (5). Option (4) is wrong because the books were already critically acclaimed.

3. (Inferential Comprehension) **(2) he seemed to understand the Navajo way so well** There is no real evidence for options (1), (3), (4), and (5).

4. (Analysis) **(4) the ones before it** This refers to the eight novels that had been written before *Talking God*. Options (1), (2), (3), and (5) do not make sense in the context.

5. (Analysis) **(2) The novel is well put together.** Navajo blankets are well-known for their fine and dense weaving, to which the reviewer compares the book's plot. There is no support for options (1), (3), (4), and (5).

6. (Inferential Comprehension) **(1) do not feel comfortable in Washington, D.C.** The suggestion that they are strangers supports this idea. Options (2), (4), and (5) are the opposite of what is said in the review. Option (3) is wrong because they are police officers.

Review: Commentary

In the commentary section, you have read criticism of fiction, poetry, and the popular arts including television, film, art, and music. You have seen how critics observe and describe these works. You also learned that the most important function of a critic is to assist the reader by offering a professional opinion of the work being reviewed. Another aspect of commentary is presenting the material in an effective and well-written personal style. Critics use various literary techniques, such as cause and effect, implications, and the use of fact and personal opinion. As you answer the review questions, be aware of the strategies you have studied.

Directions: Choose the best answer to each item.

Items 1 and 2 refer to the following review by David Hiltbrand.

WHY DID BURNETT COME BACK?

Carol Burnett, the queen of the TV comedy-variety show, returns with a plain but sturdy new series.

While she has kept the familiar theme music from her classic show of the '60s and '70s, she has changed other things. *Carol &*
(5) *Company* is more stagy than camera-oriented, more talky than slapstick. It also devotes its entire half hour to a single sketch, while *The Carol Burnett Show* was an hour-long series of skits.

Burnett, joined by guest stars (Dorothy Lyman, Alex Rocco) and a regular supporting cast headed by Terry Kiser, is still a trea-
(10) sure. She always operates at a breakneck pace, going from mousy to maniacal in a heartbeat. The material, however, often doesn't merit her dedication to it. The writing for the most part is unsurprising and listless.

Source: *People* magazine.

1. It can be concluded from this review that

   (1) Carol Burnett has lost her touch
   (2) this show is the best Burnett has ever done
   (3) this show is not as good as ones she did before
   (4) Burnett's writers are great comics
   (5) Carol Burnett is very plain looking

2. What do we learn about Carol Burnett's character from this review?

   (1) She is very lazy.
   (2) She is very energetic.
   (3) She has a lot of built-up anger.
   (4) She is quite generous.
   (5) She enjoys watching TV.

Items 3 and 4 refer to the following excerpt from a review by Jean Seligmann with Larry Wilson.

WHAT DID BROWN DO WITH HIS FOOT?

The making of *My Left Foot* was also a labor of love and commitment. . . .

Actor Daniel Day-Lewis, previously noted for his versatility in *My Beautiful Laundrette* and *A Room With a View*, was cast as

(5) Christy Brown. Before shooting, Day-Lewis spent eight weeks attending daily classes at Dublin's Sandymount clinic for cerebral palsy, watching the young patients learn to overcome many of their disabling symptoms.

Day-Lewis met Brown's large, loving family and studied

(10) carefully a documentary about Brown made in 1971. But the most astonishing aspect of the actor's immersion in his role is that he actually learned, like Brown, to write, type and paint with his left foot. In fact, some of the paintings on display at an art exhibit in the film were done by Day-Lewis with his foot. "Daniel refused to

(15) let anyone be a stand-in—or a foot in," says Pearson.

During filming, Day-Lewis would spend the day in his wheelchair, remaining in character even between takes, learning Brown's frustration by not using his hands, even to feed himself. He spoke only in the muffled, indistinct voice that Brown eventually

(20) mastered through months of instruction that didn't begin until he was 19. (He was born in 1932 to a very poor family; children with cerebral palsy today begin therapy very early, sometimes even in infancy.) The role was physically punishing; Day-Lewis required massage by a physiotherapist after each day spent twisted and cramped

(25) into the small, crude, wooden boxcar that served as Brown's wheelchair for many years. By the end of shooting, two of the actor's vertebrae had to be realigned.

Source: *Newsweek.*

---

3. Which word supports an opinion about Day-Lewis?

(1) studied
(2) astonishing
(3) refused
(4) required
(5) realigned

4. It can be concluded from this passage that Day-Lewis

(1) did not need any medical care while making the movie
(2) took his role seriously
(3) is crippled
(4) was Christy Brown's friend
(5) had an easy time playing the role

WHAT WAS WRONG WITH CHRISTINA?

"When I painted it in 1948, *Christina's World* hung all summer in my house in Maine and nobody particularly reacted to it. I thought, 'Boy, is this one ever a flat tire.' Now I get at least a letter a week from all over the world, usually wanting to know what she's
(5) doing. Actually there isn't any definite story. The way this tempera happened, I was in an upstairs room in the Olson house and saw Christina crawling in the field. Later, I went down to the road and made a pencil drawing of the house, but I never went down into the field. You see, my memory was more of a reality than the thing
(10) itself. I didn't put Christina in till the very end. I worked on the hill for months, that brown grass, and kept thinking about her in her pink dress like a faded lobster shell I might find on the beach, crumpled. Finally I got up enough courage to say to her, "Would you mind if I made a drawing of you sitting outside?" and drew her
(15) crippled arms and hands. Finally, I was so shy about posing her, I got my wife Betsy to pose for her figure. Then it came time to lay in Christina's figure against that planet I'd created for her all those weeks. I put this pink tone on her shoulder—and it almost blew me across the room."

Source: "Andrew Wyeth: An Interview."

---

5. Andrew Wyeth talks about his own work in this passage. His point of view helps the reader to understand

  (1) how painful being an artist can be
  (2) how an artwork is developed
  (3) why memory cannot be depended on
  (4) why artists get fan mail
  (5) that artists have courage

6. According to this artist, the pink tone

  (1) amazed him
  (2) was not very important
  (3) was carefully planned
  (4) was not effective
  (5) was the result of a pencil drawing

7. Why did Wyeth get all those letters about Christina?

  (1) People had seen the painting of her and were touched.
  (2) Christina had stopped writing to her fans.
  (3) People were angry at Wyeth for painting her.
  (4) People did not want to see the painting anymore.
  (5) People wanted to criticize her.

8. What emotional effect is suggested by Wyeth's reference to the faded lobster (lines 11–13)?

  (1) sadness
  (2) anger
  (3) happiness
  (4) fear
  (5) shyness

Items 9 and 10 refer to the following commentary by Pat Ordovensky.

WHAT IS NEW IN HISTORY?

The five most-used high school history books leave students feeling that democracy in the USA is a "happy accident," a new study says.

"They're full of dates and facts but very little understanding," says Albert Shanker, president of the American Federation of
(5) Teachers.

The study, by University of Massachusetts historian Paul Gagnon, looked at five textbooks published in the 1980s and used by about two-thirds of high school history students.

"There is little analysis," he says, "of the hard choices that
(10) leaders and ordinary people made and the difficult battles they fought." . . .

Missing, Gagnon says:

"Good, tough biographies of important people." The longest sketch of Abraham Lincoln is six paragraphs.

(15) The "many cultures of American society." Religious convictions that motivated many leaders are ignored.

The ideas that formed the USA and the "quarrels about those ideas."

Gagnon suggests the standard one-year U.S. history course
(20) expand to two years to give students and teachers "time to explore."

"I don't think," Gagnon says, "that students should have to ask 'so what?' so often."

Source: "History Texts Lack Insight," *USA Today*.

---

9. The author suggests that one consequence of changing the books would be

(1) unimportant to students
(2) that students will learn more about the ideas that shaped America
(3) that students will have less time to think about history
(4) a happy accident
(5) a lack of faith in democracy

10. The historian would probably agree that the space allowed for the biographic sketch of Lincoln is most similar to having

(1) six poems by Robert Frost in a poetry book
(2) sixteen pages about Martin Luther King, Jr., in a history of Black Americans
(3) six sentences about Shakespeare in a book about drama
(4) six pages about Chicago in a travel guide for the Midwest
(5) six chapters about tires in an automobile repair manual

Items 11 to 14 refer to the following excerpt from a review.

DO YOU TAKE THE D TRAIN?

The most picturesque way to get from Manhattan to a performance at the Brooklyn Academy of Music is to take the D train over the Manhattan Bridge. The slow ride over the dark water, the lights that outline the bridges and twinkle along the skyline—this is
(5) perhaps our last piece of 90-cent romance. The trip made a perfect prelude to the opening program in the three-week season of Twyla Tharp Dance, in which *Nine Sinatra Songs* was the highlight of the evening.

Tharp suggests a make-believe ballroom, with midnight-blue
(10) curtains and a faceted globe that rotates over the heads of the dancers, casting blurry diamonds into the space. To the caressing "Softly As I Leave You," Shelley Washington and Keith Young, in elegant evening clothes, float in each other's arms, a latter-day Rogers and Astaire. He releases her, she spins dreamily into the
(15) distance, then rushes back toward him, and he plucks her out of the air. The action is so easy, so tender, she seems to have no more substance than a cloud. . . .

. . . [Tharp] has given the conventions of theatrical ballroom dancing her laser-beam scrutiny and is delivering up, deadpan,
(20) both the nonsense and the beauty in them. The Sinatra songs are perfect for her purpose—egregiously sentimental now that they're heard out of their time context, and still irresistible.

Source: *New York* magazine.

---

11. Which of these statements is a fact?

(1) A Brooklyn subway ride is romantic.
(2) Shelley Washington looks weightless.
(3) Sinatra songs are irresistible.
(4) Deep-blue curtains adorned the stage.
(5) Tharp's staging is laser-beam sharp.

12. Which of the following best describes the effect of using Sinatra's songs?

(1) Older people come to watch the dancing.
(2) A mushy, romantic background is created for the dancing.
(3) The audience wants to get up and dance.
(4) The audience is reminded of the good old days.
(5) The ballroom dancing begins to seem very up-to-date.

13. The main idea of the review is

    (1) Sinatra is a wonderful singer
    (2) Tharp is a brilliant choreographer
    (3) Washington is elegantly dressed
    (4) Washington and Young are good dancers
    (5) Brooklyn is breathtaking

14. The writer of the review was most likely

    (1) a fan of Frank Sinatra
    (2) a reporter covering a pop concert
    (3) a person who enjoys riding trains
    (4) a first-time visitor to New York
    (5) a resident of Brooklyn

Items 15 to 18 refer to the following theater review.

DOES RAGGEDY ANN HAVE ROUGH EDGES?

        Finally we have a show that adults and children can view with equal distaste. *Raggedy Ann* is a musical guaranteed to bore the pants, skirts, and diapers off anyone of any age with a half-way normal brain, and it may be that the family that walks out
(5) together, stays together. . . . This is the musical that was originally produced by the Empire State Institute for the Performing Arts in Albany, and was sent to Moscow, though Siberia would have been more appropriate. Its co-producers include the Kennedy Center (it has been seen in Washington) and CBS (it has, I gather, been seen
(10) on television). Ready or not, the world is getting this show, advertised as "the musical with a heart," crammed down its throat, and I can only hope that its body will reject this transplanted organ.

Source: *New York* magazine.

---

15. Which of the following adjectives best describes the reviewer's opinion of *Raggedy Ann*?

    (1) entertaining
    (2) heartbreaking
    (3) thought-provoking
    (4) dreadful
    (5) inspiring

16. The critic reveals his judgment of *Raggedy Ann* by

    (1) contrasting it with *Peter Pan*
    (2) writing in a nasty tone
    (3) saying everyone should see it
    (4) summarizing the plot
    (5) saying that it is better on TV

17. According to this review, if you went to see this show, you probably could expect to spend most of your time

    (1) enjoying yourself
    (2) sitting on the edge of your seat
    (3) laughing
    (4) taking a nap
    (5) traveling around the world

18. Based on the passage, *Raggedy Ann* had been advertised as a musical with

    (1) clever costumes
    (2) appeal for children of all ages
    (3) lots of good feelings
    (4) two hours of nonstop laughs
    (5) songs by Cole Porter

Answers and Explanations

Commentary Review (pages 242–247)

1. (Inferential Comprehension) **(3) this show is not as good as ones she did before** The reviewer says the writing is not very good and also compares the show unfavorably to Burnett's old one, so option (2) is wrong. Options (1) and (4) are the opposite of what the reviewer says. There is no evidence for option (5).

2. (Analysis) **(2) She is very energetic.** This is suggested by "breakneck pace" (line 10). Option (1) is the opposite of what is said. There is no support for options (3), (4), and (5).

3. (Analysis) **(2) astonishing** This word suggests an emotional reaction to Day-Lewis. Options (1), (3), (4), and (5) refer to facts about him.

4. (Inferential Comprehension) **(2) took his role seriously** The actor's commitment indicates his serious attitude. Options (1) and (5) are the opposite of what is stated in the excerpt. There is no evidence for options (3) and (4).

5. (Analysis) **(2) how an artwork is developed** This passage shows that a painting comes about in stages. Options (1) and (5) may be true, but they are not revealed because of the artist's point of view. There is no support for options (3) and (4).

6. (Literal Comprehension) **(1) amazed him** This is a restatement of the last line. The pink highlight was accidental but was also important, so options (2), (3), and (4) are wrong. There is no support for option (5).

7. (Inferential Comprehension) **(1) People had seen the painting of her and were touched.** The letters reveal fascination with the woman. There is no support for option (2). Options (3), (4), and (5) suggest the opposite of the reason.

8. (Analysis) **(1) sadness** The image is of something worn out and useless. There is no support for options (2), (3), (4), and (5).

9. (Inferential Comprehension) **(2) that students will learn more about the ideas that shaped America** This is one of the elements that is missing from the current books. Option (1) is wrong because a change would be important. Option (3) refers to what Gagnon would not like to see happen. Options (4) and (5) have nothing to do with changing the books.

10. (Application) **(3) six sentences about Shakespeare in a book about drama** The famous playwright would deserve more space than that; so would Lincoln. Options (1), (2), and (4) are wrong because the numbers seem proper. Option (5) is the opposite of having too little information.

11. (Analysis) **(4) Deep-blue curtains adorned the stage.** This is something that could be seen by everyone. This factual detail about the blue curtains is given in lines 9–10 when the writer is describing the stage set. Options (1), (2), (3), and (5) describe the critic's personal feelings and do not reflect facts.

12. (Analysis) **(2) A mushy, romantic background is created for the dancing.** These older songs now seem overly sentimental but they still have romantic appeal. Options (1) and (4) may be partly true but neither is the best response. There is no support for option (3). Option (5) is wrong because the dancing does not seem modern.

13. (Literal Comprehension) **(2) Tharp is a brilliant choreographer.** The review is about Twyla Tharp. While option (1) is mentioned, the excellence of Sinatra's music is not its main idea. Options (3), (4), and (5) are details.

14. (Analysis) **(1) a fan of Frank Sinatra** From the passage it is not hard to detect an admiration for Frank Sinatra. The writer thinks his songs are "irresistible" (line 22). There is no evidence for options (2), (3), (4), and (5).

15. (Analysis) **(4) dreadful** "Dreadful" best sums up the reviewer's opinion. This is shown in lines 1–2 and by implication throughout the review. Options (1), (2), (3), and (5) are the opposite of the opinions expressed.

16. (Analysis) **(2) writing in a nasty tone** The reviewer's tone throughout is heavily insulting. Options (1), (3), (4), and (5) are not supported.

17. (Application) **(4) taking a nap** The reviewer suggests the show is boring. Options (1), (2), and (3) all suggest the show is interesting in some way. Option (5) refers to the show, not the audience.

18. (Literal Comprehension) **(3) lots of good feelings** The slogan "the musical with a heart" (line 11) means a show full of good feelings. There is no evidence for options (1), (2), (4), and (5).

Use the chart below to find your strengths and weaknesses in reading comprehension.

Skill	Area	Question	Lessons for Review
Literal Comprehension	Art	6	3
	Dance	13	1
	Drama	18	3
Inferential Comprehension	TV	1	21
	Film	4	21
	Art	7	23
	Literature	9	23
Application	Literature	10	21
	Drama	17	20
Analysis	TV	2	10
	Film	3	19
	Art	5, 8	3 and 7
	Dance	11, 12, 14	19, 20, and 22
	Drama	15, 16	20 and 14

Tests of General Educational Development

TEST _____

TEST TAKEN AT _____

TEST NUMBER

TEST ANSWERS   DO NOT MARK IN YOUR TEST BOOKLET

Fill in the circle corresponding to your answer for each question.
Erase cleanly.

① ② ③ ④ ⑤

1 ① ② ③ ④ ⑤   19 ① ② ③ ④ ⑤   36 ① ② ③ ④ ⑤   54 ① ② ③ ④ ⑤
2 ① ② ③ ④ ⑤   20 ① ② ③ ④ ⑤   37 ① ② ③ ④ ⑤   55 ① ② ③ ④ ⑤
3 ① ② ③ ④ ⑤   21 ① ② ③ ④ ⑤   38 ① ② ③ ④ ⑤   56 ① ② ③ ④ ⑤
4 ① ② ③ ④ ⑤   22 ① ② ③ ④ ⑤   39 ① ② ③ ④ ⑤   57 ① ② ③ ④ ⑤
5 ① ② ③ ④ ⑤   23 ① ② ③ ④ ⑤   40 ① ② ③ ④ ⑤   58 ① ② ③ ④ ⑤
6 ① ② ③ ④ ⑤   24 ① ② ③ ④ ⑤   41 ① ② ③ ④ ⑤   59 ① ② ③ ④ ⑤
7 ① ② ③ ④ ⑤   25 ① ② ③ ④ ⑤   42 ① ② ③ ④ ⑤   60 ① ② ③ ④ ⑤
8 ① ② ③ ④ ⑤   26 ① ② ③ ④ ⑤   43 ① ② ③ ④ ⑤   61 ① ② ③ ④ ⑤
9 ① ② ③ ④ ⑤   27 ① ② ③ ④ ⑤   44 ① ② ③ ④ ⑤   62 ① ② ③ ④ ⑤
10 ① ② ③ ④ ⑤   28 ① ② ③ ④ ⑤   45 ① ② ③ ④ ⑤   63 ① ② ③ ④ ⑤
11 ① ② ③ ④ ⑤   29 ① ② ③ ④ ⑤   46 ① ② ③ ④ ⑤   64 ① ② ③ ④ ⑤
12 ① ② ③ ④ ⑤   30 ① ② ③ ④ ⑤   47 ① ② ③ ④ ⑤   65 ① ② ③ ④ ⑤
13 ① ② ③ ④ ⑤   31 ① ② ③ ④ ⑤   48 ① ② ③ ④ ⑤   66 ① ② ③ ④ ⑤
14 ① ② ③ ④ ⑤   32 ① ② ③ ④ ⑤   49 ① ② ③ ④ ⑤   67 ① ② ③ ④ ⑤
15 ① ② ③ ④ ⑤   33 ① ② ③ ④ ⑤   50 ① ② ③ ④ ⑤   68 ① ② ③ ④ ⑤
16 ① ② ③ ④ ⑤   34 ① ② ③ ④ ⑤   51 ① ② ③ ④ ⑤   69 ① ② ③ ④ ⑤
17 ① ② ③ ④ ⑤   35 ① ② ③ ④ ⑤   52 ① ② ③ ④ ⑤   70 ① ② ③ ④ ⑤
18 ① ② ③ ④ ⑤   53 ① ② ③ ④ ⑤

Permission is granted to reproduce this form for student use.

Interpreting Literature and the Arts

Directions

The Interpreting Literature and the Arts Posttest consists of excerpts from classical and popular literature and articles about literature or the arts. Each excerpt is followed by multiple-choice questions about the reading material.

Read each excerpt first and then answer the questions following it. Refer back to the reading material as often as necessary in answering the questions.

Each excerpt is preceded by a "purpose question." The purpose question gives a reason for reading the material. Use these purpose questions to help focus your reading. You are not required to answer these purpose questions. They are given only to help you concentrate on the ideas presented in the reading materials.

You should spend no more than 65 minutes answering the questions on this posttest. Work carefully, but do not spend too much time on any one question. Be sure you answer every question. You will not be penalized for incorrect answers.

Record your answers on the answer sheet provided on page 276 or on a separate piece of paper. Be sure all requested information is properly recorded on the answer sheet. To record your answers, mark the numbered space on the answer sheet beside the number that corresponds to the question on the posttest.

Example: It was Susan's dream machine. The metallic blue paint gleamed, and the sporty wheels were highly polished. Under the hood, the engine was no less carefully cleaned. Inside, flashy lights illuminated the instruments on the dashboard, and the seats were covered by rich leather upholstery.

The subject ("It") of this excerpt is most likely

(1)   an airplane
(2)   a stereo system
(3)   an automobile
(4)   a boat
(5)   a motorcycle

The correct answer is "an automobile"; therefore, answer space 3 would be marked on the answer sheet.

Do not rest the point of your pencil on the answer sheet while you are considering your answer. Make no stray or unnecessary marks. If you change an answer, erase your first mark completely. Mark only one answer space for each question; multiple answers will be scored as incorrect. Do not fold or crease your answer sheet.

Posttest

Directions: Choose the best answer to each item.

Items 1 to 5 refer to the following passage from a play.

HOW DOES ALMA MAKE THESE PEOPLE REVEAL THEMSELVES?

MRS. BUCHANAN: You mustn't misunderstand me about Miss Alma. Naturally I feel sorry for her, too. But, precious, precious! In every Southern town there's a girl or two like that. People feel sorry for them, they're kind to them, but, darling, they keep at a
(5)   distance, they don't get involved with them. Especially not in a sentimental way.

JOHN: I don't know what you mean about Miss Alma. She's a little bit—quaint, she's very excitable, but—there's nothing *wrong* with her.

(10) MRS. BUCHANAN: Precious, can't you see. Miss Alma is an *eccentric*!

JOHN: You mean she isn't like all the other girls in Glorious Hill?

MRS. BUCHANAN: There's always at least one like her in every Southern town, sometimes, like Miss Alma, rather sweet, sometimes even gifted, and I think Miss Alma *does* have a rather appealing
(15)   voice when she doesn't become too carried away by her singing. Sometimes, but not often, pretty. I have seen Miss Alma when she was almost pretty. But never, never *quite*.

JOHN: There are moments when she has beauty.

MRS. BUCHANAN: Those moments haven't occurred when *I* looked at
(20)   her! Such a wide mouth she has, like the mouth of a clown! And she distorts her face with all those false expressions. However, Miss Alma's looks are beside the point.

JOHN: Her, her eyes are fascinating!

MRS. BUCHANAN: Goodness, yes, disturbing!

1. When Mrs. Buchanan sees Alma, she will probably

   (1) ignore her
   (2) invite her to dinner
   (3) speak politely but distantly
   (4) try to gain her friendship
   (5) laugh at her

2. When John sees Alma, he will probably

   (1) ask her to marry him
   (2) talk with her in a friendly way
   (3) tell her that he cannot see her again
   (4) tell her what Mrs. Buchanan has been saying about her
   (5) realize that Mrs. Buchanan is right

3. The words that the author italicizes serve to emphasize

   (1) Mrs. Buchanan's negative opinion of Alma
   (2) Mrs. Buchanan's fear that John will continue to like Alma
   (3) Mrs. Buchanan's anger at John
   (4) John's negative opinion of Mrs. Buchanan
   (5) John's fear of losing Alma

4. Mrs. Buchanan's own husband is most likely to be

   (1) eccentric
   (2) sentimental
   (3) beautiful
   (4) conforming
   (5) stubborn

5. Mrs. Buchanan says the things she does because she

   (1) admires beauty
   (2) feels sorry for Alma
   (3) likes talking about Alma
   (4) is sentimental and indulges John
   (5) is critical and a snob

Items 6 to 11 refer to the following poem.

HOW COLD IS REALLY COLD?

God's Backside

Cold
like Grandfather's icehouse,
ice forming like a vein
and the trees,
(5) rocks of frozen blood,
and me asking questions of the weather.
And me stupidly observing.
Me swallowing the stone of winter.
Three miles away cars push
(10) by on the highway.
Across the world
bombs drop
in their awful labor.
Ten miles away
(15) the city faints on its lights.
But here
there are only a few houses,
trees, rocks, telephone wires
and the cold punching the earth.
(20) Cold slicing the windowpane
like a razor blade
for God, it seems,
has turned his backside to us,
giving us the dark negative,
(25) the death wing,
until such time
as a flower breaks down the front door
and we cry "Father! Mother!"
and plan their wedding.

6. Which of the following phrases is <u>not</u> used by the poet to describe the cold.

    (1) like Grandfather's icehouse
    (2) ice forming like a vein
    (3) rocks of frozen blood
    (4) bombs drop in their awful labor
    (5) Cold slicing the windowpane like a razor blade

7. The speaker in the poem lives

    (1) in a city
    (2) in the country
    (3) in an icehouse
    (4) in a tent
    (5) next to a highway

8. Which of these is the speaker actually doing?

    (1) planning a wedding
    (2) swallowing a stone
    (3) slicing the windowpane
    (4) sitting in an icehouse
    (5) observing the weather

9. Which statement below best describes the mood created in lines 1–25?

    (1) The mood of the poem is upbeat and cheerful.
    (2) The mood of the poem is thoughtful and lighthearted.
    (3) The mood of the poem is gloomy and depressed.
    (4) The mood of the poem is romantic.
    (5) The mood of the poem is sarcastic.

10. According to the words used to describe the cold, the speaker thinks the cold is

    (1) a savage force
    (2) a lovely spectacle
    (3) a quiet stillness
    (4) a state of mind
    (5) a prophecy of death

11. Which of the following best describes what the poet means in lines 26–29?

    (1) The poet means that the speaker's parents were not yet married.
    (2) The poet means that flowers have extraordinary powers.
    (3) The poet means that flowers can break down doors.
    (4) The poet means that spring will follow the cold winter.
    (5) The poet means that the speaker's parents are planning to visit in the spring.

Items 12 to 17 refer to the following passage.

WHAT DOES SCROOGE SEE AND HEAR AT THE CHRISTMAS PARTY?

There was first a game of blind-man's buff. And I no more believe Topper was really blinded than I believe he had eyes in his boots. Because the way in which he went after that plump sister in the lace tucker was an outrage on the credulity of human nature.
(5) Knocking down the fire-irons, tumbling over the chairs, bumping up against the piano, smothering himself among the curtains, wherever she went, there went he. He always knew where the plump sister was. He wouldn't catch anybody else. If you had fallen up against him, as some of them did, he would have made a feint of endeav-
(10) oring to seize you, which would have been an affront to your understanding; and would instantly have sidled off in the direction of the plump sister.

"Here is a new game," said Scrooge. "One half hour, Spirit, only one!"
(15) It was a Game called Yes and No, where Scrooge's nephew had to think of something, and the rest must find out what; he only answering to their questions yes or no as the case was. The fire of questioning to which he was exposed, elicited from him that he was thinking of an animal, rather a disagreeable animal, a savage ani-
(20) mal, an animal that growled and grunted sometimes, and talked sometimes, and lived in London, and walked about the streets, and wasn't made a show of, and wasn't led by anybody, and didn't live in a menagerie, and was never killed in a market, and was not a horse, or an ass, or a cow, or a bull, or a tiger, or a dog, or a pig, or a cat, or
(25) a bear. At every new question put to him, this nephew burst into a fresh roar of laughter; and was so inexpressibly tickled, that he was obliged to get up off the sofa and stamp. At last the plump sister cried out:

"I have found it out! I know what it is, Fred! I know what it is!"
(30) "What is it?" cried Fred.

"It's your uncle Scro-o-o-oge!"

Which it certainly was. . . .

"He has given us plenty of merriment, I am sure," said Fred, "and it would be ungrateful not to drink his health. Here is a glass
(35) of mulled wine ready to our hand at the moment; and I say, 'Uncle Scrooge!'"

"Well! Uncle Scrooge!" they cried. . . .

Uncle Scrooge had become so gay and light of heart, that he would have pledged the unconscious company in return, and thanked
(40) them in an inaudible speech, if the Ghost had given him time. But the whole scene passed off in the breath of the last word spoken by his nephew; and he and the Spirit were again upon their travels.

12. The author's style is

    (1) simple and direct
    (2) dry and scholarly
    (3) wordy but lively
    (4) solemn but profound
    (5) flat and unemotional

13. In the passage, Scrooge is described as

    (1) a cheat at blindman's buff
    (2) a Spirit
    (3) a disagreeable and savage animal
    (4) a cow, a bull, or a tiger
    (5) a roar of laughter

14. In line 23, the word "menagerie" means

    (1) birdcage
    (2) den of iniquity
    (3) merry-go-round
    (4) stable
    (5) zoo

15. Why does Fred drink a toast to Scrooge?

    (1) Everyone at the party likes Scrooge.
    (2) Scrooge has given the party and set up the games.
    (3) Scrooge has made them laugh by being the object of a game.
    (4) Everyone is glad that Scrooge is dead.
    (5) He is glad that Scrooge has become lighthearted and gay.

16. From the last paragraph of the passage, you can infer that Scrooge is

    (1) invisible
    (2) all-powerful
    (3) furious
    (4) drunk
    (5) a magician

17. From his behavior at the end of the passage, you can infer that

    (1) Scrooge will never have a sense of humor
    (2) Scrooge will be able to change his grumpy ways
    (3) Scrooge will punish Fred and the others if he ever can
    (4) Scrooge will never understand why Fred toasts him
    (5) Scrooge and the Spirit will become good friends

Items 18 to 23 refer to the following excerpt from a review.

WHY ARE THE HUDLIN BROTHERS LIKELY TO SUCCEED?

At first, it's hard to believe that Reginald Hudlin won a student award at Harvard when he made a shorter version of (5) *House Party* in 1983. Or that Warrington Hudlin, who studied film at Yale, chose to make his feature debut on a project that seems as trivial as this. In 1978, (10) Warrington cofounded the Black Filmmaker Foundation, which has assisted many black filmmakers, including Spike Lee, on his debut film, *She's Gotta* (15) *Have It*.

Still, the Hudlins had a game plan. Their movie (with a sixty-percent-black production crew) would be fun, but it would (20) also be an authentic depiction of black life. Most black films are set in New York or Los Angeles, yet the Hudlins—though working in L.A.—aimed for the Middle (25) American look of their suburban neighborhood in Illinois. Strikingly photographed by Peter Deming (who won the cinematography award at Sundance), (30) the film has a unique visual snap.

For the two male leads, the Hudlins hired the rappers Kid 'n' Play (Christopher Reid and (35) Christopher Martin), who are making their acting debuts. Both are immensely engaging, with Reid, who sports an Eraserhead haircut (an *hommage* to David (40) Lynch?) proving a real find. Paul Anthony, B. Fine and Bowlegged Lou, all of Full Force, score as villains out to ruin Kid's night. . . .

Hudlin's . . . direction is remark- (45) ably fluid. The extended party sequence, with Kid 'n' Play in a rap duel, is excitingly staged. Fast and lively, the film sweeps you along on a tide of music and (50) laughs.

A genre movie has limits, but nobody seems to have told that to the Hudlins, who keep pushing against them. Stereo- (55) types about sex, drugs, drink, rock and rap are vigorously exploded. Male teens' arrogance about birth control ("It's her responsibility") is countered by (60) young women who won't buy the argument. The film's two female leads—Tisha Campbell, as a project girl, and A. J. Johnson, as her upper-class counterpart—are (65) admirably strong women who won't let their mutual yen for Kid spoil their friendship.

Despite several misguided forays into gay jokes and toilet (70) humor, the fundamental decency of the characters prevails, but without sugarcoating. There's real anger in the film. The white cops who harass Kid's father (a (75) fine Robin Harris) and any other black person they see on the street at night are buffoons, but the venom of their casual prejudice—a fact of life for blacks (80) of all classes—permeates the comedy and gives it weight.

So *House Party*, warts and all, earns its place in the Sundance lineup. While some (85) independents try to invent new forms of expression in the cinema, the Hudlins and others are showing how much can still be expressed within familiar (90) forms. Both methods are valid and necessary . . . *House Party* is a celebration of possibilities.

18. The author thinks that *House Party* is

(1) silly and funny
(2) a serious look at the issues facing black teenagers
(3) both funny and serious
(4) badly written but well acted
(5) full of stereotypes

19. The film most likely takes place

(1) over the course of several years
(2) during one week in the lives of Kid 'n' Play
(3) over twenty-four hours in the lives of some teenagers
(4) on a typical school day
(5) during one night

20. The author mentions the friendship between the project girl and her upper-class counterpart as an example of

(1) how the movie rejects stereotypes
(2) how the director develops the characters
(3) how good the acting is
(4) how funny the movie is
(5) how lively the action scenes are

21. The author does not say that the movie

(1) has a unique visual snap
(2) is set in Los Angeles
(3) is fast and lively
(4) has some bad jokes
(5) contains real anger

22. If you went to see *House Party*, you would see a film that

(1) uses new camera techniques and new forms of expression
(2) is simply an extended party sequence
(3) uses familiar forms to tell an interesting story
(4) uses rap performers to explain to the viewer what is happening
(5) stars the Hudlin brothers

23. The Hudlin brothers hired rap performers because

(1) they wanted experienced actors
(2) they could not afford regular actors
(3) they wanted to include authentic rap songs in the movie
(4) they wanted to make fun of rap groups in the movie
(5) they belong to a rap group themselves

WHY DID SUCCESS SPOIL ERNEST HEMINGWAY?

In 1928 Hemingway's mother mailed him a chocolate cake. Along with it she sent the .32-cal. Smith & Wesson revolver with which Hemingway's father had just killed himself. Hemingway dropped the pistol into a deep lake in Wyoming "and saw it go down
(5) making bubbles until it was just as big as a watch charm in that clear water, and then it was out of sight."

The story is minutely savage in its details and haunting in its outcome: perfect Hemingway. And of course, there is the water. . . . —lake water and trout stream and Gulf Stream and the rains after
(10) Caporetto and the endless washes of alcohol refracting in his brain. His style was a stream with the stones of nouns in it and a surface of prepositional ripples. . . .

. . . Ernest Hemingway's books are easier to know, and love, than his life. He wrote, at his early best, a prose of powerful and
(15) brilliant simplicity. But his character was not simple. In one of his stories, he wrote: "The most complicated subject that I know, since I am a man, is a man's life." The most complicated subject that he knew was Ernest Hemingway.

. . . His life belonged as much to the history of publicity as to the
(20) history of literature. He was a splendid writer who became his own worst creation, a hoax and a bore. He ended by being one of the most famous men in the world, white-bearded Mr. Papa. He stopped observing and started performing. . . .

Still, a long mythic fiesta between two explosions may not be a
(25) bad way to have a life. The first explosion came in Fossalta di Piave in northeastern Italy at midnight on July 8, 1918. A shell from an Austrian trench mortar punctured Hemingway with 200-odd pieces of shrapnel. . . . The second explosion came 25 years ago this sum-mer. Early one morning in Ketchum, Idaho, Hemingway (suffering
(30) from diabetes, nephritis, alcoholism, severe depression, hepatitis, hypertension, impotence and paranoid delusions, his memory all but ruined by electroshock treatments) slid two shells into his double-barreled Boss shotgun . . . the last creature Hemingway brought down was himself.

(35) Hemingway was mourned mostly as a great celebrity, his worst side, and not as a great writer, which he was.

24. According to the passage, Hemingway underwent marked changes in later life because

    (1) he had difficulty writing
    (2) he lived in Cuba
    (3) he won the Nobel Prize for Literature
    (4) he began acting out a role
    (5) he suffered serious injuries in a plane crash

25. The reviewer uses the story mentioned in the first paragraph to

    (1) explain why Hemingway's father killed himself
    (2) criticize Hemingway's behavior
    (3) introduce a discussion of Hemingway's life and style of writing
    (4) explain Hemingway's relationship with his mother
    (5) explain why Hemingway became a celebrity

26. The public reacted to Hemingway in his later years as

    (1) the most distinguished writer of his time
    (2) an expert on big-game hunting
    (3) a war correspondent
    (4) an expert on bullfighting
    (5) an international star

27. The reviewer would most likely enjoy

    (1) a play about Hemingway's life
    (2) a biography about Hemingway's later years
    (3) an early Hemingway story
    (4) a newspaper article about Hemingway's fame
    (5) a picture of Hemingway performing

28. The author uses the phrase "a hoax and a bore" (line 21) to

    (1) describe Hemingway's later style of writing
    (2) describe what became of Hemingway in his later years
    (3) describe the publicity that surrounded Hemingway
    (4) explain the kinds of things Hemingway wrote about
    (5) describe those who mourned Hemingway as a celebrity

Items <u>29 to 33</u> refer to the following passage from a play.

WHAT DECISION HAS MRS. BROOKS MADE AND WHY?

MRS. BROOKS: But, girl, this morning I made up my mind, I'm leaving Mr. Brooks.

RUBY: Gladys, it's not that bad, is it? Remember it ain't the easiest thing in the world to leave a man after all these years.

(5) MRS. BROOKS: Humph. Telling me I couldn't buy a new dress for Gail's wedding; that was the last straw.

RUBY: You know, Gladys, there is such a thing as going from the refrigerator into the frying pan.

MRS. BROOKS: Oh, Ruby, be serious.

(10) RUBY: I am just as serious as cancer. I mean, it's not as though the man won't work. Everybody knows that he ain't known to mess up a piece of money.

MRS. BROOKS: A lot of good it does me. Everything in the house is in his name. My name don't appear on nothing except the income

(15) tax deductions.

29. Which of the following best describes Mrs. Brooks's position in this passage?

(1) She appreciates the fact that Mr. Brooks has good intentions.

(2) She no longer has any patience with Mr. Brooks's behavior.

(3) She has decided to teach Mr. Brooks a lesson.

(4) She is willing to give Mr. Brooks one more chance.

(5) She likes joking with Ruby about leaving Mr. Brooks.

30. Which of the following best describes Ruby's position?

(1) She is worried about Mrs. Brooks's future.

(2) She wholeheartedly approves of Mrs. Brooks's plan.

(3) She thinks Mr. Brooks is an admirable man.

(4) She plans to help Mrs. Brooks as much as she can.

(5) She thinks that Mrs. Brooks is ungrateful to her husband.

31. The sentence "Everybody knows that he ain't known to mess up a piece of money" (lines 11–12) means that Mr. Brooks

    (1) does not know how to make money

    (2) spends money only on himself

    (3) is very neat with all his possessions

    (4) does not spend money readily

    (5) spends money on having fun

32. Mrs. Brooks made up her mind to leave Mr. Brooks because

    (1) he would not put her name on his income tax deduction

    (2) he has cancer

    (3) he refused to let her buy a new dress

    (4) he refused to let her go to a friend's wedding

    (5) he would not buy her a new refrigerator

33. From what Mrs. Brooks says, you can infer that

    (1) she has thought about leaving Mr. Brooks for a long time

    (2) she needs Ruby's approval before she will leave Mr. Brooks

    (3) she will not leave Mr. Brooks until she has found a job

    (4) she probably will not leave Mr. Brooks at all

    (5) she will move in with Ruby

WHAT ARE THE VIEWS OF THE DEAN OF MEN?

I am not unsympathetic, Jack, to your views on the war. I am
not unsympathetic to your views on the state of the world in general.
From the way you wear your hair and from the way you dress I do
find it difficult to decide whether you or that young girl you say you
(5) are about to marry is going to play the male role in your marriage—
or the female role. But even that I don't find offensive. And I am not
trying to make crude jokes at your expense. You must pardon me,
though, if my remarks seem too personal. I confess I don't know
you as well as a father *ought* to know his son, and I may seem to
(10) take liberties. . . .

I don't honestly know when I decided to go into college teaching,
Jack. I considered doing other things—a career in the army or navy.
Yes, I might have gone to Annapolis or West Point. Those appoint-
ments were much to be desired in the Depression years, and my
(15) family did still have a few political connections. One thing was certain, though. Business was just as much out of the question for me
as politics had been for my father. An honest man, I was to understand, had too much to suffer there. Yes, considering our family
history, an ivory tower didn't sound like a bad thing at all for an
(20) honest man and a serious man. . . .

After I had been dean of men for two years, I was made academic
dean of the college. In two more years, I was president of the college.
Even with as little time as you have spent with me through the
years, Jack, you have seen what a successful marriage my second
(25) marriage has been, and what a happy, active life I have had. One
sacrifices something. One sacrifices, for instance, the books one
might have written after that first one. More important, one may
sacrifice the love, even the acquaintance of one's children. One loses
something of one's self even. But at least I am not tyrannizing over
(30) old women and small children. At least I don't sit gazing into space
while my wife and perhaps some kindly neighbor woman waits
patiently to see whether or not I will risk a two-heart bid. A man
must somehow go on living among men, Jack. A part of him must.
It is important to broaden one's humanity, but it is important to
(35) remain a mere man, too. But it is a strange world, Jack, in which
an old man must tell a young man this.

34. Which of the following does the speaker believe?

    (1)   that Jack is not a real man
    (2)   that he knows Jack very well
    (3)   that he has had a happy, active life
    (4)   that Jack is not a dutiful son
    (5)   that his second marriage is a cruel joke

35. The speaker most likely sent this passage to his son in the form of a

    (1)   telegram
    (2)   short story
    (3)   newspaper article
    (4)   diary entry
    (5)   letter

36. Which statement best reflects the implications drawn from the passage as a whole concerning the speaker's relationship with Jack?

    (1)   The speaker's relationship with Jack has been a happy and active one.
    (2)   He has sacrificed his relationship with Jack to achieve other goals.
    (3)   He is sorry that he tyrannized over Jack as a young child.
    (4)   He spurns having any relationship with Jack because Jack is not a real man.
    (5)   He thinks Jack should make more sacrifices.

37. The first paragraph of the passage shows that the father is

    (1)   unsympathetic to his son's views on the war
    (2)   somewhat uncomfortable trying to communicate with his son
    (3)   trying to set the stage for some bad news
    (4)   trying to help his son with his problems
    (5)   hoping to get his son out of his life at last

38. The use of the phrase "ivory tower" (line 19) is effective because it

    (1)   emphasizes that the writer wanted to escape into a safer world
    (2)   shows how much he reveres the college where he works
    (3)   shows how he admits he has not been a good father
    (4)   reflects his opinion that Jack is not facing real life
    (5)   helps him describe his second wife

39. If Jack invites his father to his wedding, the father will probably be

    (1)   disappointed
    (2)   offended
    (3)   amused
    (4)   glad
    (5)   afraid

HOW DOES THIS MAN RELATE HIS IDENTITY TO THE PLACE HE CALLS HOME?

One of my most vivid memories is of coming back West from prep school and later from college at Christmas time. Those who went farther than Chicago would gather in the old dim Union Station at six o-clock of a December evening, with a few Chicago
(5) friends, already caught up in their own holiday gayeties, to bid them a hasty good-by. I remember the fur coats of the girls returning from Miss This-or-That's and the chatter of frozen breath and the hands waving overhead as we caught sight of old acquaintances, and the matchings of invitations: "Are you going to
(10) the Ordways'? the Herseys'? the Schultzes'?" and the long green tickets clasped tight in our gloved hands. And last the murky yellow cars of the Chicago, Milwaukee, & St. Paul railroad looking cheerful as Christmas itself on the tracks beside the gate.

When we pulled out into the winter night and the real snow,
(15) our snow, began to stretch out beside us and twinkle against the windows, and the dim lights of small Wisconsin stations moved by, a sharp wild brace came suddenly into the air. We drew in deep breaths of it as we walked back from dinner through the cold vestibules, unutterably aware of our identity with this country for
(20) one strange hour, before we melted indistinguishably into it again.

That's my Middle West—not the wheat or the prairies or the lost Swede towns, but the thrilling returning trains of my youth, and the street lamps and sleigh bells in the frosty dark and the shadows on the snow. I am part of that, a little solemn with the feel
(25) of those long winters, a little complacent from growing up in the Carraway house in a city where dwellings are still called through decades by a family's name. I see now that this has been a story of the West, after all—Tom and Gatsby, Daisy and Jordan and I, were all Westerners, and perhaps we possessed some deficiency in
(30) common which made us subtly unadaptable to Eastern life.

Even when the East excited me most, even when I was most keenly aware of its superiority to the bored, sprawling, swollen towns beyond the Ohio . . . even then it had always for me a quality of distortion. West Egg, especially, still figures in my more fantastic
(35) dreams. I see it as a night scene by El Greco: a hundred houses, at once conventional and grotesque, crouching under a sullen, overhanging sky and a lustreless moon. In the foreground four solemn men in dress suits are walking along the sidewalk with a stretcher on which lies a drunken woman in a white evening dress.
(40) Her hand, which dangles over the side, sparkles cold with jewels. Gravely the men turn in at a house—the wrong house. But no one knows the woman's name, and no one cares.

40. The main point of the first paragraph can be summed up as

    (1) the author's sadness at no longer being young and hopeful
    (2) the fun of taking a train home on vacation, instead of a plane
    (3) the author's happy memories of returning West from school
    (4) the excitement of meeting old friends on the way home
    (5) the importance of attending the best schools in the East

41. Which of the following best states the main point about the trip?

    (1) It was a difficult and disturbing journey.
    (2) It was a chance to learn about the Middle West.
    (3) It was the start of everyone's Christmas vacation.
    (4) It was an exciting way to travel in midwinter.
    (5) It made people aware of their regional identity.

42. Which of the following best sums up the main idea of the passage?

    (1) The story describes the Middle West.
    (2) The journeys home at Christmas changed the author's life.
    (3) The author's later life has been sad and disappointing.
    (4) The author and his friends were all from the Middle West.
    (5) Westerners are somehow unadaptable to life in the East.

43. Which one of the following is not a supporting detail in the first paragraph?

    (1) The students waved to each other.
    (2) Everyone clutched red tickets.
    (3) The girls wore fur coats.
    (4) People discussed invitations.
    (5) The railroad cars looked cheerful.

44. Upon returning to West Egg, the narrator will probably feel

    (1) somewhat ill at ease
    (2) surprised as if seeing it for the first time
    (3) caught up in many visits
    (4) thrilled to see the prairies and wheat again
    (5) happy to be home again

45. In the last paragraph, the narrator's description of a fantastic dream is effective because it

    (1) emphasizes how the narrator hates the Middle West
    (2) describes what happened one night in the East
    (3) emphasizes the cold, impersonal nature of the East
    (4) echoes the experience of train trips to the Middle West
    (5) emphasizes a desire to move back to the Middle West

Answers and Explanations

Literature Posttest, pages 252–267

1. (Application) **(3) speak politely but distantly** Throughout the passage, Mrs. Buchanan makes a point of being polite about Alma and not insulting her outright; therefore, options (1) and (5) are incorrect. But Mrs. Buchanan does not want to be her friend, option (4), and therefore will not be likely to invite Alma to dinner, option (2).

2. (Application) **(2) talk with her in a friendly way** John does not seem to know Alma that well, so options (1) and (4) are incorrect. Options (3) and (5) are not supported by the passage.

3. (Analysis) **(1) Mrs. Buchanan's negative opinion of Alma** Mrs. Buchanan emphasizes such words as "eccentric" and "quite" (in "not quite") to show that she does not think much of Alma. Mrs. Buchanan is not angry at, or fearful for, John in the passage, so options (2) and (3) are incorrect. Options (4) and (5) are not supported by the passage.

4. (Application) **(4) conforming** Since Mrs. Buchanan is concerned about appearances, she is not likely to be married to an eccentric man, option (1). Because she tries to convince John not to be sentimental or stubborn, she would probably not want these qualities in a husband, so options (2) and (5) are incorrect. There is no support for option (3).

5. (Inferential Comprehension) **(5) is critical and a snob** This is correct because her every word is judgmental and proud. Option (3) is wrong because she talks about Alma only to try to turn John from Alma. Options (1), (2), and (4) are not supported by the passage.

6. (Literal Comprehension) **(4) bombs drop/in their awful labor** Option (4) is descriptive language, like all the other options. However, the mention of the bombs dropping is not used by the poet to describe the cold. The poet is describing something happening far away, either to contrast with or to complement the description of the cold.

7. (Literal Comprehension) **(2) in the country** The speaker in the poem mentions that the city, option (1), and the highway, option (5), are far away. There is no mention of the speaker living in an icehouse or a tent, so options (3) and (4) are wrong.

8. (Inferential Comprehension) **(5) observing the weather** Lines 7–8 refer to the speaker's "observing./Me swallowing the stone of winter." Options (1), (2), (3), and (4) are figures of speech describing the cold or feelings of the speaker.

9. (Inferential Comprehension) **(3) The mood of the poem is gloomy and depressed.** Option (1) is wrong because the poem is filled with figurative language about the cold and death. The only hopeful part of the poem is the last four lines. Option (2) is wrong; while the poem is thoughtful, it is not lighthearted. There is no support for options (4) and (5).

10. (Analysis) **(1) a savage force** Words such as "punching" and "slicing" emphasize the force of the cold, so options (2) and (3) are wrong. Although the speaker talks about a state of mind, option (4), this is not a description of the cold. There is no support for option (5).

11. (Inferential Comprehension) **(4) The poet means that spring will follow the cold winter.** The poet is speaking figuratively. The flower represents the springtime, and the power to break down the door is the power of spring, not some power of the flower itself. Options (2) and (3) are both wrong because they are too literal, as are options (1) and (5).

12. (Analysis) **(3) wordy but lively** While wordy by today's standards, the style is full of life and feeling. It is not simple, option (1); nor is it dry, option (2); solemn, option (4); or flat, option (5).

13. (Literal Comprehension) **(3) a disagreeable and savage animal** Option (1) refers to Topper; option (2) is a separate character; option (4) lists things that Scrooge is *not*; and option (5) is something Fred gives.

14. (Inferential Comprehension) **(5) zoo** A menagerie is a place wild animals are kept, so option (5) is correct. Option (1) is incorrect; since the "animal" in question can growl and grunt, it is not a bird in a birdcage. Since the subject of the game is a live animal, option (3) is wrong. Line 23 specifically states "not a horse," thus option (4) is incorrect. Option (2) is not supported by the passage.

15. (Literal Comprehension) **(3) Scrooge has made them laugh by being the object of a game.** Everyone has laughed *at* Scrooge, not because they are grateful, option (2), or because they like him, options (1) and (5). There is no evidence that the partygoers think Scrooge is dead, option (4).

16. (Inferential Comprehension) **(1) invisible** The words "unconscious company" (line 39) and "inaudible" (line 40) imply that Scrooge is not visible to the others. There is no evidence for options (2), (3), (4), and (5).

17. (Inferential Comprehension) **(2) Scrooge will be able to change his grumpy ways** The last paragraph says that Scrooge became "gay and light of heart." From the rest of the passage, we know that Scrooge is usually grumpy and mean. Options (1), (3), and (4), which imply that Scrooge will never change, are incorrect. There is no support for option (5) in the passage.

18. (Inferential Comprehension) **(3) both funny and serious** Options (1), (2), and (4) are partly true but do not reflect the whole of the author's opinion. Option (5) is not supported by the passage.

19. (Inferential Comprehension) **(5) during one night** The only reference that the author makes to the time frame of the movie is to mention "villains out to ruin Kid's night" (line 43). We can infer that the party takes place that night. There is no evidence for options (1), (2), (3), and (4).

20. (Analysis) **(1) how the movie rejects stereotypes** The author cites the friendship between the two girls to make a point about the way the movie handles stereotypes. Options (2), (3), (4), and (5) are not discussed in relation to the girls.

21. (Literal Comprehension) **(2) is set in Los Angeles** The author says that the movie "aimed for the Middle American look of their suburban neighborhood in Illinois." Options (1), (3), (4), and (5) are things that the author *did* say.

22. (Literal Comprehension) **(3) uses familiar forms to tell an interesting story** Lines 89–90 state that the directors used "familiar forms." Options (1), (2), (4), and (5) are not supported by the passage.

23. (Literal Comprehension) **(3) they wanted to include authentic rap songs in the movie** Lines 20–21 say how the Hudlins wanted the movie to be an "authentic depiction of black life," and line 47 mentions the "rap duel." The review points out that the two rappers were making their acting debut, so option (1) is incorrect. There is no support in the passage for options (2), (4), and (5).

24. (Literal Comprehension) **(4) he began acting out a role** The changes noticeable in the older Hemingway were a consequence of a fame that was based increasingly on his image instead of his writing. Lines 19–23 support this. Options (1), (2), (3), and (5) are true but are not the cause of his behavior changes.

25. (Analysis) **(3) introduce a discussion of Hemingway's life and style of writing** The first paragraph shows his style of writing and describes an important event in his life. Options (1) and (4) are not mentioned in the passage. The first paragraph does not criticize Hemingway's behavior, option (2), or explain why he became a celebrity, option (5).

26. (Inferential Comprehension) **(5) an international star** Because Hemingway presented himself more as a celebrity than a writer (cause), people began to think of him as a star (effect). His literary skill, option (1), took second place. Options (2), (3), and (4) are factual but are not mentioned in the passage.

27. (Application) **(3) an early Hemingway story** The reviewer states a preference for Hemingway's early work in the third paragraph. Options (1), (2), (4), and (5) are about Hemingway's life, which the reviewer does not favor.

28. (Analysis) **(2) describe what became of Hemingway in his later years** The reviewer is giving an opinion of Hemingway later in his life, not his literature, so options (1) and (4) are wrong. Publicity is not being described, so option (3) is incorrect. Option (5) describes other people's opinion of Hemingway.

29. (Literal Comprehension) **(2) she no longer has any patience with Mr. Brooks's behavior.** Option (2) is correct because it is consistent with her decision to leave him. Options (1), (3), and (4) are not supported by the passage. Only Ruby makes jokes, which rules out option (5).

30. (Inferential Comprehension) **(1) She is worried about Mrs. Brooks's future.** The thrust of Ruby's dialogue is to slow Mrs. Brooks down, to caution her, so option (2) is incorrect. There is no evidence that Ruby likes or admires Mr. Brooks, so options (3) and (5) are incorrect. There is no direct evidence for option (4).

31. (Inferential Comprehension) **(4) does not spend money readily** The evidence in the passage indicates that Mr. Brooks is stingy. We do not know much else about him, so option (4) is the best answer. There is no support for options (1), (2), (3), and (5).

32. (Literal Comprehension) **(3) he refused to let her buy a new dress** The answer is found in lines 5–6. Options (1), (2), (4), and (5) are not true.

33. (Inferential Comprehension) **(1) she has thought about leaving Mr. Brooks for a long time** Mrs. Brooks refers to "the last straw," implying that this decision had been building up over time. There is no evidence for options (2), (3), (4), and (5).

34. (Literal Comprehension) **(3) that he has had a happy, active life** The speaker states this in line 25. Options (1) and (4) are not supported by the passage. The speaker admits that he does not know his son well, so option (2) is wrong. Option (5) is incorrect because he says that his second marriage is successful.

35. (Analysis) **(5) letter** The speaker is directly addressing his son, so he probably wrote him a letter. A telegram, option (1), would be much shorter. A diary entry, option (4), is private. There is no evidence in the passage to support options (2) and (3).

36. (Inferential Comprehension) **(2) He has sacrificed his relationship with Jack to achieve other goals.** There is no support in the passage for options (1), (3), and (5). Option (4) is close to the correct answer, but a reading of the passage as a whole, with its focus on sacrifice, makes it plain that option (2) is the right answer.

37. (Analysis) **(2) somewhat uncomfortable trying to talk to his son** The writer asks Jack to "pardon me" and says that he is "not trying to make crude jokes," thus showing his discomfort. Options (1) and (5) are not supported by the passage, and there is no evidence for options (3) and (4).

38. (Analysis) **(1) it emphasizes that the writer wanted to escape into a safer world** The speaker has alluded to danger in the political world and possibly some kind of scandal. The reference is not to Jack, nor about the speaker's second wife, so options (4) and (5) are incorrect. There is no evidence for options (2) and (3).

39. (Application) **(4) glad** From the passage, we can conclude that the speaker wants to be friends with his son. Though he may not understand some of his son's choices, the father takes him seriously and says that he is not unsympathetic to him. Therefore, options (1) and (2) are incorrect. The father's tone is serious, so option (3) is wrong. Option (5) is not supported by the passage.

40. (Inferential Comprehension) **(3) the author's happy memories of returning West from school** There is no evidence for options (1), (2), and (5) in the paragraph. Option (4) is simply a supporting detail.

41. (Inferential Comprehension) **(5) It made people aware of their regional identity.** There is no evidence for options (1) and (2) in the paragraph. Options (3) and (4) are supporting details.

42. (Inferential Comprehension) **(5) Westerners are somehow unadaptable to life in the East.** Options (1) and (4) are true but are secondary to the main point. There is no evidence for options (2) and (3) in the paragraph.

43. (Literal Comprehension) **(2) Everyone clutched red tickets.** The tickets were green (line 10). Options (1), (3), (4), and (5) are all supporting details.

44. (Application) **(1) ill at ease** The narrator describes West Egg as though it were a distorted painting or a nightmare, so he would probably feel ill at ease there. The narrator is remembering West Egg, so option (2) is wrong. Options (3), (4), and (5) refer to the Middle West, not West Egg.

45. (Analysis) **(3) emphasizes the cold, impersonal nature of the East** In the narrator's dream, no one knows, or cares about, one another. Options (1), (2), (4), and (5) are not supported by the passage.

POSTTEST Correlation Chart

Interpreting Literature and the Arts

The chart below will help you determine your strengths and weaknesses in reading comprehension and in the content areas of popular and classical literature and commentary.

Directions

Circle the number of each item that you answered correctly on the Posttest. Count the number of items you answered correctly in each column. Write the amount in the Total Correct space for each column. (For example, if you answered 8 literal comprehension items correctly, place the number 8 in the blank above *out of 12*.) Complete this process for the remaining columns.

Count the number of items you answered correctly in each row. Write that amount in the Total Correct space for each row. (For example, in the Popular Literature row, write the number correct in the blank before *out of 22*.) Complete this process for the remaining rows.

Cognitive Skills / Content	Literal Comprehension	Inferential Comprehension	Application	Analysis	Total Correct
Popular Literature *(Pages 36–133)* Fiction Poetry Drama	34 6, 7 29, 32	36 8, 9, 11 5, 30, 31, 33	39 1, 2, 4	35, 37, 38 10 3	_____ out of 22
Classical Literature *(Pages 134–199)* Fiction	13, 15, 43	14, 16, 17, 40, 41, 42	44	12, 45	_____ out of 12
Commentary *(Pages 200–249)* Literature Film	24 21, 22, 23	26 18, 19	27	25, 28 20	_____ out of 11
Total Correct	_____ out of 12	_____ out of 17	_____ out of 6	_____ out of 10	Total correct: ___ out of 45 1–36 → Need more review 37–45 → Congratulations! You're Ready

If you answered fewer than 45 questions correctly, determine which areas are hardest for you. Go back to the *Steck-Vaughn GED Interpreting Literature and the Arts* book and review the content in those areas. In the parentheses under the item type heading, the page numbers tell you where you can find specific instruction about that area of literature and the arts in the *Steck-Vaughn GED Interpreting Literature and the Arts* book.

Tests of General Educational Development

TEST _____

TEST TAKEN AT _____

TEST NUMBER

① ② ③ ④ ⑤

TEST ANSWERS

DO NOT MARK IN YOUR TEST BOOKLET

Fill in the circle corresponding to your answer for each question. Erase cleanly.

1 ① ② ③ ④ ⑤	19 ① ② ③ ④ ⑤	36 ① ② ③ ④ ⑤	54 ① ② ③ ④ ⑤
2 ① ② ③ ④ ⑤	20 ① ② ③ ④ ⑤	37 ① ② ③ ④ ⑤	55 ① ② ③ ④ ⑤
3 ① ② ③ ④ ⑤	21 ① ② ③ ④ ⑤	38 ① ② ③ ④ ⑤	56 ① ② ③ ④ ⑤
4 ① ② ③ ④ ⑤	22 ① ② ③ ④ ⑤	39 ① ② ③ ④ ⑤	57 ① ② ③ ④ ⑤
5 ① ② ③ ④ ⑤	23 ① ② ③ ④ ⑤	40 ① ② ③ ④ ⑤	58 ① ② ③ ④ ⑤
6 ① ② ③ ④ ⑤	24 ① ② ③ ④ ⑤	41 ① ② ③ ④ ⑤	59 ① ② ③ ④ ⑤
7 ① ② ③ ④ ⑤	25 ① ② ③ ④ ⑤	42 ① ② ③ ④ ⑤	60 ① ② ③ ④ ⑤
8 ① ② ③ ④ ⑤	26 ① ② ③ ④ ⑤	43 ① ② ③ ④ ⑤	61 ① ② ③ ④ ⑤
9 ① ② ③ ④ ⑤	27 ① ② ③ ④ ⑤	44 ① ② ③ ④ ⑤	62 ① ② ③ ④ ⑤
10 ① ② ③ ④ ⑤	28 ① ② ③ ④ ⑤	45 ① ② ③ ④ ⑤	63 ① ② ③ ④ ⑤
11 ① ② ③ ④ ⑤	29 ① ② ③ ④ ⑤	46 ① ② ③ ④ ⑤	64 ① ② ③ ④ ⑤
12 ① ② ③ ④ ⑤	30 ① ② ③ ④ ⑤	47 ① ② ③ ④ ⑤	65 ① ② ③ ④ ⑤
13 ① ② ③ ④ ⑤	31 ① ② ③ ④ ⑤	48 ① ② ③ ④ ⑤	66 ① ② ③ ④ ⑤
14 ① ② ③ ④ ⑤	32 ① ② ③ ④ ⑤	49 ① ② ③ ④ ⑤	67 ① ② ③ ④ ⑤
15 ① ② ③ ④ ⑤	33 ① ② ③ ④ ⑤	50 ① ② ③ ④ ⑤	68 ① ② ③ ④ ⑤
16 ① ② ③ ④ ⑤	34 ① ② ③ ④ ⑤	51 ① ② ③ ④ ⑤	69 ① ② ③ ④ ⑤
17 ① ② ③ ④ ⑤	35 ① ② ③ ④ ⑤	52 ① ② ③ ④ ⑤	70 ① ② ③ ④ ⑤
18 ① ② ③ ④ ⑤		53 ① ② ③ ④ ⑤	

Permission is granted to reproduce this form for student use.

Tests of General Educational Development

TEST _____

TEST TAKEN AT _____

TEST NUMBER

TEST ANSWERS

DO NOT MARK IN YOUR TEST BOOKLET

Fill in the circle corresponding to your answer for each question. Erase cleanly.

Test number column: ① ② ③ ④ ⑤

1 ① ② ③ ④ ⑤	19 ① ② ③ ④ ⑤	36 ① ② ③ ④ ⑤	54 ① ② ③ ④ ⑤
2 ① ② ③ ④ ⑤	20 ① ② ③ ④ ⑤	37 ① ② ③ ④ ⑤	55 ① ② ③ ④ ⑤
3 ① ② ③ ④ ⑤	21 ① ② ③ ④ ⑤	38 ① ② ③ ④ ⑤	56 ① ② ③ ④ ⑤
4 ① ② ③ ④ ⑤	22 ① ② ③ ④ ⑤	39 ① ② ③ ④ ⑤	57 ① ② ③ ④ ⑤
5 ① ② ③ ④ ⑤	23 ① ② ③ ④ ⑤	40 ① ② ③ ④ ⑤	58 ① ② ③ ④ ⑤
6 ① ② ③ ④ ⑤	24 ① ② ③ ④ ⑤	41 ① ② ③ ④ ⑤	59 ① ② ③ ④ ⑤
7 ① ② ③ ④ ⑤	25 ① ② ③ ④ ⑤	42 ① ② ③ ④ ⑤	60 ① ② ③ ④ ⑤
8 ① ② ③ ④ ⑤	26 ① ② ③ ④ ⑤	43 ① ② ③ ④ ⑤	61 ① ② ③ ④ ⑤
9 ① ② ③ ④ ⑤	27 ① ② ③ ④ ⑤	44 ① ② ③ ④ ⑤	62 ① ② ③ ④ ⑤
10 ① ② ③ ④ ⑤	28 ① ② ③ ④ ⑤	45 ① ② ③ ④ ⑤	63 ① ② ③ ④ ⑤
11 ① ② ③ ④ ⑤	29 ① ② ③ ④ ⑤	46 ① ② ③ ④ ⑤	64 ① ② ③ ④ ⑤
12 ① ② ③ ④ ⑤	30 ① ② ③ ④ ⑤	47 ① ② ③ ④ ⑤	65 ① ② ③ ④ ⑤
13 ① ② ③ ④ ⑤	31 ① ② ③ ④ ⑤	48 ① ② ③ ④ ⑤	66 ① ② ③ ④ ⑤
14 ① ② ③ ④ ⑤	32 ① ② ③ ④ ⑤	49 ① ② ③ ④ ⑤	67 ① ② ③ ④ ⑤
15 ① ② ③ ④ ⑤	33 ① ② ③ ④ ⑤	50 ① ② ③ ④ ⑤	68 ① ② ③ ④ ⑤
16 ① ② ③ ④ ⑤	34 ① ② ③ ④ ⑤	51 ① ② ③ ④ ⑤	69 ① ② ③ ④ ⑤
17 ① ② ③ ④ ⑤	35 ① ② ③ ④ ⑤	52 ① ② ③ ④ ⑤	70 ① ② ③ ④ ⑤
18 ① ② ③ ④ ⑤		53 ① ② ③ ④ ⑤	

Permission is granted to reproduce this form for student use.

Tests of General Educational Development

TEST _____

TEST TAKEN AT _____

TEST NUMBER

☐

① ② ③ ④ ⑤

TEST ANSWERS   DO NOT MARK IN YOUR TEST BOOKLET

Fill in the circle corresponding to your answer for each question. Erase cleanly.

1 ① ② ③ ④ ⑤	19 ① ② ③ ④ ⑤	36 ① ② ③ ④ ⑤	54 ① ② ③ ④ ⑤
2 ① ② ③ ④ ⑤	20 ① ② ③ ④ ⑤	37 ① ② ③ ④ ⑤	55 ① ② ③ ④ ⑤
3 ① ② ③ ④ ⑤	21 ① ② ③ ④ ⑤	38 ① ② ③ ④ ⑤	56 ① ② ③ ④ ⑤
4 ① ② ③ ④ ⑤	22 ① ② ③ ④ ⑤	39 ① ② ③ ④ ⑤	57 ① ② ③ ④ ⑤
5 ① ② ③ ④ ⑤	23 ① ② ③ ④ ⑤	40 ① ② ③ ④ ⑤	58 ① ② ③ ④ ⑤
6 ① ② ③ ④ ⑤	24 ① ② ③ ④ ⑤	41 ① ② ③ ④ ⑤	59 ① ② ③ ④ ⑤
7 ① ② ③ ④ ⑤	25 ① ② ③ ④ ⑤	42 ① ② ③ ④ ⑤	60 ① ② ③ ④ ⑤
8 ① ② ③ ④ ⑤	26 ① ② ③ ④ ⑤	43 ① ② ③ ④ ⑤	61 ① ② ③ ④ ⑤
9 ① ② ③ ④ ⑤	27 ① ② ③ ④ ⑤	44 ① ② ③ ④ ⑤	62 ① ② ③ ④ ⑤
10 ① ② ③ ④ ⑤	28 ① ② ③ ④ ⑤	45 ① ② ③ ④ ⑤	63 ① ② ③ ④ ⑤
11 ① ② ③ ④ ⑤	29 ① ② ③ ④ ⑤	46 ① ② ③ ④ ⑤	64 ① ② ③ ④ ⑤
12 ① ② ③ ④ ⑤	30 ① ② ③ ④ ⑤	47 ① ② ③ ④ ⑤	65 ① ② ③ ④ ⑤
13 ① ② ③ ④ ⑤	31 ① ② ③ ④ ⑤	48 ① ② ③ ④ ⑤	66 ① ② ③ ④ ⑤
14 ① ② ③ ④ ⑤	32 ① ② ③ ④ ⑤	49 ① ② ③ ④ ⑤	67 ① ② ③ ④ ⑤
15 ① ② ③ ④ ⑤	33 ① ② ③ ④ ⑤	50 ① ② ③ ④ ⑤	68 ① ② ③ ④ ⑤
16 ① ② ③ ④ ⑤	34 ① ② ③ ④ ⑤	51 ① ② ③ ④ ⑤	69 ① ② ③ ④ ⑤
17 ① ② ③ ④ ⑤	35 ① ② ③ ④ ⑤	52 ① ② ③ ④ ⑤	70 ① ② ③ ④ ⑤
18 ① ② ③ ④ ⑤		53 ① ② ③ ④ ⑤	

Interpreting Literature and the Arts

Directions

The Interpreting Literature and the Arts Simulated GED Test consists of excerpts from classical and popular literature and articles about literature or the arts. Each excerpt is followed by multiple-choice questions about the reading material.

Read each excerpt first and then answer the questions following it. Refer back to the reading material as often as necessary in answering the questions.

Each excerpt is preceded by a "purpose question." The purpose question gives a reason for reading the material. Use these purpose questions to help focus your reading. You are not required to answer these purpose questions. They are given only to help you concentrate on the ideas presented in the reading materials.

You should spend no more than 65 minutes answering the questions on this test. Work carefully, but do not spend too much time on any one question. Be sure you answer every question. You will not be penalized for incorrect answers.

Record your answers on the answer sheet provided on page 276 or on a separate piece of paper. Be sure all requested information is properly recorded on the answer sheet. To record your answers, mark the numbered space on the answer sheet beside the number that corresponds to the question on the test.

Example:
It was Susan's dream machine. The metallic blue paint gleamed, and the sporty wheels were highly polished. Under the hood, the engine was no less carefully cleaned. Inside, flashy lights illuminated the instruments on the dashboard, and the seats were covered by rich leather upholstery.

The subject ("It") of this excerpt is most likely

(1) an airplane
(2) a stereo system
(3) an automobile
(4) a boat
(5) a motorcycle

The correct answer is "an automobile"; therefore, answer space 3 would be marked on the answer sheet.

Do not rest the point of your pencil on the answer sheet while you are considering your answer. Make no stray or unnecessary marks. If you change an answer, erase your first mark completely. Mark only one answer space for each question; multiple answers will be scored as incorrect. Do not fold or crease your answer sheet.

GED Literature and the Arts— Simulated Test

Directions: Choose the one best answer to each item.

Items 1 to 5 refer to the following excerpt from a review.

WHY CAN *SUPERMAN* NOT GET OFF THE GROUND?

The film rallies when [Christopher] Reeve takes over—especially when he gets out of the drably staged scenes at the offices of the *Daily Planet*, gets into his red
(5) cape and blue tights, flies over Metropolis, and performs a string of miracles. Yet after the first graceful feat, in which he saves Lois Lane, who has fallen from a helicopter that crashed on a skyscraper, then
(10) steadies the fallen chopper (with the injured pilot inside) and gently lifts it to safety, the other miracles don't have enough tension to be memorable. . . . When Superman takes his beloved up for a joy-
(15) ride in the sky, the cutting works against the romanticism that we're meant to feel, and, with Lois reciting Leslie Bricusse lyrics to convey her poetic emotions, even the magic of two lovers flying hand in hand
(20) over New York City is banalized. Lois Lane has always been one of the more boring figures in popular mythology: she exists to get into trouble. Margot Kidder tries to do something with this thankless part, but
(25) she's harsh-voiced, and comes across as nervous and jumpy; she seems all wrong in relation to Reeve, who outclasses her. He's so gentlemanly that her lewdness makes one cringe. (We aren't given a clue to what
(30) our hero sees in Lois Lane. It might have been more modern fun if he hadn't been particularly struck by her until she'd rejected his cowardly Clark Kent side for his Superman side—if, like any other poor cluck, he
(35) wanted to be loved for his weakness.)

. . . In order to sell the film as star-studded, a great many famous performers were signed up and then stuck in among the plastic bric-a-brac of Krypton; perform-
(40) ers who get solo screen credits, with the full blast of trumpets and timpani, turn out to have walk-ons. Susannah York is up there as the infant Superman's mother, but, though Krypton is very advanced, this
(45) mother seems to have no part in the decision to send her baby to Earth. York has no part of any kind; she stares at the camera and moves her mouth as if she'd got a bit of food stuck in a back tooth. Of all the
(50) actors gathered here—all acting in different styles—she, maybe, by her placid distaste, communicates with us most directly.

Source: *When the Lights Go Down* by Pauline Kael.

1. Christopher Reeve's portrayal of Superman is described as

   (1) intelligent and insightful
   (2) courteous and well bred
   (3) crude and vulgar
   (4) boring and annoying
   (5) enthusiastic and playful

2. It would be a reasonable assumption to believe this critic might award *Superman*

   (1) **** Extraordinary
   (2) *** Excellent
   (3) ** Very good
   (4) * Good
   (5) (none) Poor

3. From the passage, which of the following can you infer is the reviewer's main point?

   (1) The special effects are stunning.
   (2) The enchantment is missing.
   (3) Lois Lane was born for trouble.
   (4) Too many stars appeared.
   (5) More good actors would have helped.

4. If you were asked to take a starring role in this film, other than the characters of Lois Lane and Superman, you would probably appear

   (1) throughout the entire film
   (2) only as a newspaper reporter
   (3) in the joyride scene
   (4) as a villain
   (5) very seldom

5. The reviewer discusses the joyride of Superman and Lois Lane as an example of

   (1) the excellent acting of Christopher Reeve
   (2) the nervous acting of Margot Kidder
   (3) a miracle that is not memorable
   (4) a time when the film rallies
   (5) the effective portrayal of love between Superman and Lois Lane

HOW ARE PERCHIK AND MENDEL DIFFERENT?

(TEVYE *notices that* PERCHIK *is eying the cheese hungrily.*)

TEVYE: Here, have a piece.

PERCHIK: I have no money. And I am not a beggar.

TEVYE: Here—it's a blessing for me to give.

(5) PERCHIK: Very well—for your sake! (*He takes the cheese and devours it.*)

TEVYE: Thank you. You know, it's no crime to be poor.

PERCHIK: In this world, it's the rich who are the criminals. Some day their wealth will be ours.

(10) TEVYE: That would be nice. If they would agree, I would agree.

MENDEL: And who will make this miracle come to pass?

PERCHIK: People. Ordinary people.

MENDEL: Like you?

PERCHIK: Like me.

(15) MENDEL: Nonsense!

Source: *The Fiddler on the Roof* by Joseph Stein.

6. From this excerpt, you can tell that Tevye is

(1) cynical
(2) greedy
(3) foolish
(4) generous
(5) crafty

7. Which of the following statements best describes Mendel's opinion of Perchik?

(1) Perchik has sound ideas.
(2) Perchik has ridiculous ideas.
(3) Perchik is a schemer.
(4) Perchik can perform miracles.
(5) Perchik is a beggar.

8. From the passage you can infer that Tevye

(1) is a cheesemaker
(2) has an easygoing attitude toward life
(3) thinks Perchik is a fool
(4) always sides with Perchik instead of Mendel
(5) does not want any more money than he has

9. Perchik thinks it is a crime to be

 (1) hungry
 (2) a beggar
 (3) rich
 (4) ordinary
 (5) nonsensical

10. With which of the following statements is Mendel likely to agree?

 (1) The rich should be forced to give money to the poor.
 (2) Ordinary people can change history.
 (3) Rich people and poor people are equal.
 (4) The rich get richer and the poor get poorer.
 (5) Everyone should try to get rich.

WHAT ARE THE THREE NEW YORKS?

There are roughly three New Yorks. There is, first, the New York of the man or woman who was born here, who takes the city for granted and accepts its size and
(5) its turbulence as natural and inevitable. Second, there is the New York of the commuter—the city that is devoured by locusts each day and spat out each night. Third, there is the New York of the person
(10) who was born somewhere else and came to New York in quest of something. Of these three trembling cities the greatest is the last—the city of final destination, the city that is a goal. It is this third city that
(15) accounts for New York's high-strung disposition, its poetical deportment, its dedication to the arts, and its incomparable achievements. Commuters give the city its tidal restlessness, natives give it solidity
(20) and continuity, but the settlers give it passion. And whether it is a farmer arriving from Italy to set up a small grocery store in a slum, or a young girl arriving from a small town in Mississippi to escape the
(25) indignity of being observed by her neighbors, or a boy arriving from the Corn Belt with a manuscript in his suitcase and a pain in his heart, it makes no difference: each embraces New York with the intense
(30) excitement of first love, each absorbs New York with the fresh eyes of an adventurer, each generates heat and light to dwarf the Consolidated Edison Company.

The commuter is the queerest bird of
(35) all. The suburb he inhabits has no essential vitality of its own and is a mere roost where he comes at day's end to go to sleep.

Except in rare cases, the man who lives in Mamaroneck or Little Neck or Teaneck
(40) and works in New York, discovers nothing much about the city except the time of arrival and departure of trains and buses, and the path to a quick lunch. He is deskbound, and has never, idly roaming in the
(45) gloaming, stumbled suddenly on Belvedere Tower in the Park, seen the ramparts rise sheer from the water of the pond, and the boys along the shore fishing for minnows, girls stretched out negligently on the shelves
(50) of the rocks; he has never come suddenly on anything at all in New York as a loiterer, because he has no time between trains. He has fished in Manhattan's wallet and dug out coins but has never listened to Manhat-
(55) tan's breathing, never awakened to its morning, never dropped off to sleep in its night. . . . The commuter dies with tremendous mileage to his credit, but he is no rover. . . .

(60) The terrain of New York is such that a resident sometimes travels farther, in the end, than a commuter. Irving Berlin's journey from Cherry Street in the Lower East Side to an apartment uptown was through
(65) an alley and was only three or four miles in length, but it was like going three times around the world.

Source: *Essays of E. B. White* by E. B. White.

11. What does the author mean when he says "Of these three trembling cities the greatest is the last" (lines 11–13)?

(1) He means that the last shall be first.
(2) He means that there are many shaky people in New York.
(3) He means that the New York of the commuter is the greatest of the three.
(4) He means that the New York of the native is the greatest of the three.
(5) He means that the New York of the settler is the greatest of the three.

12. What technique does the author use to paint a picture of the commuter?

(1) He describes the commuter's neck in great detail.
(2) He describes the commuter as a boy fishing for minnows.
(3) He uses the image of a bird that returns to its roost each night.
(4) He describes him as a loiterer.
(5) He uses exaggeration.

13. What does the author mean by the phrase "the city that is devoured by locusts each day and spat out each night" (lines 7–8)?

(1) He means that the people of New York spit a lot.
(2) He means that commuters take from the city but give nothing to it.
(3) He means that New York has an insect problem.
(4) He means that only locusts can live in New York.
(5) He means there are many poor people in New York.

14. What is the effect of the author's use of the phrase "heat and light to dwarf the Consolidated Edison Company" (lines 32–33)?

(1) He shows that the Consolidated Edison Company is run by dwarfs.
(2) He shows that the newcomers have fevers.
(3) He shows just how excited and enthusiastic the newcomers are.
(4) He shows how weak the Consolidated Edison Company is.
(5) He shows that he does not like commuters.

15. Which of the following techniques is not used by the author to describe New York?

(1) He uses examples in groups of threes to focus attention on the diversity of New York.
(2) He writes about the city as if it had feelings and interests.
(3) He uses the image of New York as a train station connecting Italy and Mississippi.
(4) He uses figurative language to restate his descriptions.
(5) He uses the descriptive word "tidal" to suggest the effect commuters have on the city's character.

16. If the author went to Paris or Rome, he would most likely

(1) walk around the city at leisure, discovering as much as possible
(2) commute to the city from the country
(3) try to meet as many natives as he could
(4) see as many museums and churches as possible
(5) plan to write a book about it

Items 17 to 22 refer to the following excerpt.

WHAT DID YOUNG FLORENCE WANT TO BECOME?

As the years passed, a restlessness began to grow upon her. She was unhappy, and at last she knew it. Mrs. Nightingale, too, began to notice that there was some-
(5) thing wrong. It was very odd; what could be the matter with dear Flo? Mr. Nightingale suggested that a husband might be advisable; but the curious thing was that she seemed to take no interest in husbands.
(10) And with her attractions, and her accomplishments, too! There was nothing in the world to prevent her making a really brilliant match. But no! She would think of nothing but how to satisfy that singular
(15) craving of hers to be *doing* something. As if there was not plenty to do in any case, in the ordinary way, at home. There was china to look after, and there was her father to be read to after dinner. Mrs. Nightingale
(20) could not understand it; and then one day her perplexity was changed to consternation and alarm. Florence pronounced an extreme desire to go to Salisbury Hospital as a nurse; and she confessed to some
(25) visionary plan of eventually setting up a house of her own in a neighbouring village, and there founding "something like a Protestant Sisterhood, without vows, for women of educated feelings." The whole
(30) scheme was summarily brushed aside as preposterous; and Mrs. Nightingale, after the first shock of terror, was able to settle down again more or less comfortably to her embroidery. But Florence, who was now
(35) twenty-five and felt that the dream of her life had been shattered, came near to desperation.

And, indeed, the difficulties in her path were great. For not only was it an
(40) almost unimaginable thing in those days for a woman of means to make her own way in the world and to live in independence, but the particular profession for which Florence was clearly marked out
(45) both by her instincts and her capacities was at that time a peculiarly disreputable one. . . .

A weaker spirit would have been overwhelmed by the load of such distresses—
(50) would have yielded or snapped. But this extraordinary young woman held firm, and fought her way to victory. With an amazing persistency, during the eight years that followed her rebuff over Salisbury Hospi-
(55) tal, she struggled and worked and planned. While superficially she was carrying on the life of a brilliant girl in high society, . . . she yet possessed the energy to collect the knowledge and to undergo the experience
(60) which alone could enable her to do what she had determined she would do. . . . While her mother and sister were taking the waters at Carlsbad, she succeeded in slipping off to a nursing institution at
(65) Kaiserswerth, where she remained for more than three months. This was the critical event of her life. The experience which she gained as a nurse at Kaiserswerth formed the foundation of all her future action and
(70) finally fixed her in her career.

Source: *Eminent Victorians* by Lytton Strachey.

17. By "a woman of means" (line 41), the author means

   (1) a woman of the streets
   (2) a wealthy woman
   (3) a mean-spirited woman
   (4) an intelligent woman
   (5) a marriageable woman

18. From this passage, you can infer that Florence's mother was

   (1) content to be a homemaker
   (2) not very intelligent
   (3) a frustrated career woman
   (4) dominated by her husband
   (5) unable to be a good mother

19. While Florence went to a nursing institution at Kaiserswerth, her mother and sister probably

   (1) approved of her journey
   (2) did not know where she was
   (3) thought that Florence had returned home early
   (4) made plans to come join her
   (5) paid for her course work

20. Florence's career hopes were

   (1) supported by her parents
   (2) considered very admirable
   (3) built around husband-hunting
   (4) greeted with shock and alarm
   (5) shared by all her friends

21. Which title might the author have given this excerpt?

   (1) A Tragic Life
   (2) Good-by, Mother
   (3) Helping Others
   (4) An Unsuitable Woman
   (5) In Spite of It All

22. The author reveals the thoughts of Mrs. Nightingale (lines 10–17) in order to

   (1) emphasize her complete lack of understanding of Florence's unhappiness
   (2) emphasize how much work there was to be done at home
   (3) show how much Florence's father needed her
   (4) show how much she hated Florence
   (5) show how lazy she thought Florence was

Items 23 to 27 refer to the following excerpt from a play.

HOW DO THESE WOMEN ACT WITH EACH OTHER?

CHICK: . . . Oh! Oh! Oh! I almost forgot. Here's a present for you. Happy birthday to Lenny, from the Buck Boyles! (*She takes a wrapped package from her bag and hands it to* LENNY.)

LENNY: Why, thank you, Chick. It's so nice to have you remember
(5)   my birthday every year like you do.

CHICK: (*modestly*) Oh, well, now, that's just the way I am, I suppose. That's just the way I was brought up to be. Well, why don't you go on and open up the present?

LENNY: All right. (*She starts to unwrap the gift.*)

(10) CHICK: It's a box of candy—assorted crèmes.

LENNY: Candy—that's always a nice gift.

CHICK: And you have a sweet tooth, don't you?

LENNY: I guess.

CHICK: Well, I'm glad you like it.

(15) LENNY: I do.

CHICK: Oh, speaking of which, remember that little polka-dot dress you got Peekay for her fifth birthday last month?

LENNY: The red-and-white one?

CHICK: Yes; well, the first time I put it in the washing machine, I
(20)   mean the very first time, it fell all to pieces. Those little polka dots just dropped right off in the water.

LENNY: (*crushed*) Oh, no. Well, I'll get something else for her, then—a little toy.

CHICK: Oh, no, no, no, no, no! We wouldn't hear of it! I just wanted
(25)   to let you know so you wouldn't go and waste any more of your hard-earned money on that make of dress. Those inexpensive brands just don't hold up. I'm sorry, but not in these modern washing machines.

Source: *Crimes of the Heart* by Beth Henley.

23. If Lenny buys Peekay a toy, which of the following is most likely to happen?

(1) Peekay will break it immediately.
(2) Lenny will criticize Peekay as she gives Peekay the toy.
(3) Lenny will tell Chick just how much the toy cost.
(4) Chick will criticize the toy.
(5) Chick will refuse to let Peekay have the toy.

24. With which of the following statements would Lenny be most likely to agree?

(1) If you can't be nice, be polite.
(2) Honesty is the best policy.
(3) Don't look a gift horse in the mouth.
(4) Every cloud has a silver lining.
(5) People who live in glass houses shouldn't throw stones.

25. The author includes the dialogue about "the polka-dot dress" (lines 16–28) as an example of how Chick

(1) shows off her knowledge of fashion
(2) tries to get Lenny to give Peekay a present
(3) shows off how well brought up she is
(4) makes Lenny feel bad
(5) shows off her knowledge of washing machines

26. Which of these is most likely to happen next?

(1) Lenny will throw Chick out of her house.
(2) Lenny will run out and buy another dress for Peekay.
(3) Lenny will tell Chick that she didn't wash Peekay's dress the right way.
(4) Lenny will offer Chick a piece of candy.
(5) Lenny will offer to adjust Chick's washing machine.

27. From the passage you can infer that Lenny

(1) has a mind of her own
(2) likes to receive candy as a present
(3) always says what others want her to say
(4) always remembers Chick's birthday
(5) does not have much money

Items 28 to 33 refer to the following poem.

WHAT IS THIS WOMAN LOOKING FORWARD TO?

How to Be Old

It is easy to be young. (Everybody is,
at first.) It is not easy
to be old. It takes time.
Youth is given; age is achieved.
(5) One must work a magic to mix with time
in order to become old.

Youth is given. One must put it away
like a doll in a closet,
take it out and play with it only
(10) on holidays. One must have many dresses
and dress the doll impeccably
(but not to show the doll, to keep it hidden.)

It is necessary to adore the doll,
to remember it in the dark on the ordinary
(15) days, and every day congratulate
one's aging face in the mirror

In time one will be very old.
In time, one's life will be accomplished.
And in time, in time, the doll—
(20) like new, though ancient—will be found.

Source: *To Mix with Time, New and Selected Poems* by May Swenson.

28. The speaker in the poem says that youth should be treated as

  (1) magic
  (2) a holiday
  (3) a dress
  (4) a doll
  (5) a mirror

29. The speaker is concerned about

  (1) hiding her youth
  (2) saving her old dolls
  (3) growing old gracefully
  (4) forgetting her youth
  (5) dressing well

30. According to the poem, what is true of age?

  (1) It must be achieved.
  (2) It must be fought off.
  (3) It must be treated like a doll.
  (4) It must be put into a closet.
  (5) It will be found.

31. To the speaker, youth is most likely

(1) the time of your childhood
(2) the time when a person is pretty
(3) the time when a person plays with dolls
(4) a state of mind
(5) the best part of life

32. The description of how to treat the doll (lines 7–12) is used in order to

(1) emphasize how precious youth is
(2) emphasize the casualness of life
(3) emphasize the uselessness of trying to fight off old age
(4) illustrate how the speaker felt when young
(5) illustrate how helpless old people are

33. How does the speaker in the poem feel about growing older than she is now?

(1) She is afraid of losing her youthful good looks.
(2) She hopes to die before she gets much older.
(3) She thinks she will enter a second childhood.
(4) She thinks she will congratulate herself.
(5) She hopes to remain young in her mind and heart.

Items 34 to 39 refer to the following excerpt.

WHY DID MICHAEL FUREY DIE?

Her hand was warm and moist: it did not respond to his touch, but he continued to caress it just as he had caressed her first letter to him that spring morning.

(5) —It was in the winter, she said, about the beginning of the winter when I was going to leave my grandmother's and come up here to the convent. And he was ill at the time in his lodgings in Galway and wouldn't

(10) be let out, and his people in Oughterard were written to. He was in decline, they said, or something like that. I never knew rightly.

She paused for a moment and sighed.

(15) —Poor fellow, she said. He was very fond of me and he was such a gentle boy. We used to go out together, walking, you know, Gabriel, like the way they do in the country. He was going to study singing only

(20) for his health. He had a very good voice, poor Michael Furey.

—Well; and then? asked Gabriel.

—And then when it came to the time for me to leave Galway and come up to the

(25) convent he was much worse and I wouldn't be let see him, so I wrote a letter saying I was going up to Dublin and would be back in the summer and hoping he would be better then.

(30) She paused for a moment to get her voice under control and then went on:

—Then the night before I left I was in my grandmother's house in Nun's Island, packing up, and heard gravel thrown up

(35) against the window. The window was so wet I couldn't see so I ran downstairs as I was and there was the poor fellow at the end of the garden, shivering.

—And did you not tell him to go back?

(40) asked Gabriel.

—I implored of him to go home at once and told him he would get his death in the rain. But he said he did not want to live. I can see his eyes as well as well! He was

(45) standing at the end of the wall where there was a tree.

—And did he go home? asked Gabriel.

—Yes, he went home. And when I was only a week in the convent he died and he

(50) was buried at Oughterard where his people came from. O, the day that I heard that, that he was dead!

She stopped, choking with sobs, and, overcome by emotion, flung herself face

(55) downward on the bed, sobbing in the quilt. Gabriel held her hand for a moment longer, irresolutely, and then, shy of intruding on her grief, let it fall gently and walked to the window.

Source: *Dubliners* by James Joyce.

34. What is the effect of the last two sentences?

   (1) They show that these people will never get along.

   (2) They contrast the stormy feelings of the woman with the quiet feelings of the man.

   (3) They emphasize the tragedy of Michael Furey's death.

   (4) They hint that the woman is not really grieving over Michael Furey.

   (5) They hint that the woman might kill herself over Michael Furey.

35. The woman and Gabriel are in

   (1) Galway

   (2) Oughterard

   (3) the country

   (4) Nun's Island

   (5) a bedroom

36. From the passage you can infer that Gabriel

   (1) is in love with the woman

   (2) was a friend of Michael Furey

   (3) thinks the woman's grief over Michael Furey is silly

   (4) is glad that Michael Furey is dead

   (5) hopes that the woman will forget about Michael Furey

37. What was the woman's response to Michael Furey's last visit?

   (1) She told him she loved him.

   (2) She sent him away.

   (3) She gave up her plans to go to the convent.

   (4) She planned to run away with him.

   (5) She rejected him and went to Gabriel instead.

38. The immediate cause of Michael Furey's death was that he

   (1) had been in ill health

   (2) was hit by lightning

   (3) swam out to Nun's Island

   (4) stayed out in the rain

   (5) walked all the way to Dublin

39. The underlying cause of Michael Furey's death was that he

   (1) had failed to become a singer

   (2) liked to go for long walks

   (3) did not want to live without love

   (4) wanted to get back at the world

   (5) suffered from a fatal disease

Items 40 to 45 refer to the following excerpt from a review.

WHAT DID THESE MEN TAKE TO WAR?

(5) Only a handful of novels and short stories have managed to clarify, in any lasting way, the meaning of the war in Vietnam for America and for the soldiers who served there. With *The Things They Carried*, Tim O'Brien adds his second title to the short list of essential fiction about Vietnam. As he did in his novel *Going After Cacciato* (1978), which won a National Book Award,
(10) he captures the war's pulsating rhythms and nerve-racking dangers. But he goes much further. By moving beyond the horror of the fighting to examine with sensitivity and insight the nature of courage and fear,
(15) by questioning the role that imagination plays in helping to form our memories and our own versions of truth, he places *The Things They Carried* high up on the list of best fiction about *any* war.

(20) *The Things They Carried* is a collection of interrelated stories. . . .

In the title story, Mr. O'Brien juxtaposes the mundane and the deadly items that soldiers carry into battle. Can openers,
(25) pocketknives, wristwatches, mosquito repellent, chewing gum, candy, cigarettes, salt tablets, packets of Kool-Aid, matches, sewing kits, C rations are "humped" by the G.I.'s along with M-16 assault rifles, M-60
(30) machine guns, M-79 grenade launchers. But the story is really about the other things the soldiers "carry": "grief, terror, love, longing . . . shameful memories" and, what unifies all the stories, "the common secret
(35) of cowardice." These young men, Mr. O'Brien tells us, "carried the soldier's greatest fear, which was the fear of blushing. Men killed, and died, because they were embarrassed not to."

(40) Embarrassment, the author reveals in "On the Rainy River," is why he, or rather the fictional version of himself, went to Vietnam. He almost went to Canada instead. What stopped him, ironically, was fear.
(45) "All those eyes on me," he writes, "and I couldn't risk the embarrassment. . . . I couldn't endure the mockery, or the disgrace, or the patriotic ridicule. . . . I was a coward. I went to the war." . . .

(50) Mr. O'Brien strives to get beyond literal descriptions of what these men went through and what they felt. He makes sense of the unreality of the war—makes sense of why he has distorted that unreality
(55) even further in his fiction—by turning back to explore the workings of the imagination, by probing his memory of the terror and fearlessly confronting the way he has dealt with it as both soldier and fiction writer. In
(60) doing all this, he not only crystallizes the Vietnam experience for us, he exposes the nature of all war stories.

Source: *New York Times Book Review*, "Too Embarrassed Not to Kill," a review by Robert R. Harris.

40. The stories in the book are about

    (1) different men in the Vietnam war

    (2) one man who has many experiences in Vietnam

    (3) the author's day-to-day life in Vietnam

    (4) some men who went to Vietnam, some who went to Canada

    (5) men who were too embarrassed to be good soldiers

41. From the excerpt you can infer that the author of the book

    (1) went to Vietnam but did not enjoy being there

    (2) wishes he had gone to Vietnam

    (3) hopes his book will be used to train future soldiers

    (4) wrote this book while he was in Vietnam

    (5) did not make many friends while he was in Vietnam

42. The reviewer mentions two stories in detail in order to

    (1) show off his knowledge of the war

    (2) explain how the stories in the book are alike and different

    (3) give examples of the characters in the book

    (4) relate these stories to the reviewer's own experience

    (5) tell why the author did not like the war

43. The reviewer thinks that *The Things They Carried* is better than most books about war because it

    (1) describes the day-to-day routines of men in war

    (2) is a collection of short stories

    (3) is about the soldiers' feelings

    (4) is not about just one person

    (5) is written by an author with a good imagination

44. How does the reviewer feel about the author's previous novel, *Going After Cacciato*?

    (1) The reviewer thinks it was better than the new novel.

    (2) The reviewer thinks it did not go far enough.

    (3) The reviewer thinks the two books should be read together.

    (4) The reviewer despises it.

    (5) The reviewer admires it.

45. The reviewer thinks that this book will help readers understand

    (1) the author's life

    (2) the war experience

    (3) certain battles in Vietnam

    (4) how to write a book

    (5) how to understand interrelated stories

Answers and Explanations

Simulated Test (pages 277–293)

1. (Literal Comprehension) **(2) courteous and well bred** The answer means "gentlemanly" (line 28). Options (3) and (4) are wrong because Lois Lane, not Reeve's Superman, is described as boring and crude. Options (1) and (5) are not supported by the excerpt.

2. (Analysis) **(5) (none) Poor** Since the writer does not recommend the film, the only rating supported by the excerpt would have to be Poor. The reviewer cites Susannah York's expression of distaste (line 51) to support her opinion. Therefore, options (1), (2), (3), and (4) are wrong.

3. (Inferential Comprehension) **(2) The enchantment is missing.** The main point is that the film lacks charm. Disappointment is implied when the reviewer writes that the miracles fall flat and that even flights over the city lack the glamour they should have conveyed. Options (1), (3), and (4) are either details or minor objections. There is no support for option (5).

4. (Application) **(5) very seldom** In line 42, big stars are described as winding up with "walk-ons," a term meaning an insignificant part. If you were a star asked to play a role in *Superman*, you too would rarely be seen, so option (1) is wrong. There is no support for options (2), (3), and (4).

5. (Analysis) **(3) a miracle that is not memorable** The reviewer says that the cutting of the film works against the effectiveness or noteworthiness of the joyride, as do the lyrics Lois Lane recites, so option (4) is wrong. The acting of Margot Kidder is mentioned later, so option (2) is wrong. Options (1) and (5) are not supported by the excerpt.

6. (Literal Comprehension) **(4) generous** The answer is found in lines 1–4, which prove that he is not greedy, option (2). There is no evidence for options (1), (3), and (5) in the excerpt.

7. (Inferential Comprehension) **(2) Perchik has ridiculous ideas.** From his responses to Perchik's statements, it is clear that Mendel thinks little of Perchik, so options (1) and (4) must be ruled out. Options (3) and (5) may be true, but there is no evidence to support them.

8. (Inferential Comprehension) **(2) has an easygoing attitude toward life** Option (2) is correct because Tevye demonstrates a pleasant and agreeable manner. Options (1) and (3) are not supported by the excerpt, and since Tevye takes no sides, option (4) is ruled out. Option (5) is the opposite of what Tevye suggests.

9. (Literal Comprehension) **(3) rich** The answer is in line 8. Options (1), (2), (4), and (5) are discussed but not described as crimes.

10. (Inferential Comprehension) **(4) The rich get richer and the poor get poorer.** This cynical view is implied by Mendel's response to Perchik's suggestion of eventual wealth. Options (1) and (2) are the ideas of Perchik, not those of Mendel. Options (3) and (5) are not mentioned in the excerpt.

11. (Literal Comprehension) **(5) He means that the New York of the settler is the greatest of the three.** In lines 1–11 the author describes three New Yorks. The third, or the last, is that of the settler, so options (3) and (4) are incorrect. Option (1) is not supported in the excerpt. Option (2) is wrong because the author does not say the people are "trembling."

12. (Analysis) **(3) He uses the image of a bird that returns to its roost each night.** This image is used in lines 34–37. The images in options (2) and (4) are mentioned in the excerpt, but the author does not say the commuter is either of these things. Option (1) is wrong; the "necks" in the excerpt are the names of towns. Although the author does use exaggeration, option (5), he does not use it to describe the commuter.

13. (Inferential Comprehension) **(2) He means that commuters take from the city but give nothing to it.** There is no support for option (1). Options (3) and (4) would make sense only if the author were speaking literally. The phrase is a figurative description of the commuters that swarm into the city daily. There is also no support for option (5), although there may be many poor people in New York.

14. (Analysis) **(3) He shows just how excited and enthusiastic the newcomers are.** The author is using this exaggeration to describe the newcomers, not the electric company, so options (1) and (4) are wrong. Option (2) makes sense only if the phrase was meant literally, but it is figurative language. Although the author may dislike commuters, option (5), such an attitude has nothing to do with the phrase.

15. (Analysis) **(3) He uses the image of New York as a train station connecting Italy and Mississippi.** Options (1), (2), (4), and (5) are used by the author in the excerpt. Trains are mentioned in the excerpt, and Italy and Mississippi also are referred to; however, the image in option (3) is never used.

16. (Application) **(1) walk around the city at leisure, discovering as much as possible** The author talks about the need to walk around at leisure to appreciate a city. Option (2) would clearly be rejected by the author. Although the author might do what is suggested in options (3), (4), and (5), those conclusions cannot be drawn from the excerpt.

17. (Inferential Comprehension) **(2) a wealthy woman** The fact that all Florence was expected to do was look after the china, read to her father, and find a husband indicates how well-off the family was. From this we can conclude that "a woman of means" is "a wealthy woman." The phrase has nothing to do with the fact that she was intelligent, option (4), or marriageable, option (5). There is no evidence for options (1) and (3) in the excerpt.

18. (Inferential Comprehension) **(1) content to be a homemaker** Florence's mother was appalled at the thought that Florence would leave home to do something else besides keep house, so option (3) is wrong. There is no evidence for options (2), (4), and (5).

19. (Inferential Comprehension) **(2) did not know where she was** The excerpt says that Florence "succeeded in slipping off" (lines 61–62) to Kaiserswerth, implying that there was something secret about the trip. Since we know that Florence's family disapproved of her career aspirations, options (1) and (5) are wrong. There is no evidence for options (3) and (4).

20. (Literal Comprehension) **(4) greeted with shock and alarm** It is made clear in lines 19–20 and 27–29 that the response to Florence's ambitions was shock and alarm, rather than support, option (1), or admiration, option (2). Line 9 makes it clear that she did not want a husband, option (3). Lines 37–45 show how unique her career hopes were, option (5).

21. (Application) **(5) In Spite of It All** The author constantly stresses the obstacles that Florence has to overcome to reach her goal. Her life was not tragic, so option (1) is wrong. Options (2) and (3) do not reflect the main idea of the excerpt. Option (4) might be an opinion others held of Florence, but it is not the author's.

22. (Analysis) **(1) emphasize her complete lack of understanding of Florence's unhappiness** The author is trying to explain how unusual Florence's behavior was. Option (2) is partly true but is not the author's reason. There is no evidence for options (3) or (4). The author is not criticizing her, option (5).

23. (Application) **(4) Chick will criticize the toy.** The excerpt does not give much information about Peekay, so option (1) is unlikely. Options (2) and (3) are more likely to describe Chick's behavior than Lenny's. There is no evidence that Chick is cruel to Peekay, so option (5) is wrong.

24. (Application) **(1) If you can't be nice, be polite.** Although Lenny seems to be hurt by Chick's cruel remarks, she is still polite. She is not honest about her feelings, so option (2) is wrong. Although she is not thrilled with Chick's gift, option (3) is not relevant to the excerpt; neither are options (4) and (5).

25. (Analysis) **(4) makes Lenny feel bad** There is no evidence that Chick really knows much about fashion or washing machines, so options (1) and (5) are wrong. She does not ask Lenny for another present; thus option (2) is wrong. Though Chick claims to be well brought up, option (3), that has nothing to do with the polka-dot dress.

26. (Application) **(4) Lenny will offer Chick a piece of candy.** Lenny has not stood up to Chick throughout the excerpt, so we can assume that she will continue to be polite by offering candy. Lenny has shown that she will not take any action against Chick, so options (1) and (3) are unlikely. Lenny says in lines 22–23 that she will not buy another dress, option (2). There is no support for option (5).

27. (Inferential Comprehension) **(3) always says what others want her to say** Option (3) is correct since Lenny usually echoes what Chick has already said. Option (1) is the opposite of option (3). Lenny says that candy is a nice gift, not that she likes it, ruling out option (2). Option (4) is not supported by the excerpt. Chick comments on Lenny's hard-earned money, but not the amount of it, so option (5) has no support.

28. (Literal Comprehension) **(4) a doll** The answer is found in lines 7–8. Options (1), (2), (3), and (5) refer to other images and symbols, not to youth.

29. (Literal Comprehension) **(3) growing old gracefully** The answer is found in lines 4–6. Options (1) and (4) are the opposite of what is said in the poem; options (2) and (5) are literal interpretations of things that are meant as symbols in the poem.

30. (Literal Comprehension) **(1) It must be achieved.** The answer is found in line 4. Option (2) is not supported by the poem; options (3), (4), and (5) refer to youth.

31. (Inferential Comprehension) **(4) a state of mind** The speaker in the poem refers to finding youth when she is old, so option (1) is incomplete. Options (2) and (3) do not reflect how the symbols are used in the poem. Since the speaker is looking forward to achieving a good old age, option (5) is wrong.

32. (Analysis) **(1) emphasize how precious youth is** The doll represents a youthful state of mind. Options (2), (3), (4), and (5) are not supported by the poem.

33. (Inferential Comprehension) **(5) She hopes to remain young in her mind and heart.** The speaker is looking forward to achieving a good old age, so options (1) and (2) are wrong. There is no support for option (3). Option (4) may be partly true, but it is not the main emphasis.

34. (Analysis) **(2) They contrast the stormy feelings of the woman with the quiet feelings of the man.** These two sentences record how the characters' actions reflect their feelings. Although we know that the woman feels that Michael Furey's death was tragic, option (3), this is not the point being made here. Options (1), (4), and (5) are not supported by the last two sentences.

35. (Literal Comprehension) **(5) a bedroom** The answer is found in line 55. Options (1), (2), (3), and (4) name places referred to by the woman.

36. (Inferential Comprehension) **(1) is in love with the woman** We can infer Gabriel's love from the information in the first paragraph. Although option (5) may be true, we cannot know that from the excerpt. There is no evidence for options (2), (3), and (4).

37. (Literal Comprehension) **(2) She sent him away.** The answer can be found in line 41, which states that she "implored of him to go home at once." Though options (1) and (5) may be true, there is not enough evidence to support them. Options (3) and (4) are the opposite of what happened in the excerpt.

38. (Inferential Comprehension) **(4) stayed out in the rain** The woman warned him that he might "get his death in the rain" (lines 42–43). Option (1), while true, was not the immediate cause of his death. Options (2), (3), and (5) are untrue.

39. (Inferential Comprehension) **(3) did not want to live without love** Options (1), (2), and (4) are untrue. Option (5) might be a contributing factor, but the woman's story makes it clear that he lost his will to live when she went away.

40. (Inferential Comprehension) **(1) different men in the Vietnam war** The reviewer discusses two stories: one about a group of soldiers, the other about the fictional version of the author's experience. Therefore, it is about more than one man, making options (2) and (3) incorrect. Options (4) and (5) are not supported by the excerpt.

41. (Inferential Comprehension) **(1) went to Vietnam but did not enjoy being there** The author writes about first-hand experiences in Vietnam, so option (2) is wrong. There is no evidence in the excerpt to support options (3), (4), and (5).

42. (Analysis) **(2) explain how the stories in the book are alike and different** The reviewer does not boast about knowledge of war or say he was ever in one, so options (1) and (4) are wrong. There is no discussion of specific characters in the first example, so option (3) is wrong. Option (5) does not explain the structure of the review.

43. (Literal Comprehension) **(3) is about the soldiers' feelings** The answer is found in lines 12–19. Options (1), (2), (4), and (5) are mentioned in the review, but not as factors that make this book better than others.

44. (Inferential Comprehension) **(5) The reviewer admires it.** The reviewer mentions that the earlier book also "captures the war's pulsating rhythms and nerve-racking dangers" (lines 10–11), and he includes both books on his "short list of essential fiction" (lines 6–7) on the war. This admiring statement is the opposite of option (4). There is no evidence for options (1), (2), and (3).

45. (Literal Comprehension) **(2) the war experience** The answer is found in lines 59–62. The book may help the reader understand the author's life, option (1), but this is not the point the reviewer makes. There is no evidence for options (3), (4), and (5).

SIMULATED GED TEST Correlation Chart

Interpreting Literature and the Arts

The chart below will help you determine your strengths and weaknesses in reading comprehension and in the content areas of popular and classical literature and commentary.

Directions

Circle the number of each item that you answered correctly on the Simulated Test. Count the number of items you answered correctly in each column. Write the amount in the Total Correct space for each column. (For example, if you answered 8 literal comprehension items correctly, place the number 8 in the blank above *out of 12.*) Complete this process for the remaining columns.

Count the number of items you answered correctly in each row. Write that amount in the Total Correct space for each row. (For example, in the Popular Literature row, write the number correct in the blank before *out of 22.*) Complete this process for the remaining rows.

Cognitive Skills / Content	Literal Comprehension	Inferential Comprehension	Application	Analysis	Total Correct
Popular Literature *(Pages 36–133)* Nonfiction Poetry Drama	11 28, 29, 30 6, 9	13 31, 33 7, 8, 10, 27	16 23, 24, 26	12, 14, 15 32 25	_____ out of 22
Classical Literature *(Pages 134–199)* Fiction Nonfiction	35, 37 20	36, 38, 39 17, 18, 19	21	34 22	_____ out of 12
Commentary *(Pages 200–249)* Literature Film	43, 45 1	40, 41, 44 3	4	42 2, 5	_____ out of 11
Total Correct	_____ out of 12	_____ out of 17	_____ out of 6	_____ out of 10	Total correct: ___ out of 45 1–36 → Need more review 37–45 → Congratulations! You're Ready

If you answered fewer than 45 questions correctly, determine which areas ar~~ numbers you. Go back to the *Steck-Vaughn GED Interpreting Literature and the A~~ and the arts in the content in those areas. In the parentheses under the item type he~~ tell you where you can find specific instruction about that area ~~ the *Steck-Vaughn GED Interpreting Literature and the A~~

GLOSSARY

apposition an arrangement of words in which one noun or noun phrase is followed by another word or phrase that gives more information

appositive a word or phrase placed after a noun or noun phrase to explain its meaning or to give more information

atmosphere the mood or emotional setting of a work of literature

autobiography a person's life story told by that person

biography a person's life story told by another person

cause a thought, word, or action that brings about a result

cause and effect the way in which one event (the cause) leads to a specific result (the effect)

character a person or animal who takes part in a work of literature

characterization the ways a writer develops a character, including physical descriptions, descriptions of thoughts and actions, and accounts of the reactions of other characters

chronological order an arrangement in order of time

comedy an amusing play that usually ends happily

commentary an expression of opinions in writing or speech

compare to examine two or more things in order to discover how they are alike or different

~ion a decision or judgment based ~mination of information

consequence the result of actions or decisions

context the ideas or descriptions that surround a word or phrase and can help to suggest its meaning

define to discover and explain a meaning

dialogue the words that a character or characters actually say

drama a story that is told through action and speech and that is meant to be performed

effect a result or condition that can be traced to a cause

essay a short piece of nonfiction usually written from a personal point of view

evaluate to examine and judge whether something is a fact or an opinion

exaggeration a statement enlarged beyond what is actual or true; used to emphasize a point

fact a statement that is based on reality and can be proven to most people's satisfaction

fiction a story based on the writer's imagination that may talk about real things but is not true

figurative language a technique that takes ordinary words and combines them in such a way as to create a vivid image—for instance, describing a parking lot as "an asphalt sea"

figuratively a way of expressing something using words normally used to demonstrate something else

figure of speech a form of expression in which words are used in an imaginative rather than literal way

formal style a serious approach to a written subject, usually using standard English and complete sentences

generalization a statement that is not specific or in detail

image a mental picture created by the imaginative use of words

imagery words used in such a way to create a mental image or picture

implication an idea that is suggested, rather than stated directly, by other facts or ideas

inference an insight based on facts and suggestions

informal style a casual approach to a written subject, often using slang words and sentence fragments

literal the ordinary or usual meaning of a word or expression

literally something presented or understood in its usual meaning

main idea the most important point or central idea of a paragraph or passage

making an inference a decision about something based on clues given by the writer

metaphor a figure of speech that uses a word meaning one thing to describe another in order to show a similarity between them—for example, "All the world's a stage,/And all the men and women merely players" (William Shakespeare)

mood the emotional background in a literary work

motivation the reason a character speaks or acts in a certain way

nonfiction writing that is based on facts about real places, real people, or events that actually took place

opinion a personal belief or viewpoint about a particular subject, not always based on facts or rational thought

phrase a group of words that make sense in themselves but do not form a complete sentence

plot the order of events in a work of literature; what happens in a story

poetry a special form of writing that is more rhythmical and imaginative than ordinary writing, often characterized by the use of figurative language. Poems may be divided into stanzas, or paragraphlike groups of lines that may or may not rhyme.

point of view refers to who is presenting the story to the reader. A first-person narrator tells the story from his or her own point of view and uses *I* and *we*. A third-person narrator is not part of the story and refers to the characters as *he* and *she*. In commentary, point of view refers to the personal interests and background that influence a person's opinions.

review a type of nonfiction that expresses a writer's opinions about the quality of something

rhythm a pattern created by the natural rise and fall in the sounds of words

simile a figure of speech that makes a direct comparison between two things using the words *like* or *as*—for example, "Like a glum cricket/the refrigerator is singing" (James Tate)

stage directions the instructions an author includes to describe actors' movements or manner, the setting, or the costumes in a play

structure the way a writer organizes or puts together a story

style the approach a writer takes in telling a story. A formal style is serious and uses complete sentences. An informal style is more like casual conversation.

summarize to express the main points about something in your own words

supporting details information that describes or explains an idea

symbol a word or phrase that has its own meaning but that is used to suggest a different, more significant meaning

theme the main idea in a work of literature, or a basic comment about life that the writer wants to share

tone the attitude a writer takes toward a subject, often suggested in the choice of words

understanding consequences the ability to recognize the relationship between causes and effects

understatement to say less than is meant in order to emphasize a point

unstated main idea a main idea that is hinted at rather than stated directly

ACKNOWLEDGEMENTS

Grateful acknowledgement is made to the following authors, agents, and publishers for permission to use copyrighted materials.

American Council on Education for the GED Answer Form AS7010. Copyright © 1987, The GED Testing Service of the American Council on Education. Used with permission.

Atheneum Publishers, Inc., for Randall Jarrell, "The Woman at the Washington Zoo" from *The Woman at the Washington Zoo*. Copyright © 1960 Randall Jarrell. Reprinted with the permission of Atheneum Publishers, Inc. Excerpt from *The Miracle Worker* by William Gibson. Copyright 1956 by William Gibson. Reprinted with the permission of Atheneum Publishers, Inc., and Flora Roberts, Inc.

Pamela Bloom for excerpt from her article "Keeping the Faith" (pp. 22–23), *Taxi*, December 1989. Reprinted by permission of the author.

Bantam Books, Inc., for excerpt from *High Hearts* by Rita Mae Brown. Copyright © 1986 by Speakeasy Productions, Inc. Reprinted by permission of Bantam Books, Inc.

University of California Press for excerpt from Theodora Kroeber, *Ishi in Two Worlds: A Biography of the Last Wild Indian in North America*, pp. 118–119. Copyright © 1961 The Regents of the University of California. Reprinted by permission of the author.

Chatto & Windus/The Hogarth Press for excerpt from *Death of the Moth and Other Essays* by Virginia Woolf. Reprinted by permission of the Executors of the Virginia Woolf Estate and the publishers. Extract from "Florence Nightingale" in *Eminent Victorians* by Lytton Strachey. Reprinted by permission of the author's estate and Chatto & Windus. Excerpt from *Cider With Rosie* by Laurie Lee. Reprinted by permission of Chatto & Windus and the Hogarth Press.

Country Journal for excerpt from "The Best Four Days in Highland County," September 1988. © Cowles Magazines.

Curtis Brown, Ltd., for "The Storm" by McKnight Malmar. Reprinted by permission of Curtis Brown, Ltd. Copyright © 1944 by Hearst Magazines, 1972 by McKnight Malmar. For excerpt from *A Separate Peace* by John Knowles. Reprinted by permission of Curtis Brown, Ltd., and Macmillan Publishing Company, Inc. Copyright ©1959 by John Knowles.

Doubleday & Company, Inc., for "My Papa's Waltz," copyright 1942 by Hearst Magazines, Inc., from *The Collected Poems of Theodore Roethke* by Theodore Roethke. Excerpt from *Blues for Mister Charlie* by James Baldwin. Copyright © 1964 by James Baldwin. Doubleday for excerpt from *How I Got To Be Perfect* by Jean Kerr. Copyright © 1978 by Collins Productions, Inc. Excerpt from *The Moon and Sixpence* by W. Somerset Maugham, copyright © 1919 by W. Somerset Maugham. Used by permission of Doubleday, a division of Bantam, Doubleday, Dell Publishing Group, Inc.

Dryad Press for "Migrants" from *Something Tugging the Line* by Roderick Jellema. Reprinted by permission of Dryad Press.

Lawrence Elliott for excerpt from *On the Edge of Nowhere* by James Huntington and Lawrence Elliott. Copyright © 1966 by James Huntington and Lawrence Elliott. Reprinted by permission of Lawrence Elliott.

Farrar, Straus and Giroux, Inc., for excerpt from "Dean of Men" (p. 264) in *The Collected Stories of Peter Taylor* by Peter Taylor. Copyright © 1940, 1941, 1948, 1949, 1950, 1951, 1955, 1957, 1958, 1959, 1960, 1961, 1962, 1963, 1964, 1967, 1968, 1969 by Peter Taylor. Copyright renewed © 1967, 1968 by Peter Taylor. Reprinted by permission of Farrar, Straus and Giroux, Inc. Excerpt from *Talley's Folly* by Lanford Wilson. Copyright © 1979 by Lanford Wilson. Reprinted by permission of Hill & Wang, a division of Farrar, Straus and Giroux, Inc.

Feminist Press for excerpt from *Salt of the Earth*. Copyright © 1953 by Michael Wilson. From the book *Salt of the Earth* by Michael Wilson and Deborah Silverton Rosenfelt (The Feminist Press, 1978). All rights reserved. Reprinted by permission.

Franklin Watts for excerpt from *A History of Art* by Norbert Lynton. Copyright Kingfisher Books Limited 1981. Reprinted by permission of Franklin Watts.

Samuel French, Inc., for excerpt from *Five on the Black-hand Side* (p. 262) by Charlie Russell. Copyright © 1969 by Charlie Russell. Copyright © 1977 (revised and rewritten) by Charlie Russell. Reprinted by permission of Samuel French, Inc.

Greenhaven Press for excerpt from *Animal Communication: Opposing Viewpoints* by Jacci Cole. Copyright 1989 and reprinted by permission of the publisher.

Thomas Griffith for excerpt from his article "What's So Special About News Magazines?" from *Newsweek*, June 26, 1989. Reprinted by permission of the author.

Harcourt Brace Jovanovich, Inc., for excerpt from *Major Writers of America Volume 1*, ed. Perry Miller, copyright © 1962 by Harcourt Brace Jovanovich, Inc., reprinted by permission of the publisher. For excerpt from "Three Pictures" from *The Death of the Moth and Other Essays* by Virginia Woolf, copyright 1942 by Harcourt Brace Jovanovich, Inc., and renewed 1970 by Marjorie T. Parsons, Executrix, reprinted by permission of the publisher. Excerpt from "The Jilting of Granny Wetherall," copyright 1930, 1958 by Katherine Anne Porter. Reprinted from "The Jilting of Granny Wetherall" in her volume *Flowering Judas and Other Stories* by permission of Harcourt Brace Jovanovich, Inc. Excerpt from "Florence Nightingale" in *Eminent Victorians* by Lytton Strachey, copyright © 1969 by Harcourt Brace Jovanovich, Inc. Reprinted by permission of the publisher.

Harper & Row Publishers, Inc., for specified excerpt from "A Mild Attack of Locust" in *The Habit of Loving* by Doris Lessing (Thomas Y. Crowell). Copyright © 1957 by Doris Lessing. From *Essays of E. B. White*: excerpt from "Once More to the Lake" copyright 1941, 1969 by E. B. White. Excerpt from "Here Is New York" copyright 1949 by E. B. White. All reprinted by permission of Harper & Row, Publishers, Inc.

A. M. Heath Company for excerpt from *Louis* by Max Jones and John Chilton.

Henry Holt & Company for excerpt from *When the Lights Go Down* by Pauline Kael. Copyright © 1986 by Pauline Kael. Excerpt from "Education by Poetry" by Robert Frost; from *The Selected Prose of Robert Frost*, ed. Hyde Cox and Edward Connery Lathem. Copyright © 1966 by Henry Holt & Company. All reprinted by permission of Henry Holt & Company.

Houghton Mifflin Company for excerpts from *Narcissa and Other Fables* by Louis Auchincloss. Copyright © 1983 by Louis Auchincloss. "God's Backside" (p. 254) from *The Death Notebooks* by Anne Sexton. Copyright © 1974 by Anne Sexton. All reprinted by permission of Houghton Mifflin Company. Excerpt from *Cold Sassy Tree* by Olive Ann Burns. Copyright © 1984 by Olive Ann Burns. Reprinted by permission of Ticknor

Dan Hurley for excerpt from his article "Those Hush-Hush Q Ratings—Fair or Foul?" in *TV Guide*, December 10, 1988. Reprinted by permission of the author.

Ari Korpivaara for excerpt from his article "Roll Over, Rambo," published in *Ms.* magazine, September 1986. Reprinted by permission of the author.

Morton L. Leavy for excerpts from *Spoon River Anthology* by Edgar Lee Masters. Copyright © 1966 by Mrs. Edgar Lee Masters. Reprinted by permission of Morton L. Leavy as attorney for Ellen Masters.

Little, Brown Company, Inc., for excerpt from *Louis* by Max Jones and John Chilton. Reprinted by permission of Little, Brown Company, Inc. For excerpt from *The Cat Who Came for Christmas* by Cleveland Amory. Reprinted by permission of Little, Brown Company, Inc.

Macmillan Publishing Company, reprinted with permission of Macmillan Publishing Company from *A Separate Peace* by John Knowles. Copyright © 1960 by John Knowles, reprinted 1961.

Richard Meryman for quote by Andrew Wyeth from "Andrew Wyeth: An Interview," in *Life*, May 14, 1965.

William Morris Agency for excerpt from *Fiddler on the Roof* by Joseph Stein. Copyright © 1964 by Joseph Stein. Used by permission of William Morris Agency as agent for Joseph Stein. Excerpt from *Don't Drink the Water* by Woody Allen. Copyright © 1967 by Woody Allen. Used by permission of William Morris Agency. "Close Ties" copyright © 1981 by Elizabeth Diggs. All rights reserved. Used by permission of William Morris Agency. The first professional production of *Close Ties* was by The Long Wharf Theatre, New Haven, Connecticut on February 3, 1981.

Reprinted from *Black Elk Speaks*, by John G. Neihardt, by permission of University of Nebraska Press. Copyright 1932, 1959, 1972 by John G. Neihardt. Copyright © 1961 by the John G. Neihardt Trust.

New Directions Publishing Corporation for "The River Merchant's Wife" from *Personae* by Ezra Pound. Copyright 1926 by Ezra Pound. For excerpt from Tennessee Williams, *The Eccentricities of a Nightingale* (p. 252). Copyright © 1948, 1964 by Tennessee Williams. All reprinted by permission of New Directions Publishing Corporation.

Newsweek magazine for excerpts from issues of June 19, October 2, October 23, and December 25, 1989, and January 15 and 29, 1990, copyright © 1989, 1990 by Newsweek, Inc. For excerpt from "When a Bear Is a Dog," by Jack Kroll. Condensed from *Newsweek*. Copyright 1986 by Newsweek, Inc. All rights reserved. Reprinted by permission.

New York magazine for excerpt from "Romance and Other Disturbances" by Tobi Tobias. Copyright © 1984 by News America Publishing, Inc. Excerpt from Theater Commentary by John Simon, copyright © 1987 by News America Publishing, Inc. All reprinted with the permission of *New York* magazine.

The New York Times Company for excerpts from "Adventure—The Unending Challenge" by Maurice Herzog and from "Too Embarrassed Not to Kill" by Robert R. Harris. Copyright © 1953/1990 by the New York Times Company. Reprinted by permission. For excerpt from "Three Traditions, Two and a Half Heirs," by David Kirby of October 12, 1986, *Book Review*. Copyright © 1986 by The New York Times Company. Reprinted by permission. Excerpt from Art review by John Russell of October 12, 1986, and excerpt from review of *Wanderlust* by Jill Gerston of August 3, 1986, *Book Review*. Copyright © 1986 by The New York Times Company. Reprinted by permission.

North Point Press for "Traveling at Home" excerpted from: *A Part*, copyright © 1980 by Wendell Berry. "The Wheel" excerpted from: *The Wheel*, copyright © 1982 by Wendell Berry. Published by North Point Press and reprinted by permission. All rights reserved.

Harold Ober Associates, Inc., for excerpt from *The Young John Adams*. Reprinted by permission of Harold Ober Associates, Incorporated. Copyright © 1949 by Catherine Drinker Bowen. Copyright renewed 1977 by Ezra Bowen. For excerpt from "Up in the Old Hotel" by Joseph Mitchell. Reprinted by permission of Harold Ober Associates, Incorporated. Copyright 1959 by Joseph Mitchell.

Overlook Press for "Miami" from *The Book of Fortune* by Daniel Mark Epstein. Copyright © 1982 by Daniel Mark Epstein. Reprinted by permission of Overlook Press.

Oxford University Press, London, for excerpt from "A Christmas Carol" (p. 256) by Charles Dickens. For excerpt from *A Doll's House* by Henrik Ibsen, translated by James McFarlane, from *Four Major Plays* (Oxford University Press, 1981). Reprinted by permission of Oxford University Press.

Merrill Penitt for excerpt from his article "Empty Nest" in *TV Guide*, December 31, 1988. Reprinted by permission of the author.

Paramount Pictures for excerpt from *Star Trek: Doctor's Orders* by Diane Dwayne. Copyright © 1990 and reprinted by permission of Paramount Pictures.

People Weekly for Ralph Novak, David Hiltbrand, and Lorenzo Carcaterra/*People* Weekly, copyright © 1990 The Time, Inc. Magazine Co. All rights reserved.

Putnam Berkley Group, Inc., for excerpt from *The Unkown Country* by Bruce Hutchinson, published by Coward, McCann.

Random House, Inc., for "Man on Wheels" copyright © 1968 by Karl Shapiro. Reprinted by permission of Random House, Inc. Excerpts from *Collected Poems, 1940–1978* by Karl Shapiro, by permission of Random House, Inc. "To be of use" copyright © 1972 by Marge Piercy. Reprinted from *Circles on the Water*, by Marge Piercy, by permission of Alfred A. Knopf, Inc. Excerpt from *A Raisin in the Sun* by Lorraine Hansberry. Copyright © 1958 by Robert Nemiroff, as an unpublished work. Copyright © 1959, 1966, 1984 by Robert Nemiroff. Reprinted by permission of Random House, Inc. For "Velvet Shoes" by Elinor Wylie. Copyright 1921 by Alfred A. Knopf, Inc., and renewed 1949 by William Rose Benet. Reprinted from *Collected Poems of Elinor Wylie* by Elinor Wylie, by permission of the publisher. Excerpt from *The Glass Menagerie* by Tennessee Williams. Copyright 1945 by Tennessee Williams and Edwina D. Williams and renewed 1973 by Tennessee Williams. Reprinted by permission of Random House, Inc. Excerpt from *The Children's Hour*, by Lillian Hellman. Copyright 1934 by Lillian Hellman Kober and renewed 1962 by Lillian Hellman. Reprinted by permission of Random House, Inc. Excerpts from *Ragtime* by E. L. Doctorow. Copyright © 1974, 1975 by E. L. Doctorow. Reprinted by permission of Random House, Inc. From Act I of *Don't Drink the Water* by Woody Allen. Copyright © 1967 by Woody Allen. Reprinted by permission of Random House, Inc. Excerpt from *Space*, by James A. Michener. Copyright © 1982 by James A. Michener. Reprinted by permission of Random House, Inc. For "Harlem" copyright 1951 by Langston Hughes. Reprinted from *The Panther and the Lash: Poems of Our Time* by Langston Hughes, by permission of Alfred A. Knopf, Inc. Excerpt from *The Odd Couple* by Neil Simon. Copyright © 1966 by Nancy Enterprises, Inc. Reprinted by permission of Random House, Inc., and DaSilva & DaSilva, attorneys. For excerpt from *Burr: A Novel* by Gore Vidal. Random House, Inc., for excerpt from

Obscure Destinies by Willa Cather. Copyright 1960, published by Alfred A. Knopf. Reprinted by permission of Random House, Inc.

Reiman Associates, Inc., for excerpt from "Windmills" in *Country*, Premier Collector's Edition. Reprinted by permission of the publisher.

Flora Roberts, Inc., for excerpt from *Painting Churches* (p. 24) by Tina Howe. Copyright © 1982 by Tina Howe. Reprinted by permission of Flora Roberts, Inc.

Rollins Joffe Morra & Brezner, Inc., for excerpt from *The Floating Light Bulb* (p. 14) by Woody Allen. Copyright © 1981 by Woody Allen. Reprinted by permission of Rollins Joffe Morra & Brezner, Inc.

St. Martin's Press, Inc., for excerpt from *Huysman's Pets* by Kate Wilhelm. Published by Bluejay Books, New York. Copyright © 1986 by Kate Wilhelm. Reprinted by permission of St. Martin's Press, Inc.

Saturday Evening Post for excerpt from "Forty-Five Seconds Inside a Tornado," in the issue of July 11, 1953. Reprinted by permission of the *Saturday Evening Post*.

Charles Scribner's Sons for excerpt from *Wind in the Willows* by Kenneth Grahame. For excerpt from *The Great Gatsby* (p. 266) by F. Scott Fitzgerald. Copyright 1925 Charles Scribner's Sons. Copyright renewed 1953 by Frances Scott Fitzgerald Lanahan. Reprinted with the permission of the publisher. Excerpt from "A Day's Wait" from *Winner Take Nothing* by Ernest Hemingway. Copyright 1933 Charles Scribner's Sons; copyright renewed © 1961 Mary Hemingway. Reprinted with the permission of the publisher.

Simon & Schuster, Inc., for excerpt from *Contact* by Carl Sagan. Copyright © 1985 by Carl Sagan. Excerpt from *Lonesome Dove* by Larry McMurtry. Copyright © by Larry McMurtry. Excerpt from "Marty" in *Television Plays* by Paddy Chayefsky. Copyright © 1955 by Paddy Chayefsky, renewed 1983 by Susan Chayefsky. Reprinted by permission of Simon & Schuster, Inc. For excerpt from *The Clue in the Old Album* by Carolyn Keene. Reprinted by permission of Simon & Schuster, Inc.

The Society of Authors for extract from *The Devil's Disciple* by George Bernard Shaw. Copyright © 1941 by George Bernard Shaw. Reprinted by permission of The Society of Authors.

Alexander Speer for excerpt from *Talking With . . .* by Jane Martin. Copyright 1980 by Alexander Speer, as Trustee. All rights reserved.

Sports Illustrated for the article "In Pool, the Shark Still Leaves a Wide Wake" by Steve Rushin, June 6, 1988. Copyright © 1988, Time, Inc. All rights reserved.

Straight Arrow Publishers, Inc., for "Independents' Day" (pp. 258–259) by Peter Travers from *Rolling Stone*, March 22, 1990. Copyright © 1990 by Straight Arrow Publishers, Inc. All rights reserved. Reprinted by permission.

Estate of May Swenson for "How to Be Old" by May Swenson, © 1963 and reprinted by permission of the Estate of May Swenson.

Time, Inc., for excerpt from "A Quarter-Century Later, the Myth Endures" (p. 260). Copyright © 1986 Time, Inc. All rights reserved. Reprinted by permission from *Time*.

TV Guide magazine for excerpt by Art Durbano. Reprinted with permission from *TV Guide* magazine. Copyright © 1990 by News America Publications, Inc., Radnor, Pennsylvania.

INDEX